All really great advertising emanates from a really great idea with a motivated champion determined to bring it to life. Creating Brand Loyalty makes a powerful and articulate case for the client to be that champion throughout the creative process. Recommended reading for all marketing professionals.

> David H. Brenner, Senior Vice President
> New Business Ventures, Amway

Business is war. Today, there are more worthy opponents armed with more information and resources than ever. Creating Brand Loyalty is a timeless Zen weapon without limitation. It will expand your mind, management capabilities, and capacity to create new solutions for increasing brand value and building your business.

> Ron Hirasawa, CEO & Chairman
> General Products & Services Corporation

Participants from around the world at the Johnson & Johnson School of Advertising have welcomed the practical approach and hands-on experience Richard and Mike have brought to our company. Their contribution has been invaluable and a joy.

> Richard Cook, Executive Director
> Johnson & Johnson School of Advertising

In real estate the key is location; in marketing it's positioning. And nobody communicates the power of positioning and how to identify and translate it into action better than Czerniawski and Maloney. For years I've been sending my staff to their Strategic Positioning and Ad College seminars. Their message is universally applicable and essential to approaching any market strategically. Creating Brand Loyalty will become required reading—as it should be for anyone looking to maximize his or her advertising dollar.

> Richard Strup, Senior Vice President
> Corporate Strategy and Miller International
> Miller Brewing Company

Czerniawski and Maloney really get it. Everything starts with a powerful brand positioning. Now you can get it. This book tells you how to develop one and then convert it into high-impact advertising. A marketer couldn't ask for more.

> Dwight Riskey, Senior Vice President
> Frito-Lay International

Czerniawski and Maloney have combined their extensive marketing and consulting experiences to produce an engaging advertising guide full of practical advice and real-world examples.

> Brad Moore, President
> Hallmark Hall of Fame Productions

Great advertising is the responsibility of the client as much as the advertising agency. Unfortunately, too many clients don't internalize this shared responsibility or just don't have the expertise to contribute. Mike and Richard know how to help clients become true partners in the process of developing effective advertising. They translate their broad experience and personal insight into practical application.

> Bill Weintraub, Senior Vice President, Marketing
> Coors Brewing Company

Building a dynamic brand is the core driver for the most successful long term growth businesses. Both Richard and Mike are extraordinary marketers who have built major international brands and contributed to the success of a wide array of leading companies. This book captures their strategic insights and is a tremendous, thought-provoking work that will help all of its readers to build stronger brands for the future.

Bill Atchinson, General Manager, Celestial Seasonings

This book will help both clients and agencies significantly improve the impact of advertising, taking it from ordinary to great. These approaches have helped me in many situations.

Jerry Noonan, Senior Vice President, Marketing and
Product Development, Poloroid Corporation

From concept development to creative execution, Creating Brand Loyalty is a valuable and practical tool for producing powerful advertising.

W. Leo Kiely III, President, Coors Brewing Company

One of the most important pieces of work one ever undertakes as guardian of a brand is positioning. Richard and Mike have developed a straightforward, common sense approach to positioning which results in building a brand that has a real competitive advantage. A worthwhile read for anyone committed to creating brand greatness.

Nannette Gardetto, Executive Vice President
Gardetto's

In Creating Brand Loyalty, Czerniawski and Maloney provide marketers with invaluable advice for building strong, enduring brands. They also show you how to develop and nurture successful client-agency relationships.

Joseph Doyle, President/CEO
BGMHealth communications

Creating Brand Loyalty addresses the most important issue in a marketer's life—brand positioning. The concept of Power Positioning is the link to great advertising. Improved brand power can only result through the application of disciplines presented in this book.

Frank A. Sajovic, Executive Vice President, Marketing
Pharmavite Corporation

The primary responsibility of a marketer is the building and development of the brand. It's a company's most important asset. Richard and Mike share a lifetime of knowledge, demonstrating how to do it with excellence. Their book is a must read for anyone interested in building the value of his or her company.

Dave Ellis, General Manager, Xerox Corporation

It is refreshing to see a book about marketing that has practical application and is written by individuals who have "been there, done that". If you are interested in a book that provides practical marketing advice with a process and tools to execute it with excellence, Creating Brand Loyalty is a must read.

Shelley Spencer, Vice President, Global Category
Director, OTC, Bristol-Myers Squibb Company

Richard and Mike's book is the perfect roadmap for developing the "Power" Brand Positioning and bringing it to life in the marketplace.

Ellen S. Hoenig, Vice President, Consumer Marketing
U.S. Pharmaceutical Group, Bristol-Myers Squibb

CREATING BRAND LOYALTY

CREATING BRAND LOYALTY

The Management of Power Positioning and Really Great Advertising

Richard D. Czerniawski

Michael W. Maloney

American Management Association

New York • Atlanta • Boston • Chicago • Kansas City • San Francisco • Washington, D.C.
Brussels • Mexico City • Tokyo • Toronto

Special discounts on bulk quantities of AMACOM
books are available to corporations, professional
associations, and other organizations. For details,
contact Special Sales Department, AMACOM,
an imprint of AMA Publications, a division of
American Management Association,
1601 Broadway, New York, NY 10019.
Tel.: 212-903-8316. Fax: 212-903-8083

This publication is designed to provide accurate and
authoritative information in regard to the subject matter
covered. It is sold with the understanding that the
publisher is not engaged in rendering legal, accounting,
or other professional service. If legal advice or other
expert assistance is required, the services of a competent
professional person should be sought.

Library of Congress Cataloging-in-Publication Data

Czerniawski, Richard D.
    Creating brand loyalty: the management of power positioning and
really great advertising / Richard D. Czerniawski, Michael W. Maloney.
        p.   cm.
    Includes index.
    ISBN 0-8144-0501-0
    1. Advertising—Brand name products.   2. Brand loyalty.
I. Maloney, Michael W.   II. Title.
HF6161.B4C94   1999
658.8'343—dc21   99-26211
                                                            CIP

Printing number
10 9 8 7 6 5 4 3 2 1

Contents

Acknowledgments

The material for this book comes squarely out of our experiences in branding, positioning, marketing, advertising (in short, business-building) over the past 25 years. So, as we thoughtfully consider to whom we owe rightful gratitude and acknowledgement, the list of people who have shaped our experiences grows long indeed. In fact, the names are too many to mention.

But there is still a way to acknowledge credit well-deserved: by saluting those larger groups for whom we've had the great privilege to work—and from whom we've learned so much. We are both extremely fortunate to have begun our business careers with one of the finest learning organizations in the world, Procter & Gamble. From these early experiences we not only took away tried and true thinking disciplines, but we also gained a life-long passion for excellence in brand marketing, in general, and for advertising, in particular.

Our follow-on experiences in heading up business and marketing teams at world-class companies such as Johnson & Johnson, The Coca-Cola Company, and Frito-Lay fed our natural competitive spirits and exposed us to new paradigms in crafting competitive brand positionings and creating brand loyalty. So, we are indeed grateful for all these special opportunities and the training we received from our managers at these extraordinary companies.

But, in fairness, we owe an equal thanks to our consulting-practice clients of the past 15 years—many of whose company names appear throughout our book. We have been consistently blessed with wonderful clients who keep us ever-challenged (with tough new product launches, old and new brand positioning, and ad campaign development assignments). Importantly, they have also given us the freedom to be creative and forward-thinking in all our endeavors.

There are two clients who deserve special acknowledgment, Peter Larson, chairman and chief executive officer of the Brunswick Corporation, and Richard Cook, Executive Director of The Johnson & Johnson School of Advertising. Peter, while serving as a company group chairman at Johnson & Johnson, recognized the urgent need for training marketing managers in brand building and advertising. As such he got the ball rolling and introduced us to Richard Cook. Peter, we are most thankful for your vision and for opening a significant door for us.

When Richard Cook began development of the J&J school more than six years ago, he selected us from a field of consultants, academicians, and training specialists to develop a practical, skill-based program—to share our learnings, experiences and, yes, passion for the creation of Power Positioning and really great advertising. That relationship continues, and more than any of our experiences, our teaching at the Johnson & Johnson School of Advertising has inspired us to write this book. To Richard we say, fondly, thank you for your unfailing confidence in us.

And there is yet one other person deserving of our special thanks—not a client, but our own longtime associate and friend, Lori Vandervoort, who not only runs the administrative side of our consulting business day in and day out, but also painstakingly pulled together our rough drafts and retrieved the permissions and artwork for the ads appearing in this book. Lori, we share our pride in publication with you.

We also tip our caps to Ellen Kadin, senior acquisitions editor at AMACOM, and a devoted Mets fan. While the conventional wisdom these days seems to be that "advertising books don't sell well" (unless your name happens to be David Ogilvy), Ellen went to bat for us. In fact, she has pinch-hit for us a number of times and always come through with a clutch hit!

Thanks, too, to the folks at Interactive Composition Corporation for their thoughtful editing and preparation of our manuscript for publication.

Finally, while this book comes out of our many business experiences, we would undoubtedly still be staring at blank pages had not our families—our wives and our children—given us such enthusiastic encouragement to "just do it." To each of them—June, Barbara, Brian, Katie, Brendan, Christina, and Melissa—we give our biggest, and most heartfelt, thanks.

Richard D. Czerniawski   *Michael W. Maloney*

Foreword—The Client's View

We all respect great brands—as consumers and marketers, and for reflecting favorably on their owners as good companies for which to work and invest. But their greatest impact is in the marketplace where they distinguish and elevate the underlying products into uniqueness and differentiation, transcending price and guiding purchasers through the myriad of choices offered by similar products. The best of the breed, power brands like Sea Ray boats and Mercury engines here at Brunswick, literally bring consumers in the retailers' doors with our brand names on their lips.

Building a brand through Power Positioning lifts products above what Richard Czerniawski and Michael Maloney properly characterize as the current times as "the age of sameness." Regardless of whether the product is undifferentiated or unique in its features and attributes, it's a strategically sound and pre-emptive positioning, consistently delivered in all the elements of the marketing mix, that makes the brand unique and important. Ultimately, it is this positioning strength that lifts the brand over others in the same category and provides that most important of all consumer responses—brand loyalty.

Beyond the product, there is no doubt that advertising is one of the most important marketing mix elements in seeding the positioning and enabling the brand to take root. In this age of sameness we are highly unlikely to create brand loyalty without also managing the development of great advertising. And, while Wall Street has figured out and placed premium value on leading brands, business schools seem to have misread the message. Newly minted MBA's have increasingly become trade promotion specialists and advertising purchasing agents. They lack an integrated, competitive vision for the brand. And, they buy advertising like any other commodity, getting exactly what they sow: mediocrity in marketing communications.

The development of brand positioning and truly great advertising requires knowledge, keen insights, and a rather demanding skill set. Those of us who grew up in an earlier age, learning how to nurture the development of leadership brands and produce great advertising, from an even earlier generation who understood its value, have failed to effectively pass on our knowledge and develop the needed skills in today's generation of marketing managers. We are, therefore, at least equally responsible for the erosion of customer loyalty and what passes for advertising in this age of sameness.

The good news is that it doesn't have to be this way. The potential to create strong brands and great advertising is more available today than it has ever been before. New technologies, media, and distribution channels offer more ways to identify, connect with, and satisfy customer needs. We are left only with the question of whether we possess the knowledge and skill set to develop a strategically positioned brand and a specific message worth delivering.

The essential knowledge and skills can be learned. But first we have to accept the fact that we are all students (throughout our careers and lives) and seek out those who do it best and learn from them. This is the underlying reason why you should read and employ the principles espoused in this book. Richard and Mike have a rich and enviable set of client and consulting experiences from their contribution to the success of leading brands such as Coke, Folger's coffee, Reach toothbrush, Doritos, Band-Aid brand adhesive bandages, and Tropicana orange juice. They know what works and, importantly, how to teach it. They offer a guide to the best practices and thinking in the industry.

Richard and Mike will also challenge you to change the way you think about brand positioning, advertising, and what it takes to create customer loyalty. Going beyond the (same) research that you and all your competitors possess, it is the thoughtful strategic decisions on positioning and marketing mix strategies that can put your brand in a position to capture the "high ground" with the customers of its segment or category. In my 30 years in the business I've never seen the generation of leadership brands and truly great advertising without sound strategic thinking, processes to guide that thinking and, ultimately, direction. (Positive accidents may happen but I've never seen one in this area.)

Finally, another essential part of the process of building brands lies in effectively working with creative people and resources including your advertising agency. Ken Roman, the former chief of Ogilvy and Mather, said it best: "Clients get what they deserve (in their advertising)." Effective clients understand their responsibilities in unearthing the essence of the agency's creativity, a very rare material. In reading this book you will gain valuable insights on how to work with creative people and agencies in a special way that yields great ideas, strategies, and advertising.

While those of my generation took many years to learn these essential truths about building brands and developing great advertising, **Creating Brand Loyalty** packages all the key lessons. I know from experience that these lessons work. It also provides you with a toolbox to guide and, at the same time, assess your thinking. At the end of the day, internalizing and practicing the lessons Richard and Mike share will be a giant step toward producing excellence in brand building through Power Positioning and the development of really great advertising. Your customers will thank you with the growing sales and the higher profits that come from creating brand loyalty.

Peter N. Larson
Chairman and Chief Executive Officer
Brunswick Corporation

Foreword—The Creative Director's View

I have been involved in creating advertising for what seems like a hundred years—as intern, art director, copywriter and finally creative director for at least half a dozen large global and small advertising agencies. I have worked on over a thousand products and/or services, some inherently unique (the easy ones), most inherently parity. I have worked with some of the world's largest and most marketing-sophisticated corporations with huge advertising budgets, and with small, local enterpreneurs about to spend their first advertising dollar. I have worked with prolifically innovative creative people as well as some who hadn't had a fresh idea in their lives. And over the years I have learned that none of these things are key to marketing success or failure. Instead, the single most essential ingredient in a product's marketing mix, the one that controls all the others, the one that compensates for all weaknesses and capitalizes on all strengths, is none other than the product's marketing manager. She or he is the leader of the marketing team, creator and guardian of the "brand," impresario of its presentation to the public, and the determiner of its eventual success or failure. The exact title may vary by company, but to all advertising agencies these people are known as "the client."

I agree 100% with Peter Larson's reference to the axiom: "A client gets the kind of advertising he or she deserves" (although I respectively disagree with his attribution of its origin). Whenever I see a lousy ad (and I seem to be seeing more and more of them lately than ever before) I never blame the creative people who did it. I always blame the client who let them do it. The client should have known it was lousy. Nine times out of ten it was lousy because it lacked even a hint of strategy. Chances are the creative team went directly to the execution. And execution can never cover up for the lack of a strategy. The consumer may enjoy the commercial, but the product will never enjoy customer loyalty because the ad gave them no reason to buy it over other products in the category. Allowing advertising to be developed and run without a strong strategy statement is the failure of the marketing manager.

Often the marketing manager pays with his or her job. The marketing manager is responsible for working with the creative director to develop the advertising that contributes to establishing the brand, which ultimately creates and builds customer loyalty. The advertising strategy is the single most important step in differentiating the brand and its advertising in the minds of customers. Parity products with parity advertising are doomed to failure. To me, they are the result of laziness. I have always believed there is no such thing as a parity product—only parity marketing managers and parity advertising agencies. They both get paid to "un-parity" products. This book tells you how.

One of the most important steps in developing a sound strategy is for the marketing manager and creative director to agree on the target customer. Unless both are absolutely clear as to who the most likely potential prospect for the product is, how can the advertising be tailored directly to them and their specific needs? As a creative practitioner I want to know everything I possibly can about the person I'm trying to convince to buy a product. The most effective advertising is written person-to-person, so this is a must. The responsibility for gathering this information belongs to the marketing manager. Believe me, *the best friend a smart creative director can have is a smart marketing manager to work with.*

Once the advertising strategy has been crafted, the job of the marketing manager is not over. The marketing manager must be directly involved in the advertising. He or she must be sure that in its execution the advertising does not lose its strategic focus or allow the executional technique to overpower the strategy. This is where the Campaign Idea comes in. The late, great Rosser Reeves called it the "U.S.P." (Unique Selling Proposition). I call it the "Unique Advantage." This book defines the basic principle to a far greater degree with its integration of key copy words with core dramatization . . . be it the visualization of the benefit, use of a spokesperson, and such. Any advertising not built around a Campaign Idea is not advertising at all and is a complete waste of a client's money. No marketing manager can afford to squander a company's precious and always scarce marketing funds.

By the way, when I say the marketing manager should be deeply involved in the advertising I don't mean for this person to write the copy or suggest the layout or plot the storyboard or take-over the TV shoot or edit the footage. He or she cannot perform any of these functions as well as professionals. He shouldn't even try! Besides, that would make him the worst client and will result in the worst execution of strategic advertising you can imagine. Strategy without execution is as bad as execution without strategy—well, not quite. Remember, *the best friend a smart marketing manager can have is a smart creative director to work with!*

Creative people are brought up to believe they're something special. They believe that God gifted them with a rare talent that only they possess—certainly not account executives and absolutely, positively, definitely not clients. Don't you believe it! It took me almost half my career to realize fully the arrogance and, most of all, the falsehood of this belief. This is not to imply that all the marketing managers I have come across are brilliant. There are smart ones and not-so-smart ones, just as this is true among creative people. However, with the coming of this book there is no longer an excuse for a not-so-smart marketing manager. What I have learned the hard way over so many years in advertising one can learn by reading, working through, and understanding this book. It's all here. And it's all the real stuff. After having spent a lifetime learning this business, I had the privilege and joy of working closely with Richard and Mike recently and realized how much I could still learn. You live and learn. What I learned from reading this book is: *The best friend a smart, aspiring marketing manager or creative director can have is this smart book to work with!*

Hank Seiden
Chairman
The Seiden Group

Introduction

Competition has exploded. It's all about more, more, more. There are significantly more products and services today than ever before vying to meet every conceivable customer need. Everywhere you turn, you find new competitive entries and more pernicious competition. Worse yet, an end to competition does not appear to be in sight. The explosion continues to develop at what seems like geometric rates.

Yet to borrow from an old expression: the more things change, the more they stay the same. This "age of proliferation" does not appear to offer consumers meaningful differentiation. It really has all the characteristics of, and feels like, an "age of sameness." The result has been the erosion of customer loyalty. The customer's evoked set of acceptable products and vendors has expanded with product selection varying from one purchase occasion to another. Marketers have become more dependent upon price promotions and incentives to bolster sales.

Breaking out of this age of sameness requires the development of "brand loyalty." A brand goes beyond the tangible elements of a product or service to include the special bond we marketers establish for it in the minds and hearts of our customers. This leads to a unique kind of loyalty, what we refer to as brand loyalty. Brand loyalty is enjoyed by such revered names as Hallmark cards, Tylenol, Coca-Cola, and Tide laundry detergent, among many others.

Creating brand loyalty calls for the skillful development of brand positioning and effective advertising. Unfortunately, few marketers have a meaningful way to gain these specialized and needed skills. Instead they are left to their own devices, shackled by outdated processes, mired in management practices that lead to adversarial relationships, forced to repeat the mistakes of their predecessors, and enslaved to tactics that are contraindicative to creating brand loyalty. All of this contributes, in turn, to the demise of ad effectiveness, customer loyalty, and overall business health.

This book deals with winning customer preference by creating brand loyalty through the development of Power Positioning and, not just great but *really great advertising.* Our program is geared toward instructing marketing managers (and even ad agency people) on how to **become more effective brand builders and managers of advertising development.** It takes a client advertiser (i.e., brand marketing manager), not an ad agency (i.e., creative director), approach. It is rooted in strategy, not executional tactics. Importantly, it deals with "how" versus "what" the marketer should think. In this age of sameness we firmly believe that how one thinks is the essential strategic weapon to winning in the marketplace.

This book is built upon our many years of client experiences in successful brand building through the development of strategically sound positioning and compelling advertising at leading companies such as Procter & Gamble, Johnson & Johnson, Frito-Lay and The Coca-Cola Company, to name just a few. It is an outgrowth of our immensely popular **Strategic Positioning & Ad College,** which we have conducted for marketing leadership in business centers throughout the world, such as in Rome, Paris, Shanghai, Hong Kong, London, Mexico City, Los Angeles, and New York.

The marketer who reads this book and utilizes the many available tools will learn how to:

- fulfill the four core responsibilities of the effective client brand builder and advertiser
- establish Power Positioning to meaningfully differentiate any product or service and motivate customer preference through the creation of brand loyalty
- develop and communicate sound strategic and competitive ad direction for, among other things, a surefooted creative exploratory

- establish a creative process that can cut development time in half and improve the quality of the creative product
- inspire breakthrough advertising
- create superiority impressions even with parity products, and
- develop winning campaigns capable of lasting 10 years or longer

For the earnest marketing professional, the book goes beyond imparting information to begin development of needed skills to be a stronger competitor in the marketplace. It is loaded with simple tools you can use as levers to work with your marketing and agency teams to develop competitive strategies and compelling creative. We hope it will serve to encourage development of the brand building marketing leadership needed to achieve customer loyalty and take competition to a new level for success and advancement in an age of sameness.

PART ONE

Pre-Production

Chapter 1
"What Think?" About Advertising

CHAPTER 1

"What Think?" About Advertising

"What do you think?" or the shorthand version, "What think?" is a question we frequently encounter regarding advertising and other marketing management issues. Undoubtedly, you have been asked "What think?" on more than one occasion. Perhaps, it was in a room full of managers senior to you during an agency copy presentation. Or, perhaps, it was while passing your general manager in the hall, when she stopped to ask you "What think?" with regard to a new competitive campaign.

The areas of interest and the locales are many. My partner, Mike, tells of a time when he was passing his general manager while entering the rest room. When Mike exited he found his general manager waiting to inquire "What think?" regarding new competitive advertising.

The person asking the question may be veiling his intention to espouse his opinions. Regardless, it is an invitation to express your feelings and, hopefully, add value to the subject under discussion. Certainly, one would hope that a well thought-out, appropriate, and intelligent response will encourage many more such inquiries and opportunities to contribute.

In our work with clients we are fortunate to be asked "What think?" regarding a varied palette of advertising and issues. We, too, like to ask the question of our clients and do so as a standard practice. This is a good time to hear from you. What do you think about the following television ad for Kellogg's Frosted Flakes Cereal? You may already be familiar with it. The ad goes something like this:

A priest appears sitting stoically in a chair with a microphone placed on a low table before him. His face is shaded so we cannot make out his identity. The words "Joseph—Priest" are supered on the frame. He contritely states, *"Everyone calls me Father, and I love a kid's cereal."*

The ad cuts to a box of Kellogg's Frosted Flakes Cereal and a self-assured, powerful voice-over announces, *"Brave adults wrestle with the notion that Frosted Flakes is just for kids."*

Next we cut to "Lisa," a zookeeper, who fidgeting in her chair, says, *"I work with tigers, I never thought I'd love one."*

We then cut to a shot of the priest enjoying Kellogg's Frosted Flakes Cereal. The announcer says, *"That delectable taste, that incredible crunch, no wonder adults never outgrow the taste."*

Finally we meet "George," a judge, sitting in his majesterial robes. At wit's end, with head shaking, he admits, *"U-h-h, I'm guilty, guilty, guilty."*

Tony the (animated) Tiger appears and reassures everyone that *"It's no crime. Frosted Flakes have the taste adults have grown to love. They're G-r-r-eat!"*

A photo-board is presented for a closer examination.

Rather than tell you our impressions, take a moment to review the photo-board and narrative presented earlier. Jot down what you think about it.

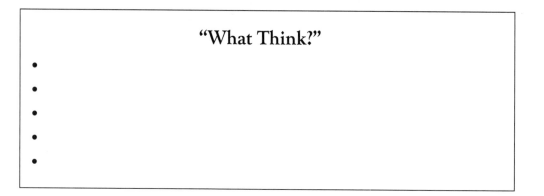

"What think?" Most managers to whom we pose this question note what they don't like. In our society we are conditioned to find fault, criticize versus employ critical thinking skills. As per "likes" or "dislikes," they really

Kellogg's Frosted Flakes Cereal
(Silhouette Testimonials—"Joseph" Priest)

JOSEPH: Everyone calls me, Father. And I love a kids' cereal.

MALE ANNCR: Brave adults

wrestle with the notion that Kellogg's Frosted Flakes

is just for kids.

LISA: I work with tigers.

I never thought I'd love one. MALE ANNCR: That

delectable frosting,

that incredible crunch.

No wonder adults never outgrow the taste.

GEORGE: Oh, I'm guilty, guilty, guilty.

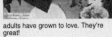

TONY: It's no crime. Frosted Flakes have the taste

adults have grown to love. They're great!

have no basis in the assessment of advertising *unless* they are related to one's judgment regarding the perceived effectiveness of the ad.

Among the most frequent comments are those dealing with executional issues. Concerns are expressed about the casting or roles portrayed, the absence of reality, the size or number of package shots, the length of the copy, and so forth. Managers focus on executional issues, bypassing the more important strategic issues. We typically receive few comments dealing with brand positioning, ad strategy, benefit point-of-difference, Campaign Idea, and those other elements which we will discuss throughout this book, that are at the heart of really great advertising and the sound assessment of it.

"How" Not "What"

In our Strategic Positioning & Advertising College sessions, when we ask the question "What think?" we really don't care what the participants think. Instead, we are attempting to get at *how* they think about brand- and advertising-related issues. "What" refers to judgment. Everyone is entitled to her/his own judgment. It is what truly contributes to the bigger picture mosaic that we seek when we develop brand positioning and advertising. On the other hand, "how" relates to the quality of thinking. It transcends corporate, category, cultural, and even country boundaries.

Your judgment is, well, yours. It grows from your experiences and springs from your perceptions. "How" gets to "the way," the process. It can be learned. "How" is a lever to be used to employ your judgment in a more productive manner. Consider the track-and-field event pole vaulting. For years 16-feet was an insurmountable barrier. Try as they might, no competitor could manage to clear the 16-foot mark. Then along came the fiberglass pole. Nothing else in the sport changed. Today, with the aid of the fiberglass pole, competitors are vaulting better than 20-feet, on a consistent basis. Similarly, "how" becomes your fiberglass pole. It serves as a lever to ensuring the development of really great advertising . . . and powerful brand building. All of this goes toward creating brand loyalty in an age of sameness.

Universality of Brand Positioning and Advertising

Often, we encounter managers who feel their situation is unique. They have special ground rules and jargon that evidences their uniqueness. We may not speak the language of your situation but we do speak the language of "brand positioning" and "advertising." Like music, it is the same worldwide. Consider for a moment the C note, or an F sharp, or G chord. They are identical whether you play them in Chicago, Beijing, or Paris. What differs is the type of music one plays. The arrangement of notes and pauses will differ if you are playing jazz or classical or rock or country-western. The instrumentation will vary based on the sound you wish to create. So a jazz piece may feature the saxophone, classical the violin or piano, rock the electric guitar and country western the harmonica.

Like music, the basic principles for brand development and great advertising are the same worldwide. However, how you put those principles to use will reflect the culture of your country, category, and company. The principles are universal. The application will depend upon your unique situation to encompass market factors, regulatory issues, company values, category practices, and so on. It will also depend upon your unique brand of creativity.

What to Expect

Our goal is to enable you to become a brand builder and great advertiser, leading to the creation of brand loyalty. In order to help you grow and develop, we will be taking a disciplined approach and sharing a common language, which are critically important. In our approach, we want to ensure we are assessing the most relevant and impactful elements of the brand and its advertising: brand positioning, the advertising strategy, the Campaign Idea and, yes, we will also delve into executional elements. Execution is listed last here because it should proceed from, and grow out of, the strategic elements. If it doesn't it is unlikely that you will be able to manage the development of effective advertising and create brand loyalty.

A common language is essential to ensure we are on the same page with colleagues within our companies and with our agencies. My partner, Mike, and I are former military pilots. In flying we shared a common language with air traffic controllers, crew, and members of other military branches. Specificity and commonality are important in military aviation to ensure precision and avert disaster. When we refer to "brand positioning," client and agency should have a similar understanding. The work should be directed at developing a creative and competitive positioning, not defining the word!

The "Brand"

A brand is significantly more than a product. The product comprises mere physical attributes and dimensions. It is nothing more than an interchangeable commodity. It is coffee, razor blades, credit cards—the label we give to whole categories.

The brand, on the other hand, reflects the special relationship and bond we forge with our customers. It is a constellation of values that goes beyond physical attributes to include intangibles (that have tangible value) and, importantly, customer perceptions. It is what distinguishes Starbucks from the commodity coffee, Gillette Sensor from razor blades, and American Express Platinum Card from credit cards. Establishing a brand becomes the foundation for a franchise, encouraging brand loyalty, and desensitizing customers to the lure of competitive price promotions and incursions. In fact, branding is so powerful that Wall Street and corporate America place a significant premium on "brands" such as Coca-Cola as opposed to "products" such as soft drinks.

The Role of Advertising

The most significant contributor to the development of a brand, beyond the product itself (in the splendor of all of its tangible and intangible elements), is brand positioning and advertising. The positioning charts the relationship we want to establish with potential customers. Advertising, on the other hand, is a critically essential plank for establishing in the minds of your customers how and what to think about your offering in the absolute and relative to other products in the marketplace. Advertising contributes to the development and establishment of the brand. Really great advertising helps establish great brands and, of course, brand loyalty.

This book will show you how to create brand loyalty through thoughtful strategic positioning, imprinting the positioning with customers and the development of great advertising. The emphasis is both on brand positioning and advertising. It gets to the heart of the matter as it relates to the core responsibilities of the effective brand builder and client advertiser.

Responsibilities of the Effective Brand Builder and Client Advertiser

There are four core responsibilities of the effective brand builder and client advertiser. The first is establishing the strategic vision for the development of the brand: **brand positioning.** The second is providing clear ad development direction based upon a customer insight that will enable the marketer to realize the overarching marketing objective: **ad strategy.** The third is providing and nurturing an effective and efficient process that will leverage creative development against the ad strategy: employment of **Campaign Ideas** and Applied Strategic Advertising Process (**ASAP**). Fourth is **coaching** the agency (and, for that matter, all resources) to success. Each is briefly discussed below and detailed in subsequent chapters.

1. *Brand Positioning Statement*—This is the starting and ending point for marketing. It provides the blueprint for the development and franchise building of the brand. Therefore, positioning should precede the development of all sub-strategies such as pricing, distribution and packaging, to name a few of the many marketing mix elements.

We define brand positioning as **the way we want customers to perceive, think, and feel about our product or service relative to competitors.** It is the specific piece of turf we want to occupy in the potential customers' minds and, even, hearts as they view the market landscape before them. Positioning is composed of six essential elements: target customer group, need, competitive framework, benefit, reason-why, and brand character. While most managers have some understanding of positioning, few have a real appreciation for this basic concept in establishing a brand and creating brand loyalty. The few products that have a Brand Positioning Statement evidence this. If you do not, you could be shortchanging the potential for your product, leaving it rudderless to float wherever minor eddies carry it and susceptible to competitive forces. Also, many of those marketers who do have a positioning statement view it as a window to advertising communications as opposed to the bigger role of establishing a brand and subsequent loyalty.

2. Ad Strategy—The ad strategy provides guidance and direction for the development of the brand's advertising campaign. Additionally, it provides a common basis upon which to assess all agency advertising submissions. It consists of the **who, what,** and **why** in addressing a specific brand marketing issue or objective.

An effective ad strategy is built upon a meaningful **customer insight.** This requires an understanding of customer and competitive purchase dynamics and attitudes. The key customer insight is strategic-based and must lead to a change in behavior that enables the brand to achieve its desired purchase behavior and marketing objectives.

3. *Process to Leverage Creative Development*—Most processes are outmoded, ineffective, and inefficient practices that have, well, just been "the way things have always been done around here." The client takes care of the strategic side (which is most often non-existent or simply not bought into by agency or top client management) and the agency is responsible for coming-up with the creative genius (which is lacking when clear ad direction is missing). A process designed to improve the likelihood of efficiently developing great advertising needs to be anchored in discipline, have clear client and agency roles, and deliver a lot of creative options that are tied to the ad strategy. Toward this end, we propose the **Applied Strategic Advertising Process (ASAP)** to make the process more effective. In ASAP, the agency

Break the breakout cycle®!

Neutrogena Cleansing Bar washes your skin clear.
It carries away acne-causing dirt and excess oil
without over-drying and irritation. Without the
pore-clogging residue most soaps leave behind.

Take your skin beyond clean…
all the way to clear! Neutrogena.

Neutrogena®

FOR ACNE-PRONE SKIN

Dermatologist-recommended. In the Neutrogena section of your store.

"Since I found out

about my osteoporosis,

I've been afraid to

walk to my mailbox

when it rains."

FIGHT YOUR FEAR.

INTRODUCING FOSAMAX.

THE FIRST HORMONE-FREE TREATMENT FOR OSTEOPOROSIS PROVEN TO REBUILD BONE.

Knowing you have osteoporosis doesn't have to mean you'll never be able to do the things you want to do, like to do, live to do.

Because now there's FOSAMAX – a breakthrough new treatment that's hormone-free and proven to restore lost bone in many women past menopause.

Is FOSAMAX right for you? Ask your doctor. It should be used with caution if you have certain stomach or digestive problems, and should not be used if you have certain disorders of the esophagus (the tube that connects your mouth with your stomach), are unable to stand or sit upright for at least 30 minutes or have severe kidney disease, low levels of calcium in your blood, or are pregnant or nursing. And like any prescription drug, FOSAMAX may cause side effects, most commonly stomach and muscle/bone pain. Generally, the side effects are mild and usually have not stopped people from taking it. However, some patients may develop serious reactions in the esophagus.

But if you're like most women with osteoporosis, FOSAMAX could be an exciting new option for you. And a way to build back your bone strength, as well as your confidence.

ASK YOUR DOCTOR
CALL FOR INFORMATION
1 800 799-4936

FOSAMAX

MERCK

(alendronate sodium tablets)

Please see the Patient Information on the next page and discuss it with your doctor.

Every four minutes, someone dies of diabetes complications. In the time it takes to make a phone call, you can find out how to prevent it.

The statistics are bad. Each year, more than 150,000 people die from diabetes complications. Fortunately, new evidence indicates that with frequent monitoring and tight control of blood glucose, many complications can be dramatically reduced. Find out what the American Diabetes Association has to say about the latest developments in preventing complications. Just fill out and return the coupon below or call our toll-free number.

They say the simple things in life are best. That's especially true when it comes to blood glucose monitoring. And that's why LifeScan offers two ways to make monitoring simple.

The ONE TOUCH® BASIC® System is the value-priced meter for people who simply want an accurate reading quickly and easily.

The ONE TOUCH® II System takes simple monitoring a step further with a 250-test memory with date and time, and an automatic 14-day test average.

PRESS POWER, INSERT STRIP.   APPLY SAMPLE. NO WIPING. NO TIMING.   ACCURATE RESULTS IN 45 SECONDS.

Whichever you choose, you'll be using the blood glucose monitoring system that's recommended by more physicians, diabetes educators and pharmacists. And by using Genuine ONE TOUCH® Test Strips, you ensure the accuracy that LifeScan is known for.

You'll also receive the assurance of our 30-day, money-back guarantee. As well as our 24-hour, toll-free customer service.*

ONE TOUCH® Brand Systems. Simple solutions to your most basic needs.

MY NEEDS ARE BASIC.
WHAT I WANT MOST
IN A MONITORING SYSTEM
IS SIMPLICITY.

For diabetes and life.

LIFESCAN INC.

a Johnson-Johnson company

©1995 LifeScan Inc. Milpitas, California 95035
*Call LifeScan Customer Services, 1 800 227-8862, for more information.
AW054-299

BEST SELLERS

WITH MORE THAN THREE MILLION ONE TOUCH® METERS SOLD, IT'S HARD TO KEEP US ON THE SHELF.

Fact is, with more than three million ONE TOUCH® meters and over two billion test strips sold, our numbers speak for themselves. Loud and clear. Which makes LifeScan the market leader. So you can take stock in the fact that our experienced sales team is fully prepared to help you manage your category in a way that will build both sales and profits. Plan now to book your orders. Call your local sales team representative or 1 800 524-7226 for assistance.

Simple to Demonstrate, Recommend and Sell.

- Number One Market Share – provides you with the highest sales potential in the category

- Number One HBC SKU in Dollar Sales – provides you with the highest dollar sales potential in the category

- Number One Consumer-Preferred Blood Glucose System – provides you with the highest consumer appeal in the category

- Number One Low-Priced Meter – ONE TOUCH® BASIC® System provides expanded market opportunities in the low-price category

- Number One Full-Featured Meter – ONE TOUCH® Profile™ System offers more tracking features than any other home monitoring system

- Number One Test Strip – best-selling Genuine ONE TOUCH® Test Strips for both best-sellers

For diabetes and life.

a Johnson-Johnson company

Presenting the 10 calorie,
fat free cookie.

(Actual size)

Presenting 10 calorie, fat free Jell-O.

(Actual size)

Even fat free snacks can be
loaded with calories. So why
settle for just a bite? Sugar Free
Strawberry Kiwi Jell-O Gelatin.

Sugar Free

JELL-O

Strawberry Kiwi

SHOULDDDDDDDDDDA,
SHOULDDDDA, **CLICK**, **CLICK**
SHOULDABOUGHT, **CLICK**,
SHOULDABOUGHTA,
CLICK, **CLICK**, **CLICK**,
SHOULDABOUGHTAMARINER,
SHOULDABOUGHTAMARINER,
CLICK, **CLICK**,

TRYING TO START SOME TROUBLE? SHOULD'VE GONE WITH THE COMPANY THAT PIONEERED OUTBOARD EFI TECHNOLOGY FOR QUICK, DEPENDABLE STARTS. SHOULDA BOUGHT A MARINER.

PEAK PERFORMANCE. *EFI provides instantaneous response and quicker acceleration.*

QUICK, DEPENDABLE STARTING. *Mariner EFI gives you quick, turn-key starts in any weather conditions.*

SMOOTH AS SILK. *Whether at idle or top speed, EFI provides smooth, quiet operation.*

JUST IN CASE. *Electronic protection system provides audible and visual warnings, plus automatic RPM reduction should engine over-rev or over-heat.*

NyQuil: *Fisherman And His Goldfish*

MAN: Oh, Izzy, this cold. I'm so stuffed up. (MUSIC) It feels like I'm underwater, too.

(MUSIC) (SFX: MAN SNEEZES IN & OUT)

(SFX: MAN COUGHS IN & OUT) This sneezing and coughing could last all night.

My eyes won't shut either.

I need NyQuil for relief so I can rest,
SUPER: USE AS DIRECTED

'cause I have plans in the morning. What, I can't say. MALE ANNCR: With NyQuil he gets relief, so he'll

sleep and wake up

to a good morning.

(MUSIC) (SFX: FISH GASPS IN & OUT)

MAN: Don't look. MALE ANNCR: NyQuil.

The nightime sniffling, sneezing, coughing, aching, stuffy head, fever, so you can rest

and have a good morning medicine. (MUSIC OUT)

Orthoxicol: *Take Control*

(SFX: WATER BUBBLING IN)

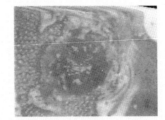

(SFX: WATER BUBBLING OUT) FEMALE ANNCR: Feeling blocked up?

Trust Orthoxicol for control of colds

and flu.

(SFX: WATER DRAINING, DEEP BREATH IN & OUT)

Take Orthoxicol. Take control.

SUPER: USE CAPLETS ONLY AS DIRECTED.

Orthoxicol: *Take Control*

(SFX: COUGHING IN & OUT)

FEMALE ANNCR: Dry, tickly cough.

Trust Orthoxical for control of coughs,

colds and flu.

(SFX: ELECTRIC STATIC IN & OUT)

SUPER: IF SYMPTOMS PERSIST CONSULT YOUR DOCTOR

Take Orthoxical. Take Control.

SUPER: USE CAPLETS ONLY AS DIRECTED

and client focus on Campaign Ideas. This is our currency for the development and assessment of advertising.

4. *Coach the Agency to Success*—Too many clients believe one of their primary responsibilities is to evaluate the agency's submissions. This word "evaluate" is drenched in criticism, finding what is wrong versus what is right with an idea. Instead of evaluating we should be involved in coaching. ASAP provides you with ample opportunity to coach. It doesn't come down to a question of buying or not buying advertising, but what ideas you want to explore and learn more about. Effective coaches do it in a manner that others understand and are motivated to achieve. In other words, they bring out the best in their players.

Broaden Your Knowledge and Enhance Your Skills

Creating the brand loyalty that comes from the development of great brands and even effective advertising doesn't just happen. It takes exceptional marketing managers who know and dutifully undertake their responsibilities. And, it takes skills. All of which can be yours through the instruction in this book and with some hard work. This book addresses:

- **Critical Areas of Brand Building and Advertising—**We take a client perspective. Brand building and great advertising flow from sound strategic marketing. So, Part I, **Pre-Production,** serves as a pathfinder for the book turning on the notion of how to think. Part II, **Building a Brand Through Power Positioning,** deals with brand positioning and each of its essential elements. Importantly, it introduces the concept of *Power Positioning* to ensure the brand positioning becomes competitive, ownable, and enduring in the marketplace. Part III, **Managing Really Great Advertising,** defines what we mean by really great advertising. It covers the ad strategy and fundamentals of effective advertising such as the Campaign Idea, executional development and practices to make your advertising more compelling. Part IV, **Processes That Work,** provides a process to leverage creative development, practices for managing and enhancing the client–agency relationship, and principles for making the creative meeting productive. Finally, Part V, **Post-Production,** provides a check on your personal development and suggests ways to further enhance your brand building and advertising management skills.

As you will see, we deal with these major elements in a progressive manner. One cannot expect to play Carnegie Hall without first going through a building process. You start out learning the language of music, becoming familiar with the musical instrument and engaging in hours of practice directed at developing your talents. Likewise, one cannot do a professional job of brand building and leading the process to creating great advertising, without first establishing a competitive positioning and understanding one's role in its creation.

- **Skills**—Our educational systems are failing in large part because they fill our heads with facts and don't teach young people how to think and do anymore! Being able to define "positioning" won't make you more effective, but developing the skills to create a brand positioning will. In our family, each of my daughters learns how to drive using an automatic transmission. When they become familiar with the rules of the road, and the vehicle, my wife and I move them on to a stick shift. Recently, my 15-year-old told me she was going out with my wife to drive the stick shift. When I asked her if she knew how to drive it she responded with a resounding "Yes!" "How so?" I asked. Well, her older sister told her how to handle the stick and clutch. No sooner had she gone out the door that I could hear the screeching of the automobile, smell the burning of the clutch and was greeted, in turn, by the deafening silence of a stalled car. It is easy to understand the words, yet more difficult to put them in practice.

Likewise, much of what we will share with you will appear rather easy. However, few will ever master or become versatile in the principles. Just as my daughter has learned the skills to drive a stick shift through patience and practice, we set out to help you develop skills, not just learn principles. This book is, we hope, not a textbook. Instead, it is geared to putting you on the road to developing skills. So, you'll be asked to develop a brand positioning and ad strategy statement, and put your learnings into practice. My 15-year-old is now quite skillful at driving a stick shift. In time, with practice, you can grow to become a more skillful brand builder and advertiser.

- **Toolbox**—We have provided you with a toolbox filled with tools we have found effective in focusing our thinking and developing our skills. Apply these tools against your own specific brand, service, or business. The more you use them, the more proficient you will become in developing the needed skill set to be an effective brand builder and advertiser. Importantly, use of the toolbox will serve to improve the likelihood of your developing a great brand and great advertising.

One other note about the toolbox: feel free to modify the tools. If you find that you need a needle nose pliers versus the standard type, you would undoubtedly use it (if it were available to you). If you find a specific tool doesn't quite work 100% for you, modify it so it better meets your needs.

Beginner's Mind

Here's a story that is relevant to the journey we are about to embark upon together. It deals with a philosophy professor who wanted to learn more about Zen. A student arranged for the professor to meet with the foremost Zen master in all of Japan, perhaps in the entire world.

The professor went to the Zen master's humble abode where he was greeted by the slight, still, gentle personage of the master. At once the professor, who had an encyclopedic mind, began spilling out everything he had learned about the subject of Zen. The master invited the professor into his home to sit and share some tea. As the Zen master brewed the tea, the professor continued to talk and talk. The Zen master, listening patiently, began to pour the tea and the professor continued telling him all that he knew of Zen. While the professor spilled his facts the Zen master overfilled the cup and spilled the tea. Soon, the kimono of the talking professor became wet, snapping him to the realization that the Zen master was overfilling the cup. "Look, look what you are doing. You are overfilling the cup," cried the professor. The Zen master stopped pouring, looked up and responded, "Just as this cup is overflowing so is your mind with opinions and worthless facts. If you truly want to learn Zen you must first empty your mind so we may refill it."

This story is our invitation to you to empty your mind of opinions, preconceived notions, and beliefs, and to be open to new learnings. It is by emptying your mind and embracing the Buddhist concept of Beginner's Mind that you will gain fresh new perspectives.

By the time you have completed reading this book, working the exercises, and using the tools we present, you will not only be able to more professionally assess the Kellogg's Frosted Flakes Cereal TV ad we shared with you earlier but the positioning of any brand, in the absolute and relative to yours, and advertising from any category, in any medium.

We are now ready to tackle brand positioning and its importance in creating brand loyalty in an age of sameness. With Beginner's Mind we move on to the next chapter!

PART TWO

Building a Brand Through Power Positioning

CHAPTER 2

Positioning—The Foundation for the Brand

"It's job number one!"

As we mentioned at the start of this book, we take a client (i.e., brand marketing manager) perspective to the subject of branding and advertising. A client's perspective is one that is rooted in sound strategic marketing management.

So, What's Positioning?

The answer to this question is rather interesting. Managers will state that positioning is: your target audience; or your benefit; or, perhaps, it is what you want customers to think about you (such as the image); and so forth.

We all have a passing knowledge of positioning. After all, we've been positioning ourselves and others virtually all of our lives. We get a poor grade on a test at school and we begin to think of ways in which we might explain this unpleasant piece of news to that critical and demanding species of beings we refer to as our parents:

- The (unreasonable) teacher tested us on things he did not teach us and weren't even in the textbook!

- This test doesn't count very much, it's only 20% of my grade.
- I can make it up with extra-credit assignments.
- The teacher drops our lowest grade, so this test won't even count.
- Everybody in the class failed the exam—even Jane Witney, the class brain!

The way we serve up this unfortunate occurrence is limited only by one's imagination (which is typically in direct proportion to the perceived penalties), applied in context to his/her parents' hot buttons.

We are positioning all the time. How are you going to explain to your spouse why you were two hours late to celebrate your anniversary with a romantic dinner at that exclusive restaurant reserved six months in advance? Or, how will you propose an assistant for promotion, particularly one with whom your boss is not particularly fond? Or, how will you deal with potential objections you anticipate from a penny-pinching customer to a price hike that you are about to take? Positioning is a full time job. It's also **job number one** when it comes to sound strategic marketing, brand building, and the development of great advertising.

When we think about positioning we are really getting at how we want an intended audience (be it one or many) to perceive our situation. More precisely, we define brand positioning as **the way we want customers to perceive, think, and feel about our brand versus competitive entries.** It's the specific piece of turf we want to occupy in potential customers' minds and hearts as they view the market landscape before them. Positioning can be simply captured in the statement on page 19.

Positioning involves six elements (which will be treated in detail in subsequent chapters devoted to each one). These are:

- Customer Need
- Target Customer Group
- Competitive Framework
- Benefit
- Reasons-Why
- Brand Character

While most managers have some understanding of positioning, few have a real appreciation for the basic concept of brand positioning. They are distant admirers as opposed to committed practitioners. This is evidenced

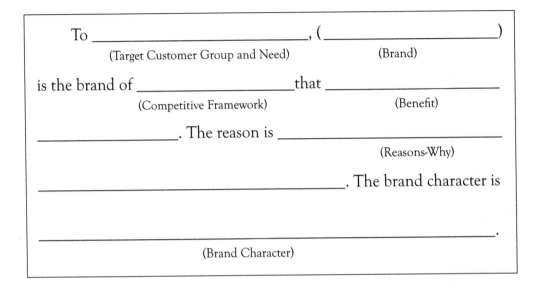

To _____, (_____)
         (Target Customer Group and Need)   (Brand)

is the brand of _____that _____
        (Competitive Framework)   (Benefit)

_____. The reason is _____
                                  (Reasons-Why)

_____. The brand character is

_____.
             (Brand Character)

by the few brands that have clear-cut positioning statements. Unfortunately, we are all too busy in our "right-sized" environments to do anything but execute. And, there's precious little time to even execute. Moreover, those that do "position" limit it to advertising versus establishing the brand. But, if you don't have a Brand Positioning Statement for your product you could be short-changing its potential. Worse yet, you could be rudderless, leaving your product to float wherever the changing currents take it.

Brand positioning asserts the reason-for-being for the brand among select customers versus competitive products or services. It should **serve to provide a blueprint for the development and franchise building of the brand.** Therefore, brand positioning should precede the development of all substrategies such as pricing, distribution, and packaging, to name just a few of the many marketing mix elements and planks. Brand positioning that firmly takes hold in the marketplace becomes your equity. It creates value for the brand that goes beyond the mere physical properties of the product, sales, and/or market share position.

Those companies without an established brand positioning will, more often than not, chase their tails squandering precious support dollars to introduce new marketing, promotion, public relations and advertising campaigns on an annual basis that go nowhere with customers. What's more, the brand will lack the integrity needed in its marketing mix elements to establish a meaningful basis for positively influencing customer preference, ultimately leading to confusing customers and diluting its efforts.

Still Waters Run Deep

An iceberg makes an interesting metaphor regarding the importance and role of brand positioning. Unlike what was shown in the blockbuster movie "Titanic," those unfortunate ships, and their crews, meeting their demise by a collision with an iceberg, are struck by what they cannot see. No, this isn't about the fog that, in the movie, obscured the vision of the crew. Nor is it the night that blinded the crew and passengers to the danger that lay before them. Instead, the ship is more likely to collide with that part of the iceberg that lies below the sea. The largest mass of an iceberg, about 85–90%, lies below the sea, where the human eye cannot see. Similarly, the largest and most important driver in creating the brand is its competitive brand positioning. The various marketing mix elements, and in particular the communications, are what make the positioning real, just as the tip of the iceberg makes its mass real. Without a competitive brand positioning, however, one does not have an iceberg. One merely has floating surface ice.

Brand positioning establishes in **strategic language** the **competitive reason** for customer selection of your brand versus that of your competition and the unique relationship you hope to enjoy.

- *Strategic Language*—One of the areas we find most vexing to clients is the specificity of wording one's positioning. Clients, rightfully so, scrutinize the words they use to coin their brand positionings. However, most often the effort goes wrongfully in arriving at the customer language for the basic brand proposition. Customer language is the province of resource providers such as the advertising agency, not the marketing team. The agency can do it better, much better! (If not, you are either on the wrong side of the business or you had better get yourself a new creative team.) Instead, exacting efforts should go into the strategic thinking and its articulation.

- **Competitive Reason**—The marketer needs to go beyond mere product classification to identify a meaningful way to differentiate the nascent brand versus competition. (More on this subject when we get to the "benefit" in chapter 7.)

Positioning Example—Tide provides an instructive example regarding the use of the Brand Positioning Statement. Here's an example of an inferred brand positioning for Tide laundry detergent:

To <u>moms with active children and husbands . . . who have heavy duty</u>
(Target Customer Group and Need)
<u>cleaning needs and want to keep their clothes and their families</u>

<u>looking their best,</u> <u>(Tide)</u> is the brand of <u>laundry care detergent</u>
     (Brand)   (Competitive Framework)
<u>products</u> that <u>is best for your clothes (cleaning, protecting fabrics</u>
                    (Benefit)
<u>etc.) and you.</u> The reason is <u>a) special formulations with heavy duty</u>
                      (Reasons-Why)
<u>cleaners (e.g., grease releasers), special fabric protectors (e.g., color</u>

<u>guard), etc., and b) endorsement by authorities.</u> The brand character is

<u>strong ("a rock"), traditional, dependable, commanding yet practical.</u>
(Brand Character)

We've known Tide for years as being the "heavy duty cleaning detergent." Tide has been positioned as getting out the dirt that families get into. This brand positioning for Tide has been played out in all its marketing mix elements. It has been emphatically reflected in its advertising. But, today Tide has evolved to more—going beyond dirt and even clean. This is made possible by changes in the product's formulation and introduction of line extensions.

Going Beyond the "Age of Sameness"

We live in an "age of sameness." Or, at least whatever advantages we enjoy can soon be neutralized by determined and creative competitors. When you observe one brand versus another in the same category, you see a basic sameness. Think for a moment about your brand, your company. Chances are your product's physical attributes are not dissimilar from competition. Pricing, distribution, terms, and other important elements are also on par with those of other brands and companies. Not even knowledge is sacrosanct from this encroachment of sameness. Look at your marketing colleagues, or even yourself. Chances are high that marketing managers in your company have experience working with other companies. So, too, your product research and development, sales, and purchasing managers have a knowledge and experience base that was imported from some other company or companies.

This theme of "how you think" that we introduced earlier is important to revisit. In this age of sameness "how you think" can be the critical difference in gaining a sustainable, competitive advantage. It could represent your company's and product's strategic weapon in creating brand loyalty.

But first there is a myth that needs to be dispelled. The myth is that creativity is for people in certain functions. Creativity is for agency people and, more specifically, agency creatives. Moreover, the myth extends to confining creativity to select uses. For example, it's okay to be creative when transforming strategic language into customer language. It is not only acceptable but also highly desirable to be creative in developing language that will appeal to, and resonate with, customers. For other people, or at other times, we give lip service to creativity but do not put our money where our mouths are. Imagine the reaction if the company's chief financial officer is labeled as "creative." Now how is it that he is able to afford a new Porsche?

If we are to break out of this age of sameness we need to be extraordinarily creative in the way we think. Creative strategic thinking is a requisite for every marketing manager. It is absolutely essential in the development of a competitive brand positioning. We need to be creative strategists who can envision a future and a game plan to get us there. Each of the six essential elements of brand positioning provides us with an opportunity to ply our creative strategic thinking. Each provides us with an opportunity to develop a brand and, in that manner, set our product or service apart from the competition in a way that is meaningful to our customers. Anyone can easily fill out the Brand Positioning Statement. But, it is the creative strategist that will create a positioning to build a brand and enable a competitive advantage to be gained and sustained in the marketplace. Strategic discipline must be married to creative strategic thinking for the ultimate success.

KEY PRINCIPLES

Summary

✔ Positioning is job number one when it comes to sound strategic marketing, brand building, and the development of great advertising.

✔ We define brand positioning as the way we want customers to perceive, think, and feel about our brand versus competitive entries.

✔ Brand positioning is composed of the following six elements: customer need, target customer group, competitive framework, benefit, reason-why, and brand character.

✔ Brand positioning should serve to provide a blueprint for the development and franchise building of the brand. Therefore, brand positioning should precede the development of all sub-strategies such as pricing, distribution, and packaging, to name just a few of the many marketing mix elements.

✔ Brand positioning establishes, in strategic language, the competitive reason for customer selection of your brand versus that of your competition, and the unique relationship you hope to enjoy.

✔ In this age of sameness, "how you think" can be the critical difference in gaining a sustainable competitive advantage. It could represent your company's and product's strategic weapon in creating brand loyalty.

✔ If we are to break out of this age of sameness we need to be creative strategists who can envision a future and a game plan to get us there. Each of the six essential elements of brand positioning provides us with an opportunity to ply our creative strategic thinking.

✔ Strategic discipline must be married to creative strategic thinking for the ultimate success.

CHAPTER 3

Prospecting for Pay Dirt—Customer Needs and Knowing When to "Lead with Need"

Gary Davidson (the first president of the American Basketball Association, co-founder of the World Hockey Association, and founder of the World Football League) was once aptly described by a sports columnist as "always eager to meet the demand for something nobody asked for."

Steve Rushin
Sports Illustrated,
April 16, 1994

Customer Needs and the Brand Positioning

Understanding, developing, and evolving—even *creating*—customer needs (such as the entrepreneur Gary Davidson did, more than once) is at the core of every successful business venture. This is no less true when it comes to crafting a winning brand positioning. In fact, it can rightly be said that if brand positioning is the starting point for achieving really *great advertising*, then customer needs are the starting point for constructing that winning brand positioning.

More often than not, however, we find our interaction with *real customer needs* to be pretty limited. If we are working on an established business (especially a large one), we may only review the known "category needs" when a bi-annual Usage & Attitude or Market Segmentation Study comes in. More than likely, we take for granted that the inherent needs-structure of our category has been well established and is unlikely to change much anyway.

But the truth is that—much like the tectonic earth-plates under our feet—a category's needs-structure is shifting, evolving, and emerging in some fashion all the time, whether we perceive it or not. Marketers who spend even a little time working in new products know this to be the case. (In fact, they are probably the closest to being customer need "experts" in an organization—or at least they *should* be.) And, if you talk with new products people about customer needs, you learn a number of key operating principles:

1. You have to *stay current* with shifting and emerging needs by using an assortment of methods: (a) **talking to customers** on a regular basis; using qualitative sessions—incorporating short-period diaries, product sorts, and laddering techniques—to take frequent snapshots of the need-state terrain; (b) **using intuition**, based on past experiences as a customer to "guesstimate" underlying need shifts and swings; (c) **borrowing from other categories** for parallels and insights. (Most package goods companies are using the same research companies to do their need-state spade work; so many of the output models are similar anyway.); and (d) **fielding occasional quantitative studies**, especially ones that allow for trend-tracking.

2. To build the most compelling, competitive brand positionings you must link up both *physical (functional) and psychographic (emotional) needs*. Take a look at Starbucks' amazing success in revolutionizing America's coffee business. At the heart of their business proposition—*and* their brand positioning—lies a consciously crafted means of addressing emerging functional and emotional coffee-customer needs:

Functional Needs:

"I want a bolder, more robust tasting coffee"; "I'm looking for more ways to 'mix' my coffee drinks"; "I'd love to drink coffee that's truly authentic."

Emotional Needs:

"I look at coffee time as a true social time . . . and I'd like it to be more of an experience"; "What I'm seeking is 'coffee entertainment.'"

Imagine what Starbucks would have been without satisfying the truly "differentiating" emotional needs—just a stronger cup of coffee! And think, too, how much more competitive they've made themselves vis-à-vis traditional canned coffees by addressing the emotional dimension of coffee drinking!

3. If at all possible, you want to know the *relative order of importance* among a given set of physical and emotional needs, plus how well you and your competition *deliver against the important needs.* To know these things with any certainty usually requires a thorough, quantitative study; but you *can* get directional answers from some careful probing in qualitative research. Whichever method is used, the idea is **not** just to look for performance "gaps" (between important needs and customer satisfaction levels); rather, the idea is to "go prospecting" within the implied need-state structure to look for hidden veins that might pay off:

A client in the sanitary protection business recently recognized that achieving a parity performance on the top two physical needs of the category was all their core competencies would allow. So, how to find a way to win on some other meaningful customer need? This client elected to move further down the emotional needs hierarchy, and focused against an emerging 1990s mindset best described as "Feeling more like your natural self." This represented a need that their brand positioning could incorporate; it also represented a need ranked lower on the general category list, but considerably higher on an opportunistic segment (the twenty-something segment), *within the category's list. Prospecting, in this case, led to a perceived emotional advantage among that segment.*

4. Finally, remember that, more than anything else, *innovation is what makes the relative order of importance rankings change* within a given slate of customer needs. For years, fat-free cookies and chips were "off the radar screen" of snack buying customers' need-states. Certainly the anti-cholesterol and less-fat-in-your-diet news of the 1980s contributed to elevating a lower-in-fat need among customers. But it wasn't until products like Snackwell's and the likes of Baked Lays that this need became so important to so many snack customers. In other words, once customers were convinced they could have their snacking indulgence *and* their dietary health needs met simultaneously, they were no longer willing to settle for indulgence alone.

These operating principles are equally useful, whether you are creating a brand positioning for an all-new product or category, or whether you are looking to re-position a longstanding brand that needs to become more competitive (that's trapped in that "age of sameness"). In fact, taking the time to lay out the "known" or perceived current need-states on a map is an essential warm-up exercise for any new positioning work. You can then have customers confirm or deny the accuracy of that map.

A good example of the effectiveness of this kind of exercise can be seen in some recent work by a major cracker and cookie manufacturer in Mexico. Using progressive qualitative research (one-on-one interviews and focus groups), this client derived an updated understanding of its "need-state architecture." More specifically (as illustrated in the chart on page 30), the manufacturer learned that 11 elicited need-states formed six need-state "camps."

These need-state camps became the foundation for their first *Portfolio Positioning.* Once—with heavy users' inputs—they were able to link up distinct

Cookie Need-States and Camps

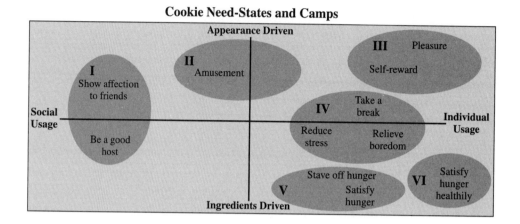

product traits (from among their wide variety of cookie products) with each of the six need-state camps, they had the bedrock material for each brand's benefits and reasons why, or, each brand's *positioning nucleus* (see table below).

However customer needs are determined and delineated, they play a critical, first-step role in any serious brand positioning effort. There *is* one

Cookie Need-State Product Trait Linkages

More Emotional _____ More Rational

Need States	Indulge Myself	Change My Mood		Share Good Times With Friends	Feed Me	
		Amuse Me	Comfort Me		Satisfy My Hunger	Good For Me
Product Traits	1. Very sweet 2. Chocolate 3. Layers of ingredients 4. You can taste the fat	1. Colorful 2. Shapes 3. Play-value Sizing & Portions	1. Lighter • Texture • Portion 2. Mild sweetness good with beverages	1. Good pieces • Sized for handing around 2. Fillings and special flavors	1. Heavier texture 2. More bulk density/ grams per piece	1. Food-value ingredients • Wheat • Grains 2. Less sugar 3. Plain looking (dough-like)

"watch-out" to keep in mind as you prospect and map your category's needs: *don't confuse* **customer needs** *with* **manufacturer needs.** In other words, make sure you meet the needs of the intended heavy user, and not merely pay them lip service. From time to time it happens that a company's core competencies (or even their asset base) constrains them from meeting a category's basic needs. Instead of investing in new competencies or assets, they may infer customer needs that are merely wishful thinking.

Something like this happened a couple of years ago in the U.S. beverage market. A key player wanted to enter the sports beverage segment, wherein meeting the most basic category need of *fast-drinking* requires a still, or non-carbonated, formulation. But this manufacturer had a carbonated-only asset base. Their entry: a slightly carbonated isotonic drink. The results: a very limited slice of the marketshare pie.

Customer Needs and Advertising

The value of understanding and leveraging customer needs is not limited to brand positioning development. As with any of the other six key elements of a brand positioning, customer needs also play a pivotal role in a brand's advertising. When this happens, the brand's copy is said to *lead with need*.

What are some of those times when, for added competitiveness, you might want your advertising to lead with need?

Grow the Category—The dominant share leader of the cup-of-noodle category in Japan launched a major, new advertising campaign in 1993 (after being off-air for several years). The copy words were limited to a very simple query, "HUNGRY? Cup-of-Noodles . . . by Nissin" executed in a clever prehistoric-parody format. The results were impressive growth for the brand . . . *and the cup-of-noodles category.* It was precisely what Nissin intended. Having lost significant category ground to new domestic and imported "mini-meals" and snacks (like Pringles), they realized it was time to reclaim some of those casual eating occasions. And what better way to do that than to reclaim ownership of the most basic category need—satisfying big, on-the-go hunger? Leading with need . . .

Make a Need Part of Your Equity—In a parity game with a number of competitors, one way to get a leg up is by appearing to *own* a key need. Doing this effectively requires two things: 1) a creative, ownable way to express the need in question; and 2) a steady investment against that expression over time. There's an oral care brand in Procter & Gamble's stable that has done both of these quite nicely—Scope Mouthwash. They have cleverly taken one of the most basic mouthwash need-states—freshening bad breath upon awakening—and re-written it in their own (copyrighted) style: *"morning breath."* And what they have steadfastly done over the years is remind prospects that (only) Scope fights morning breath. Does Scope *beat* Listerine in satisfying this need? No . . . but you sure do get that impression. Leading with need . . .

Establish a New Segment—This is literally the juncture where new-products marketing and customer needs should intersect. And this only makes sense when you consider that creating a new segment almost always depends on: 1) gaining a foothold with a small set of lead adopters (who are probably ahead of most people in understanding the emerging needs underpinning the new segment); and 2) broadening that user base by *educating the masses* on what the lead adopters already know. Arm & Hammer baking soda toothpaste is not only the number five share brand of dentifrice in the United States now, but it is also the father of a segment that all leading brands now have entries in. How did such a segment amass such a following? Simple: Arm & Hammer took time to educate prospects about the need for a "more thorough kind of clean"—more like the feel of your teeth just after a hygienist's cleaning. Leading with need . . .

Expand the Target Group—It is usually a good assumption to make that different demographic/psychographic target groups probably have a different hierarchy of need-states. Although there will always be common needs across a number of target groups, the relative importance of each may be quite different. Going after a new target market is not unlike establishing a new target segment: highlighting the basic, most important need-state(s) helps a great deal in attracting new business. Neutrogena obviously understood this principle when it introduced and advertised its translucent amber Acne-Prone Skin Bar for teens; intentionally, the teen bar *looked* identical to the base brand bar (the one used for years by their moms). So it was essential that in initial advertising teens learned the difference between the two. As the brand expressed in its print ad headlines: "Break the breakout cycle." The teen bar had all the gentleness of the original (that is, it met the gentle cleansing need), and it met an even more important other need among teens—it helped control acne breakout. Leading with need . . .

Leverage News or Trends (for example, to Create a New-Use Occasion)—Once in a great while it happens that a new study is released, or an old ingredient gets new life thanks to suddenly realized, beneficial properties, or some new trend fits a given brand's profile. When that happens, the given brand may find itself with a real or perceived advantage—more specifically, a need-state advantage. Of course, such advantages are not always merely opportunistic or fortuitous. Some brand marketers (and their respective R&D partners) work long and hard to deliver them.

Take the case of Bayer Aspirin. Long regarded as the generic name in aspirin, Bayer had also once been the leading analgesic brand as well. But the advent of Tylenol, Advil, and Aleve (not to mention Excedrin and others) took its toll on the Bayer brand's standing. Well into the 1980s, Bayer was struggling to compete in the expanding "pain reliever wars." But behind the scenes, they were diligently seeking a way back to the forefront—by exploring other needs that pure aspirin (i.e., Bayer) might satisfy **that other analgesic compounds could not.** By the mid-nineties, Bayer had found the need: helping to prevent heart attacks (a fast-emerging need among an aging baby boomer population). Clinical studies showed that aspirin—along with proper diet and exercise—could reduce the *risk of a second heart attack by up to 50%.* But in their advertising, Bayer cleverly made satisfying the literal need more applicable to the mass market by including people who had never had a first heart attack.

The results were a significant increase in sales and a new marketplace respect for a timeless brand. Well into the late 1990s, Bayer's selling line continues to be: *"Powerful Pain Relief . . . And So Much More,"* with the "so much more" being its preventive efficacy against heart attacks.

In a similar vein, Tums Antacid Tablets have more recently leveraged news to add another important need-satisfaction to their brand bundle. With the rise in the incidence and awareness of osteoporosis (particularly among middle-aged and older women), the need for *calcium supplements* has grown dramatically. Enter Tums with its calcium-rich formula. No longer merely an antacid, Tums is suddenly a legitimate calcium supplement. In their advertising, they compare Tums' calcium levels to those in a quart of milk. Tums is now the *only* antacid that can also deliver required calcium levels. In the process, the brand also created a nifty additional use occasion. Leading with need . . .

KEY PRINCIPLES

Summary

✔ The first step is to re-examine customer needs in any brand positioning work (new product development, established brand re-positioning, portfolio positioning).

✔ Check customer need hierarchy for changes on a regular basis—the need-state landscape is always shifting.

✔ Address both the functional and emotional need-states when aiming to craft a more compelling and competitive brand positioning.

✔ Through quantitative or qualitative methods, try to understand the relative order of importance and comparative brand satisfaction levels for each key need.

✔ There are times when leading with need makes sense for a brand's advertising: Category Growth; Need-Ownership for an Edge; Segment Establishment; Target Expansion; and Leveraging News and Trends to Create a New-Use Occasion.

CHAPTER 4

Sighting the Right Bull's-Eye
Target Customer

---

*"We're chasing our tails for 18- to 49-year-old idiots when 10,000 people
are turning 50 every day."*

*Former CBS president Howard Stringer
on the folly of network TV ignoring older
viewers. (Chicago Tribune, April 17, 1996)*

***T**hink about it*. It's the heading for the column in which the above quote appeared. Think about it. Mr. Stringer makes a rather provocative comment that suggests a number of issues worth surfacing.

- It identifies a penchant for defining target groups by demographics (i.e., age, gender, income, and education, and so on). In this case, it is 18- to 49-year olds.
- Moreover, it makes us aware of the practice of defining our target in the same manner as we have always done, or the way our competitors define it. This practice of chasing after 18- to 49-year-olds has probably been in place for many years, decades even, without question. Also, it represents the age demography shared by all major network competitors.
- The statement evidences the lag inherent in the way many companies compete. Here is a significant trend in demography, the aging of America

that is going largely ignored by the TV networks. It is ignored in programming. It is ignored in casting. And, it is likely to remain largely ignored until that time when it has either grown much larger and powerful, and/or some competitor demonstrates it is able to successfully cater to this rapidly emerging population. Then, the others will follow, perhaps even to the point of ignoring their franchise base. This sets up the pendulum effect of swinging mindlessly back and forth from one target customer group to another. Or it can lead to the development of multiple targets (which the networks may more easily serve than marketers can with a single product or service).

- We may also infer the absence of meaningful segmentation. There are undoubtedly a wide variety of segments of viewers who may be more precisely defined, contributing to a brand positioning that differentiates one network station from another. Also, the identification of more precisely defined segments should encourage the development of programming that better caters to the specific needs of a given segment.

- In Mr. Stringer's quote, the term "idiots" brings into focus two other important factors in defining the target customer group: current habits and mindset. In the case of idiots one gets the impression that the target is certainly not very intelligent (to say the least), and their viewing habits may be well served by the mindless drivel broadcast by the networks.

How we go about defining the target customer group has significant implications in the positioning and establishment of a brand. There needs to be a better way to define the target group other than demographics (the media target), past practices (the way it was), or competitive behavior (the herd effect).

Defining the Target Customer Group

We define the target customer group as the **most likely prospects** who have a **similar set of needs and concerns** that **our product or service can satisfy.** In this way, we focus against all potential users of the product in a manner that will be relevant to them. We urge clients to go beyond defining the target by demographics, past practices, or the way competition is doing it.

1. **Most Likely Prospects**—The focus on *most likely prospects* comprises two major issues. First, we must decide what is the most important constituency to the successful creation of brand loyalty. Second, it requires us to identify who is most likely to purchase, use, or recommend our intended brand within a given constituency.

• **Most important constituency**—Is it the purchaser or the gatekeeper? Is it the ultimate user? Is it the key influencer or one whom recommends the brand? For example, in the introduction of the Reach toothbrush brand three major constituencies presented themselves. One is the dental professional who represents a key influencer in consumers' purchase behavior and the success of Oral-B (a premium-priced product). A second is the retail trade which is responsible for pushing the product out to and upon consumers via distribution (i.e., making it available), merchandising, and pricing. Brands such as Pepsodent and Tek toothbrushes owe their success to aggressive trade activity which resulted in pricing to the consumer of eight or even ten toothbrushes for only $1.00. The third is the consumer. No toothbrush brand had been able to establish a loyal franchise (i.e., create brand loyalty) by going directly to the consumer.

In the case of the Reach toothbrush brand we chose to target the consumer constituency. While we recognized the importance of the dental professional community in establishing the success of Oral-B toothbrushes and enabling the premium pricing the brand enjoyed, qualitative research uncovered that Reach would encounter significant, pernicious resistance. This traced to the fact that the design of the Reach toothbrush did not comply with perceived standards of efficacy and safety. The standards were established in the late 1940s for a straight (versus angled) design, one level of bristles (Reach had bi-level bristles), and soft bristles (Reach was a combination of soft outer bristles to clean along the gum line and medium hard inner bristles to scrub teeth clean). The standards established before the introduction of the Reach toothbrush brand were perceived by dental professionals as sacrosanct. So they blindly adhered to them even in the face of clinical evidence which demonstrated the superior cleaning ability of the Reach toothbrush.

The trade did not represent a viable lead constituency since they believed they made the market for toothbrushes. Accordingly, they required deep cut feature pricing in order to push brands out to consumers at the previously disclosed eight or ten toothbrushes for $1.00 retail. This requirement undermined the establishment of brand loyalty with consumers and, importantly, made it impossible to achieve internal corporate profitability hurdles.

Instead, we believed the Reach toothbrush had a design that meaningfully differentiated itself from all competitors in the eyes and minds of consumers. The brush's unique design features translated to consumer perceptions of superior cleaning and cavity prevention efficacy. These were benefits for which we strongly believed consumers would be willing to pay a premium price versus brands hawked at retail and even those few (most notably Oral-B) which were being dispensed free and recommended by dental professionals.

- **Who Within the Constituency**—Within each of these major constituencies we need to choose further. For example, if we choose to go with the dental professionals (i.e., key influencers) we have further choices to make. Do we target dentists? Or dental hygienists who order the product and dispense it to patients? If we go with dentists, should we select a specific specialty such as orthodontists? Or periodontists?

In our case of marketing to the consumer constituency, we had to choose between toothbrush purchasers, gatekeepers, and users. There is overlap. A purchaser can also be the gatekeeper (for a household) and user. In fact, we chose moms, who by their role in the household of the mid-1970s put them in the position of purchaser, gatekeeper, and user of toothbrushes. Mom chose and bought for the family. When she did buy she purchased 2.7 toothbrushes per purchase occasion. What mom bought determined what dad, children, and she used to practice good oral hygiene!

2. *Similar Set of Needs and Concerns*—In order to identify the *most likely prospects* it is essential to also understand and capture their *needs and concerns*. This enables us to go beyond mere demographics to capture all potential users of a product. The needs and concerns are the bait with which we hope to capture a similar band of prospects.

Returning to the Reach toothbrush case history, we had to identify who would be willing to pay a premium price for a toothbrush. After all, all moms do not share the same needs and concerns. In peeling back the onion, we identified those moms most likely to purchase as desiring to do their absolute best to protect their families teeth against cavities and avoid costly, painful dental visits. These moms ensured their children had regular check-ups at the dentist's office, purchased and used a fluoride toothpaste (most likely Crest, which had the endorsement of the American Dental Association), and even had dental floss on hand for occasional usage.

Another interesting example is diet Coke. Prior to its introduction, women (particularly dieters) comprised the low-cal soft drink segment almost entirely. We believed the market was ripe for, and could be expanded with, a better-tasting, low-calorie cola entry. Instead of going only after women, we set out to attract males as well—not just dieters but anyone who appreciates great taste in a cola. The key copy words behind the Campaign Idea "Just for the taste of it" coupled with the lower case "d" in the trademark diet Coke (which has since been changed to a capital "D") evidenced a broader target defined by mindset and not mere demographics such as gender.

3. *Our Brand Can Satisfy*—Obviously, we need to be able to satisfy the needs and concerns of the target customer group. Had Reach toothbrush not demonstrated its superior efficacy in product design features and attributes, as well as better check-ups, it would have ultimately failed with consumers. Had diet Coke not had a unique, full-bodied great cola taste it would not have been able to grow the low-calorie segment, increase the composition of male consumers, nor achieve the leadership position in this same segment. The product has to deliver to the target, or you will fail miserably!

Beyond Demographics

Demographics are inadequate as the sole element in defining the target customer group. Demographics represent at best a media target. They assist us in identifying specific media, vehicles, and programming in which to reach our target. But, by themselves, demographics do not help us identify the most likely prospects for our brands, nor do they assist us in creating a compelling message.

If we were to specify our target as 25–34-year-old males we expose ourselves to a wide range of socioeconomic backgrounds and mindsets. There is a vast difference in need-mindsets between a 25- and a 34-year old, particularly if they occupy different lifestages (e.g., single versus married). This need-mindset difference is compounded by race, education, occupation, values, and such.

Imagine for a moment that we are marketing men's clothing. The typical target definition might be males 25 and older, with incomes greater than $25,000, who have some college. Now consider two males, both 34 years of age. Both have annual incomes of $35,000. Both have college experience. One is a garbage collector in Valley Stream, Long Island. The other is a high school French teacher in Winnetka, Illinois. It is very likely these two will be miles apart, not just in geography, but in interests, needs, values, taste, and such. A simple demographic description is insufficient for defining the target group in positioning our clothing line. We need to know more.

Balancing Size and Message Relevancy

Defining the target customer group represents a balancing act. We are balancing the size of the group with our ability to deliver a meaningful message. Imagine that we are selling to one person and one person only. If we are attempting to sell to just one person, we can learn about that person in great detail and then craft our message to appeal to him or her. We increase the probability that we will offer benefits and communicate in a way that is relevant and will lead the one to act in a manner consistent with our goal.

If we increase the target from one to 20, then our message may be expected to lose some of its power with the many, because the needs of the one may not be the same as the needs of the many. Worse yet, in trying to be for everyone we could suffer the consequence of being for no one. For most consumer products, the message is being developed for millions of people. This makes the task of creating a relevant message significantly more challenging.

Defining the target represents a balancing act of yet another kind, the balance between efficiency and effectiveness. The larger (and more diverse) the target customer group, the more efficient we are in reaching customers. On the other hand, the message can be expected to be diluted and miss the mark. Remember playing as a child on a seesaw? As one side goes up, the other side comes down. If we attempt to sell too many divergent mindsets, the weight of the effort will pull us down and send the message above the heads of the target customer group. We may enhance efficiency, as measured by cost-per-thousand consumers reached with our message, but we sacrifice effectiveness. Instead, we prefer to get our efficiency from being effective.

An example of the illusion of efficiency is found in the use of television advertising by large consulting companies. Somewhere along the line someone at these consulting companies was impressed by the efficiency of selling through television spots. The lure of reaching thousands of adult males, ages 35–59, can be very compelling from an efficiency standpoint. But think about it. How many adults per thousand are in a position to hire a consulting company? One that will undoubtedly cost six figures each month? How many of those, at that point in time, are actually in the market for the services of these consulting companies? Not to be overlooked, how many of these will hear the message they need to act in a 30-second TV spot? Our guess is as good as yours. Our guess, and we'll wager yours is too, that the answer to these questions is not many. So the bargain of delivering a message at the cost of, say, $9.50 per thousand, really turns out to be folly. The cost of getting the right one to act will be significantly more.

The same argument could be used for looking at the efficiency of 10- or 15-second TV spots. In talking with Brad Moore, a friend and former associate from our early days at Procter & Gamble who is currently president of Hallmark Productions, Inc., we learned that his company will employ the message length needed to tell its story. If that takes two minutes of prime time, he will use a 2-minute spot. His belief, which we advocate, is that six or eight or more 15-second TV spots will not do the business any good if the brand's story cannot be told in that time length. Again, it comes down to balancing efficiency and effectiveness. What may appear to be inefficient on a cost-per-spot basis (i.e., 2-minute versus 15-second) is effective and therefore more efficient on a cost-per-conversion basis.

Roping customers by a similar set of needs and concerns not only transcends demographics but assists us in telling our story in a way that is relevant. It helps us to be more effective. In being effective we put our companies in a position to be truly efficient on the basis it matters most: conversion of customers to our brand, creating brand loyalty, realizing premium margins, and profitability.

Examples of Target Mindsets

A number of successful companies reflect a target customer group in their advertising that is based upon a mindset relating to needs versus demographics. Here are a few:

Crest Toothpaste	Moms concerned about their families' oral health care, particularly the avoidance of cavities for their children.
Pepsi-Cola	People who think young!
American Express	Prestige-conscious, frequent travelers who crave recognition, attention, and special service.
Michelin Tires	Highly anxious, safety-conscious parents of young children.
Microsoft	Computer users who want to avoid mistakes and be covered with the standard in technology.

You can probably think of many more examples. In fact, it is a good idea to do so. Take a few minutes to leaf through one of your favorite magazines and look for three examples of brands that reflect a target customer group with a need mindset.

Brand	**Need Mindset**
• _____	_____
	_____
• _____	_____
	_____
• _____	_____
	_____

Microsoft is an interesting example. Microsoft has outdone IBM in setting the standard for computer operations and dethroned the blue chip company in achieving the pre-eminent position in the computer industry (software, of course). In its heyday, IBM practiced FUD, which stands for Fear, Uncertainty, and Doubt. Whenever a competitor was about to introduce a new, advanced computer technology, IBM would announce their intention to introduce, in the near future, an IBM solution. Customers, perceiving IBM as the industry leader and standard, would forgo the competitive offering based on their fear, uncertainty, and doubt that it would perform up to the level of IBM.

Similarly, Microsoft is playing this game based upon their leadership role. A few years ago when IBM introduced OS-2 software, Microsoft announced their intention to introduce, in the near future, a product they had in development—Windows Chicago. Never mind the fact that the introduction of Windows Chicago (i.e., Windows 95) faced repeated delays and was introduced many months following the OS-2 launch. It had the effect Microsoft wanted to achieve. Namely, customers eschewed the IBM offering in anticipation of Windows 95. The reason Microsoft is able to achieve this desired effect is that it preys on a customer mindset that holds the company as the standard and does not want to make a wrong decision (i.e., Fear, Uncertainty, and Doubt). (As you know, Microsoft has since introduced Windows 98, and Windows 2000 is on the drawing-board.)

One of our favorite examples of targeting to a need-mindset is American Express. They have been able to expand their target audience without diluting their message. In the beginning there was the "green" American Express Card. It was targeted at prestige-conscious frequent travelers. In time as demand for the card grew, its value was being undermined by its popularity. If everyone else on the planet has a green American Express Card, then its possession does not distinguish the bearer in a meaningful way. In other words, ego gratification is lost. So, what did American Express do to forestall the situation from unfolding? It introduced a gold card to distinguish the top spenders. As the ranks of gold cardholders began to swell, American Express introduced the platinum card. In this way the American Express Card maintains its appeal with prestige-conscious frequent travelers while expanding its cardmember base.

Components of a Target Customer Group Definition

A good target customer group definition is made up of three components: 1) demographics; 2) current usage habits; and 3) need-mindset. These are evident in a print ad for Dewar's Scotch. The ad shows a beautiful young woman, in a playful pose, making direct eye contact with the reader. The headline reads, *"Okay, so she's coming over for dinner. What are you gonna offer her, a nice cold one?"*

How would you define the target using each of the three components?

Demographics:

_____

_____

Current Usage Habits:

_____

_____

Need Mindset:

_____

_____

As for **demographics,** the ad appears to be talking to young, single males probably in the range of 21–34 years of age. These young men probably have some college, white-collar jobs and the means to be living on their own. The cues are: the young woman and how she is dressed; the fact that the target has finally managed to get her to join him; and the reference that she is "coming over for dinner." (We assume it's the target's pad and he has the ability to put together something meaningful, even if it is takeout!)

The **current usage habits** are that the male is a beer drinker. Why else would he even considering offering her "a nice cold one." This ties to the demographics in that younger men tend to prefer and drink beer versus a hard liquor such as scotch. Liquors are an acquired taste and suggest a more sophisticated palate. With the exception of micro-brews and imported beers, they are also perceived to be more upscale, worldly, and as previously mentioned, sophisticated.

The **need mindset** is to favorably impress this young woman to win her over. One may infer from the headline that if the target fails to convey the right message about himself then he will lose her.

Pulling it all together we could define the target as *25–34-year-old male beer drinkers who are on the make and would like to impress others with their seeming sophistication.* You might choose to pull together the definition somewhat differently. But it conveys the basic elements and how they work together.

There is undoubtedly more that we might say about each component of the target definition. But this should demonstrate that there is more to the target than mere demographics. Of the three components, we believe that the most important component is the need mindset. The other two components help us put the need mindset into context.

The need mindset is the bait for attracting the attention of the target. It sets up the benefit that pays off the need mindset and serves to differentiate your brand from competitive products in a meaningful way. Establish the need mindset and the benefit becomes self-evident. We will talk more about this in Chapter Six, on the fourth essential element of positioning, the benefit.

Be Precise

Peter Drucker, distinguished professor and prolific author of management books and thinking, said something to the effect that the 30-second commercial is the most crafted message in our society. Think about it. Thousands of hours go into the development of one spot. There are the hours for the development of the positioning, customer research, briefing the agency, creative development, pre-production, production, editing, and on and on and on. In order to be effective, the spot must communicate a relevant benefit in a clear yet provocative manner.

We expect the advertising to be clear. But marketers often communicate in a less than clear fashion. We tend to be imprecise in our word choice and direction. Chalk it up to time pressure, intellectual laziness, poor training, indecision, and so on. It still has the same ill-effect. Clear positioning starts with a clear definition of the target group.

Kellogg's Frosted Flakes cereal has been running two campaigns. One is directed at young children, the other at adults. However, if we are not precise about each target we run the risk of undermining the brand positioning and advertising message. Let's take the adult target. It is, in our judgment, strategically brilliant. The brand isn't just targeting adults (with a reasonable set of demographics) but instead, those adults who:

- Grew up eating Kellogg's Frosted Flakes cereal
- Perhaps purchase the brand for their children and have it available in their pantries
- No longer eat Kellogg's Frosted Flakes cereal (or eat it infrequently) because they think it's a kid's cereal; but if they were to eat it they would like it (as they did when they were children).

Accordingly, we might define this target as *adult cereal eaters who grew up on Kellogg's Frosted Flakes cereal and may currently purchase the brand for their children but no longer eat it themselves (frequently), even though they still favor its taste, because they believe it is for children and lack the permission to indulge.*

The company calls attention to this target in an earlier campaign using tongue-in-cheek executions showing reluctant adults, who are protected from identification, confessing their love for the brand. Execution aside, the target is strategic. The target is precise. Omit any one of the aforementioned factors and we change the target and, very likely, the approximately 15-year success the brand enjoyed with this target and flanker campaign.

Target Customer Profile

If you think about your favorite television series, one that has lasted for years, you'll probably note the integrity of the main characters. When we speak of integrity we are referring to predictability of behavior for any given situation. You know how Kelsey Grammer will respond as Frasier when confronted with either characters or various situations. That is character integrity.

This doesn't happen by accident. The screenwriter has probably put together a biographical sketch of the character, taking him from cradle to grave. Both the screenwriter and actor have immersed themselves in the character. They become Frasier. Unless they are schizophrenic, the integrity of the character will be present.

Similarly, we need to know and understand our target customer group equally as well. Certainly, you will find a diversity of people within your target group. However, there is always a core that represents the ideal or what we refer to as the **bull's-eye customer.** This customer is ideal for your product. He or she reflects the values, practices, attitudes, and need mindset that make your product and the benefits it delivers a perfect match.

Often, when we refer to the bull's-eye target customer in our seminars, someone will counter that he doesn't want to limit his target—for fear of limiting sales potential. While experience shows that a sure way to fail is to try to be everything to everyone, this concept shouldn't limit sales potential but enhance it. Specifically, it enables the marketer to really understand the bull's-eye mindset and establish a positioning and story to allow her or him to capitalize on more sales opportunities with the most appropriate prospects. Also, it establishes the bridge for the marketer regarding those factors, which meaningfully differentiate the brand from competition, and paves the road to the story, which gets to the heart of the matter for customers. Some of the most successful creative directors will tell you it helps to have someone specific in mind when writing and developing advertising. The message and voice will ring more true.

In order to get at the bull's-eye customer we have developed a **Target Customer Profile.** This tool addresses specific questions about the bull's-eye customer in a way that fosters deeper insights into values, practices, attitudes, and mindset of the customer. Importantly, it makes the customer real, as opposed to some abstraction out there in the marketplace (versus in here at company headquarters). As such, it provides meaningful focus for all marketing mix elements. In fact, one company has put together a biography of the bull's-eye customer using words, music, and pictures. Everyone refers to this fictitious customer by name. When an issue comes up the executive team asks how the named customer would respond. And, because they have done their homework, they can predict the customer's response.

Here's an example of a completed Target Customer Profile for the Tide bull's-eye consumer. We have inferred this customer from observing Tide marketing efforts and business development over the years.

TARGET CUSTOMER PROFILE
(TIDE RETAIL CONSUMER EXAMPLE)

NAME: *Mary Beth Williams*

GENDER: *Female*   **AGE:** *38*

MARITAL STATUS (Married to / # years): *John (8) - 2nd marriage*

CHILDREN (AGES): *Tricia (17), Billy (15), John Jr. (18), James (15), Melissa (6), Rob & Ed (4)*

OCCUPATION: *Full-time caretaker, part-time bookkeeper for husband John's roofing business*

EDUCATION: *Regina High School*

PERSONAL AUTO: *Ford Bronco*

CURRENTLY WORKING ON: *Picking up after the children!*

MY FAVORITE LEISURE ACTIVITY IS: *I don't have time for leisure*

I STAY HOME TO WATCH (ON TV): *Roseanne, Home Improvement, As The World Turns*

LAST GOOD BOOK I READ: *I don't have time to read books!*

THE NEWSPAPERS/MAGAZINES I USUALLY READ INCLUDE: *People, Reader's Digest, Good Housekeeping, Enquirer*

MY FAVORITE MUSIC / PERFORMER IS: *Classical Rock (The Eagles)*

THE LAST VACATION I TOOK WAS: *Last summer we drove to and camped in Yosemite*

I LOVE TO SHOP FOR: *Earrings*

MY FAVORITE SHOPPING PLACE IS: *Flea Markets and Garage Sales*

(continued ...)

WHAT MY FRIENDS SAY ABOUT ME (WHEN I'M NOT IN THEIR PRESENCE) IS: *If she doesn't slow down she is going to drive herself into the ground*

IF I COULD CHANGE ONE THING ABOUT MYSELF IT WOULD BE: *I would have gone to college*

A REALLY GOOD EVENING TO ME IS: *Go out alone with John to either a movie or dinner (just get away from the house and kids).*

MY DREAM IN LIFE IS: *To win the lottery and not have to do a damn thing.*

THE REASON(S) I CHOOSE *Tide*
(VERSUS COMPETITIVE BRANDS) IS: *Tide gets even the dirtiest clothes clean (and I can tell you my husband and the twins really get their clothes dirty) without damaging the fabric so we all can look our best. Also, I can usually buy it on special.*

Now it's time for you to gain experience in using this tool. Use the format provided on page 51 to identify the bull's-eye customer for your brand.

Target Customer Profile—Practical Tips

Here are some practical tips for pulling together a sound Target Customer Profile. Check your work for each of the following:

1. *Be as specific as possible*—You know this person. When we know someone we can be specific. The more specific we are, the easier it will be to develop the brand's positioning and its advertising. Also, as previously mentioned, it will aid in the development of all marketing mix elements and decisions. Leaving out sections suggests we don't know our customer. If we don't, it is time to find out more. And now, having completed the profile, we know what we need to learn.

2. *Look for brand name connections to shed further insights into the target*—In the Tide example we learn that Mary Beth Williams drives a Ford

TARGET CUSTOMER PROFILE

NAME: _____

GENDER: _____ AGE: _____

MARITAL STATUS (Married to / # years): _____

CHILDREN (AGES): _____

OCCUPATION: _____

EDUCATION: _____

PERSONAL AUTO: _____

CURRENTLY WORKING ON: _____

MY FAVORITE LEISURE ACTIVITY IS: _____

I STAY HOME TO WATCH (ON TV): _____

_____

LAST GOOD BOOK I READ: _____

THE NEWSPAPERS/MAGAZINES I USUALLY READ INCLUDE:

_____

MY FAVORITE MUSIC/PERFORMER IS: _____

_____

THE LAST VACATION I TOOK WAS: _____

_____

I LOVE TO SHOP FOR: _____

MY FAVORITE SHOPPING PLACE IS: _____

_____

(continued...)

WHAT MY FRIENDS SAY ABOUT ME (WHEN I'M NOT IN THEIR PRESENCE) IS: _____

IF I COULD CHANGE ONE THING ABOUT MYSELF IT WOULD BE: _____

A REALLY GOOD EVENING TO ME IS: _____

_____

MY DREAM IN LIFE IS: _____

THE REASON(S) I CHOOSE _____

(VERSUS COMPETITIVE BRANDS) IS: _____

_____

_____

Bronco, watches *Roseanne* and *As The World Turns* on TV, and reads *Reader's Digest* and even the *Enquirer*. These connections help us establish habits and attitudes. They allow us to be in resonance with our customer.

3. *Reflect the customer's attitudes and habits, not yours or the agency's!*—We are profiling the customer, not ourselves. We tend to be more upscale, and urbane (particularly if you are an agency creative living in a condominium off Central Park South in Manhattan) . . . not the bull's-eye customer. At a meeting with a marketing director for a canned meat product we pulled together a Target Customer Profile. The marketing director stepped back and snickered that the bull's-eye target couldn't possibly be correct. He said that no one in his neighborhood fits the profile we had created. We pointed out that his neighborhood was filled with doctors, lawyers, and business moguls like himself, who wouldn't be caught dead eating 49-cent canned meat (unless it was their mission in life to market it). He lived in a neighborhood where the mean price of a home is over $400,000 . . . in an obscure part of the world no less. His target customer more likely lives in a

home valued at $50,000, is blue-collar, significantly older, and so on. Do we need to say more?

4. Give the consumer's reason for selecting your brand, not the conventional wisdom of the manufacturer—It is important to know why the customer selects your brand versus competitive offerings. Sometimes we think we know the answer to why they choose our brand when we really don't know. Manufacturers' responses tend to be more rational and are made to fit with their world perfectly. Customer responses tend to appear somewhat less rational and fit with their world—the real world!

5. Check for consistency in attitudes and habits to ensure integrity of the profile—We ought to be able to get an accurate picture of the bull's-eye customer and predict her or his behavior based upon a deeper understanding of the customer. If we find (unexplainable) inconsistencies, then we have not accurately defined the target nor will we have the precision needed to provide proper direction and to aid decision making.

6. Confirm with (qualitative) research—Check it out! We like to use this tool at, and following, focus groups. We either fill these out for the alternate customers (i.e., ours and various competitors) as the groups progress, or we have the respondents fill out a profile on themselves before the focus group begins. Focus groups give you a better feel for the customer than the endless pages of statistics presented in quantitative research. Certainly, using both types of research should add more understanding. When our research work is complete we pull together the many profiles and construct the one bull's-eye based upon everything we learned. (This is not an amalgam of diversity but a crystallization of lifestyle, attitudes, habits, and needs of the bull's-eye target.)

Target Considerations in Advertising

A review of a broad spectrum of advertising from alternate categories and alternate countries leads us to the adoption of a few additional considerations when dealing with advertising. Among those worthy of note is:

- **The advertising does not need to show the target to be effective**—A print ad for Volvo aimed at parents does not show a visualization of adults but, instead, the object of the parents' affection—children. Another ad, a TV spot for Dove Soap, demonstrates Dove's superior mildness versus competitive brands such as Ivory through a litmus test. Nowhere in the spot will one find a beauty shot of a woman's soft skin. In fact, there are no people to be found in the ad. But the spot effectively communicates that "Dove is mildest. Bar none."

- *Alternate target constituencies require separate Target Customer Profiles and positionings*—At a given point in time, Lifescan, the marketer of glucose testing systems for diabetics, has three separate print campaigns. One is aimed at the trade. Another focuses on the consumer. The third campaign is directed at the health care professional. Each ad addresses different needs and pays the brand off with linking benefits. For example, the trade ad is geared to the retailer's need for sales productivity. The consumer ad deals with simplicity and accuracy you can depend upon. The health professional ad is designed to help doctors help diabetics . . . and avoid complications. If you have multiple constituencies with different needs, benefits, and reasons-why, then you, too, will need to develop separate Target Customer Profiles and positionings.

- *The creative marketer can develop new classifications of customers*—These may be key influencers to a purchase. They may be the person(s) administering the product. This is akin to creating a new market. It is going where competitors do not (currently) tread. A case in point is an ad for Depends, incontinence diapers, which is directed at the caregiver. It shows an adult daughter of around 50 years of age with her mother who appears 70 years plus in age. Typically, marketers of incontinence diapers directed their efforts at the user.

- *Talk to your customer in a manner that will strike a responsive chord*—We see so many poor examples of ads that attempt to talk to customers in a manner that is stilted, expected, overbearing, pretentious, and patronizing. Remember that we are talking with human beings through our advertising. An ad to health care professionals does not need to be in some prescribed format (boring). Get the need mindset and benefits right. Then use language, layout, ideas, visuals, and so on, that capture the target customer's attention and win her or him over to your way of thinking. Luvox, an Rx anti-depressant medication, talks to doctors as if they were consumers. The ads are inviting and refreshing.

KEY PRINCIPLES

Summary

✔ The target customer group is composed of the most likely prospects that have a similar set of needs and concerns that our brand can satisfy.

✔ It is important to identify the customer constituency and the key target within that grouping when selecting a target.

✔ Demographics are inadequate as the sole element in defining the target customer group. Demographics represent, at best, a media target—not a creative or decision-making target.

✔ Therefore, the definition of the target customer group needs to go beyond demographics. A good definition is made up of three components: a) demographics; b) current usage habits; and c) need mindset.

✔ The need mindset is the most important of the three components. It is the bait for attracting the attention of the target. It assists us in telling the brand's story in a way that will be relevant.

✔ Defining the target customer group requires balancing the size of the group with our ability to deliver a meaningful message. We are also balancing efficiency and effectiveness.

✔ The best way to achieve efficiency is to first be effective. In being effective, we put our brand in a position to be truly efficient on the basis it matters most—conversion of customers to our brand, strengthening brand loyalty, realizing premium margins and profitability.

✔ Be precise in defining your target customer.

✔ The bull's-eye customer is the ideal for your product. She or he reflects the values, practices, attitudes, and need mindset that makes your product and the benefits it delivers a perfect match.

✔ Remember, trying to be all things to all people is a sure way to fail.

✔ Use the **Target Customer Profile** tool to develop a better understanding for the brand's bull's-eye customer. Reflect the customer's attitudes and habits . . . not yours or the agency's.

✔ Confirm the bull's-eye customer with (qualitative) research. Check it out!

✔ Alternate target constituencies require separate **Target Customer Profiles** and, most likely, brand positionings.

✔ Talk to your customers through all your marketing mix elements, including your advertising, in a manner that will strike a responsive chord.

CHAPTER 5

Setting the Competitive Framework for a Competitive Edge

*I hadn't been working at the company for long when one of the new products people handed me a plain white bag containing one of their promising new items. "Try these HUT (home use test samples)—they're terrific," she said. "What are they?" I asked. "They're sweet, crunchy, and really addictive ... we're calling them **granola snacks**—to compete with all those semi-sweet new snacks." "No thanks," I replied, "I can't stand granola."*

Competitive Framework and Brand Positioning

The real-life interchange above illustrates what—at its most basic level—the competitive framework of a brand's positioning is supposed to do: *enable* the intended customer to quickly discern: (a) what *kind* of product is being presented, and (b) what *other products* it can substitute for among their share of requirements. In this example, *designating* the new snack "granola" was merely one execution of the product's competitive framework. And, in the case of this example, you can also see how quickly customers can "compute" their trial (or purchase) decisions based on their perception of the framework.

Sometimes you may see *competitive framework* referred to as *frame-of-reference*. They are similar terms, but the former seems the more practical of the two, especially when building or re-tooling a brand positioning. It is more practical for a couple of reasons:

1. Not only should a *competitive framework* signal to customers, but it should also make clear to manufacturers (and their agencies!) what the *expected source of volume* is for the brand, or, what products the brand *competes with*.

2. In addition, thanks largely to a tremendous amount of new product innovation lately, traditional "hard and fast" category boundaries have broken down. There is a true blurring of the categories: shampoos are now conditioners, as well as hair-nutrients; pretzels aren't salty snacks, they're baked better-for-you (BFY) snacks; antacids are now even more—they're acid blockers; and self-tanners are (with moisturizers added) therapeutic skin care.

Quite simply, manufacturers across many categories are more often gambling for higher stakes by trying to get customers to perceive their brands as substitutes for a broader set of products.

So, "competitive framework" is the operative phrase these days. Now, how do you put it into action for your business, for your brand positioning? A real useful place to start is by diagramming where your current competitive framework sits in the marketplace, along with as many other possibilities as you can think of—as in the longstanding and now classic *Tree Diagram* for Jell-O brand:

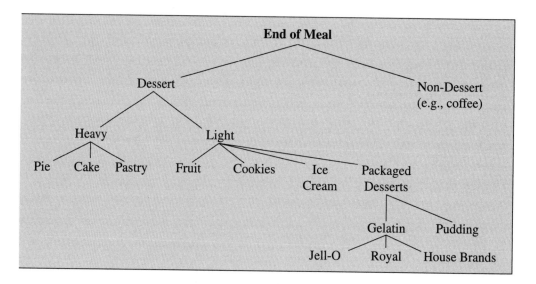

A good way to draw a diagram like this is somewhat counter-intuitive: start in the lower right-hand corner of a blank page, and work your way up and left/center as the possible segments, or markets, open up. In this fashion, Jell-O's most immediate competitive framework is all other brands of gelatin, which is only one of the sub-sets underneath a broader framework called "Packaged Desserts," which are only one of the sub-sets underneath the even broader framework called "Light Desserts," and so on.

Over time, the Jell-O brand sees opportunity in competing for a broader set of substitute products. But there's a catch in this opportunity: *the product line has to deliver on the key benefit(s) of the broader set.* For Jell-O, competing effectively with, say, "Pie Desserts," means that their line has to include some pie-like items. Enter Jell-O Instant Pudding & Pie Filling. To be taken seriously as an alternative to the more snack-like cookies and brownies, Jell-O has to go them one better, as in recent print-ad direct comparisons between their *Sugar-Free* line and piecemeal-like portions of fat-free, devil's food cookies and chocolate brownies (that look suspiciously like Snackwell's). Such comparisons derive their legitimacy from a simple "trump card": a 10-calorie serving of fat-free, *Sugar-Free* Jell-O fills a bowl; but even the best fat-free cookie or brownie can only get to 10 calories by reducing to one-fourth or one-fifth its size. If you're counting calories, which serving would *you* rather have?

As already noted, what with on-going manufacturer innovation and "category blurring," these kinds of tree diagrams are usually not permanent. Rather, they typically reflect only the way the *market is currently structured.* So it's important to update them on a regular basis, and especially whenever a market re-structuring occurs—which is also when the largest opportunities for growth usually occur.

Consider the contact lens market, for example. Virtually all the major players in that market today are framing themselves against each other: Acuvue Disposable Extended Wear versus Bausch & Lomb Disposable Extended Wear contacts. In some instances, one of the manufacturers may use minor innovation to be the first with a totally new frame. 1-Day Acuvue is a product that says very literally in its branding what its framework is: the first *daily* disposable contact lens. While such moves are intriguing and somewhat opportunistic, they still represent minor re-structures of the vision correction market. A major re-structuring has yet to occur—something akin to having contact lenses legitimately substitutes for **spectacles** (which would no doubt require reliable delivery of a bi-focal benefit, for instance).

In this contact lens example it's pretty clear that the onus of the *framework re-structuring* is largely on the manufacturers' shoulders. But sometimes the customer herself **re-groups products**, effecting a significant re-structure for the manufacturers! Look at what has happened to the traditional salty snack market over a period of just the past eight years. In 1990, the brand manager on Rold Gold pretzels was doing well to compete against other leading pretzel brands, (such as Snyder's), and maybe some of the bigger share chip and cheese puff brands, for his share of mind and inventory.

Competitive Framework
(A Recent Restructuring Example)

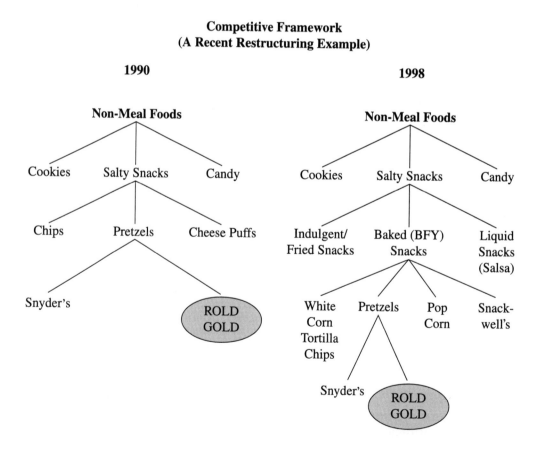

But by 1998, that same manager's competitive landscape had shifted dramatically, thanks in great part to customers' changing perceptions about **kinds of snacks** available to them. While customers used to make purchase decisions largely on the basis of *snack form and flavor*, (i.e., tortilla chips vs. potato chips vs. pretzels), by 1998 they were more and more purchasing *indulgent snacks* vs. *better-for-you snacks* vs. even *liquid snacks* (like salsa). Of course, snack manufacturers (and their able marketers!) helped to create the "better-for-you" snack segment; but it was the customer who began the re-grouping of previously "non-direct-compete" items like white corn tortilla chips, pretzels, and popcorn—perceiving such snacks to be less oily and more wholesome.

Designating the Positioning

As already mentioned, this diagramming exercise is an excellent place to begin to position, or re-position, a brand. But diagramming *alone* is insufficient for developing a stronger, more competitive brand positioning. Assuming that the exercise leads to broader volume sources for the brand, what must follow is the *creation of a broader designator* for the brand. Ideally, this *designator* should be incorporated into the Brand Positioning Statement as Pepcid AC has done in creating the designation "acid controller." Such a move not only identifies the intended competitive set (antacids); it elevates Pepcid AC above the set as the only controller.

To _____ (Target)_____ Pepcid AC	
Is the brand of COMPLETE ACID RELIEVER/ACID CONTROLLER	
That _____ (Benefit) _____	
Because _____ (Reason-Why) _____	
The (Brand Character) is _____	

Here are some other examples—from a wide range of categories—of the kinds of *"positioning designators"* that are being created (from an equally wide range of change bases) for added volume potential and heightened competitiveness versus brands' direct competition:

Brand	Frame was	Frame is now	Change Basis
• JELL-O	*Gelatin*	*Light Dessert*	*Line Extensions*
• PERT	*Shampoo*	*Conditioning Shampoo*	*New Formula*
• ENSURE	*Hospital Supplement*	*Nutritional (Everyday) Supplement*	*Advertising*
• EXCEDRIN	*Pain Relievers*	*Headache Medicines*	*Advertising & Packaging*
• BOSTON MARKET	*Fast Food Chicken*	*Fast Food Home-Cooked Meals*	*New Menu & Trademark*

You can see at once some of the inherent advantages of these evolved frameworks. Ensure significantly **broadens** its competitive set—it becomes more than an institutional supplement, it's now an on-the-go meal in itself. Excedrin consciously **narrows** its set to the largest volume segment within pain relievers, however, hoping to become the number one pain reliever for headaches, and to eventually be the "world's headache medicine of choice." In short, the role of the *Competitive Framework Designator* is a powerful one, both within the Brand Positioning Statement itself, and in subsequent customer communications.

Competitive Framework and Advertising

Not only does the "CF" make your brand positioning more inherently competitive, but it can also be expressed in a number of ways in your advertising to create the impression of a competitive edge. Here's a short checklist of some **ways to frame:**

Versus a Contiguous Category—The Pepcid AC competitive framework is a good example of this approach. Because the new brand effectively prevents heartburn from ever happening, it can reasonably frame itself against the closest-in category, antacids. In its introductory advertising campaign, Pepcid AC mentioned two or three times that "it's *not* an antacid," and it also made a visual comparison to Tums. Such an approach makes especially good sense when trying to establish a totally new segment (acid controller)—and trying to make an old one obsolete!

Similarly, a few years back, when Taco Bell was launching its low-fat Border Lites menu, it ran direct comparisons of the brand's fat content per item versus—**not** another taco chain competitor—but versus Burger King's "Whopper." And why not? Heavy-customers of fast foods want variety, and what better way to attract new Border Lites users than by having the largest-consuming group (burger eaters) re-think their high-fat habits?

Versus Your "Old" Self—This approach is among the oldest in the book, but it can still have competitive impact, particularly if your brand needs repositioning but remains essentially at parity performance to your competition. Of course, to convincingly frame against your former self, you need some kind of **news.** Car manufacturers have had considerable success with this approach; after all, they almost always have new features year-to-year. In fact, much of Mustang's revival can be traced to advertising that taps into the equity of the brand's *sixties' classicness.* Using the selling idea "It is What It Was and More," Mustang advertising directly compared classic features of the original design to those of the updated 1990s models. And it worked—both for "early boomers" seeking to re-live their "first car" experience and for twenty-somethings who want what's timeless, but also contemporary.

Versus the Gold Standard—This is yet another framing approach that has worked for many years. It tends to require a direct, visual comparison of some kind, as well as some kind of **superiority claim.** One could argue that the well-known Pepsi Challenge represents the ultimate gold standard framing—communicating a superior taste (at least on a sip basis) versus the world's best-known brand, Coca-Cola.

Another more recent example lies in another beverage category—orange juice. In select markets, Minute Maid *Frozen Orange Juice* once compared its "real orange flavor" to the taste of Tropicana's Pure Premium *Ready-to-Serve Orange Juice*, claiming a "win." By far the leading share brand in the markets where this comparison aired on television, Pure Premium makes a logical "gold standard." But what makes the framing provocative (and engaging!) is the notion of equating a **frozen concentrate** flavor with that of a **ready-to-serve** one. Truly a powerfully competitive, direct approach.

It seems that wherever there are "marketing wars" going on, the gold standard framing approach tends to thrive. The whole idea behind Burger King's recent comparison of their "new and improved" fries versus McDonald's fries comes out of the on-going "burger wars." Burger King defended its direct-comparison/we-taste-better approach on a simple premise: "It's because they have the gold standard and we don't." But underneath their public explanation was a more conscious, even "deadlier" strategy: using the competitor's enormous strength and size in french fries against them.

But there are many clever ways of framing against a gold standard *without* resorting to direct, "face-to-face" comparisons or even leveraging the weight of superiority claims. Maybelline's Avent alpha-hydroxy cosmetics call themselves "A Makeover, not Make-Up." And Maxwell House's Espresso Roast Coffee is touted as being as rich as "coffee-house coffee." In both instances the brands are attempting to frame themselves against that ideal in the customer's mind. And, in the case of Espresso Roast, the brand is also attempting to reasonably siphon some coffee-house occasions from—who else? Starbucks.

Versus the "Rat Pack"—An off-shoot of the direct framing or comparison, the "rat pack" is nothing more than roping together a number of your competitors on the basis of **some shortcoming they have in common.** That shortcoming need not be the "lead" need on a category's hierarchy, but it *must* be of sufficient relevance to provoke customers' thinking. Tylenol has used this approach in television and print—mainly as a way to counter a barrage of direct comparisons from other analgesics. In the process, the brand has highlighted the longstanding point-of-difference its formulation (acetaminophen) offers: no upset stomach. The main competitors—Advil, Bayer, and Aleve—all fall into a sub-category of analgesics that *can* cause stomach upset. Hence, Tylenol's opportunistic pulling together of the "stomach upset rats."

Versus the Outrageous (with a winning benefit)—No doubt the most creative of all these framing alternatives, this approach really requires a stretch in thinking (for the advertiser and the customer!). It's based on the simple premise that "You may be stuck with parity performance you cannot change, but maybe you can change your competition." Take the introduction of Honda's 4-wheel drive Passport. The challenge for Honda is a common one: how to imply a "better choice" when you're number four or five to enter the market (behind Jeep, Ford Explorer, Chevy Blazer, whoever)? Framing against this crowd of high-performance, popular "household names" has got to be a losing proposition. No "rat pack" in this bunch.

So what does Passport elect to do? Leapfrog totally out of the obvious and frame against Porsche. And not just any Porsche, but a 911 at that!! But here's the catch: the framing is based on the winning, all-terrain maneuverability that Passport offers over the Porsche 911 and all its speed. Crazy? Maybe a little, but it sure provokes the customer who's thinking about buying an Explorer or Cherokee to size up the Passport too.

Competitive Framework Exercise

You can actually use these same ways of framing in your advertising to gather some competitive framework options for strengthening your *positioning*. The idea is simple: using the five ways (plus any others you come up with) as a checklist device, try to identify as many **potential** competitors as you can for each. Don't worry if some are more useable than others; the idea is to get your thinking out on the table. Here are a couple of examples: one that might have been done for an established brand, Jell-O, and one for an entirely new product (a purely fabricated "non-narcotic, pain-site-targeted Rx analgesic").

Remember, this is only a first step in getting to the actual competitive framework you'll include in your Brand Positioning Statement. Once you have compiled a stretch-the-boundaries list of possible competitive sets, you'll

Competitive Framework Exercise

	Jell-O	New Rx Analgesic
1. Vs. Contiguous Category	Puddings; pie fillings; custards	Over-the-counter pain relievers; topicals
2. Vs. Old Self	Original Jell-O; old-fashioned desserts	NA (it's new!)
3. Vs. Gold Standard	Sherbet; ice cream	Tylenol; narcotics
4. Vs. "Rat Pack"	High-calorie desserts	N-Saids; narcotics
5. Vs. Unexpected	Indulgent pastries	Acupuncture; herbals

next want to assess a number of key variables before selecting the optimal ones for your brand. For example, how capable is your product in performing against, say, an Rx Tylenol or the leading Rx and OTC N-Saids; and the relative volumetric potential of seeking business from topical analgesics or something as "fringe-y" as acupuncture?

But once you *do* decide on the set of products that you intend to compete with (and that you intend your customers to replace with your brand), you need to do two other things: (1) translate the competitive set into a term within your Brand Positioning Statement, and (2) translate that *strategic terminology* into an easy handle ("designator") for your customers. We don't know for sure what Pepcid AC wrote in their initial Brand Positioning Statement, but we have reasonably inferred the following:

STEP 1 **Identify competitive set:**	**STEP 2** **Translate this set into positioning terms:**	**STEP 3** **Give the customer an easy way to understand the set (designate it):**
• *Antacids—all forms, but especially tablets* • *Emerging OTC "acid blockers"*	*Pepcid AC is the brand of complete acid reliever*	*"Acid Controller"*

Perspective Is Everything: A Story

There's really no magic in out-thinking your competitors when it comes to pushing the boundaries of your brand's competitive framework. All that's required is an open-mined perspective, along the lines of that in the following tale:

> Two monks from different holy orders were arguing heatedly over a rather practical matter: whether it would be proper to smoke while praying. The one, hard-line thinking monk insisted that to do so would be offensive; the other, more open-minded monk saw no real harm in it. Because they could not agree, they decided to ask their superiors. When they had done this, they met again to compare answers. The hard-liner confidently asserted: "It's as I knew it would be—my superior said emphatically, "one must never smoke while praying." "That's funny," the open-minded monk replied, "I asked my superior if it would be all right to *pray while smoking,* and he readily agreed that praying at any time is a good thing."

Being able to see your brand and its potential competition with such flexible perspective as this can make all the difference.

KEY PRINCIPLES

Summary

✔ The competitive framework is the *enabler* of the Brand Positioning Statement—it enables (1) the customer to see what products yours can be substituted for; and (2) you—the manufacturer/marketer—to identify the primary sources of volume for your brand.

✔ Per its name, the competitive framework must be inherently *competitive.* That means it should stretch out customers' thinking beyond the immediate, direct-competitor brands in the category. For this to succeed, your brand must be able to meet all the important needs of the broadened framework, which in turn often requires product improvements or line extensions (à la Jell-O Pudding & Pie Filling items), but may be finessed by advertising alone (Ensure—Complete & Balanced Nutrition; Excedrin—The Headache Medicine)

✔ Whether consciously constructing (or re-tooling) a brand positioning or not, it's a good idea to periodically *tree-diagram* out the various ways of setting the competitive framework in your category. What with continuous innovations and changes in customer perceptions, the framework architecture of any category keeps evolving, and the biggest opportunities for the alert marketer happen when fundamental re-structuring occurs in the market.

✔ Creating a *designator* that will comprise the breadth of your brand's competitors is part and parcel of your brand positioning. And, it may well give you an edge—if even for just a short time (remember Pepcid AC's Acid Controller).

✔ When it comes to communicating the competitive framework in your advertising, there are a number of approaches you might want to consider (especially if your brand lacks meaningful superiority):

1. Versus a Contiguous Category   4. Versus the Rat Pack
2. Versus Your Old Self   5. Versus the Outrageous
3. Versus the Gold Standard

✔ Use these same approaches to identify competitive set options for your brand positioning.

CHAPTER 6

Building Better Benefits for a Compelling Payoff

"So, what's in it for me?"

The "benefit" is the fourth essential element in developing a brand positioning. The benefit is the principle driver in the customer's purchase decision. It is the customer's payoff for purchasing and using your brand of products and/or services. It addresses the customer's questions: "So, what's in it for me?" and "Why should I purchase your product?"

Types of Benefits

The positioning benefit provides customers with the basis for choosing your product or service. Therefore, it needs to be competitive. Moreover, it should be the most meaningful customer benefit you want to and can own, in the minds and hearts of your customers.

There are a number of benefit types. There are *product, customer,* and *emotional* benefits. The Reach toothbrush provides us with an illustration of the three types of benefits.

- **Product**–Reaches better (than competitive toothbrushes) to clean places other brushes can miss.
- **Customer**–Results in cleaner, healthier teeth.
- **Emotional**–Gives you the confidence that you are doing your best to keep your teeth cleaner and healthier.

Notice the difference among the benefit types. The *product benefit* gets at what the product itself does. It is probably the most frequently used benefit type in positioning and advertising. Sometimes it's the only benefit you need, such as when your product is establishing a new segment or category—or, when the product benefit enables different customers to take away a customer benefit that is particularly meaningful to them (from among an array of potential customer benefits). Unfortunately, its frequency of use is more likely a function of the lack of sophistication of the marketer. The product benefit is the lowest-order benefit and, in many cases, will fail to evoke brand loyalty particularly with parity products.

The *customer benefit* addresses the reward inherent in the product benefit to the customer. In the Reach toothbrush example the customer benefit is cleaner, healthier teeth. The customer benefit builds a bridge for customers in translating the product benefit into something more meaningful to them. Additionally, it can serve to differentiate one product from another. You may arrive at the customer benefit by simply addressing the following question regarding the product benefit: "So, why is that important to me?"

The *emotional benefit* is, in reality, another form or classification of customer benefit. "Feelings" and "beliefs" as opposed to performance factors characterize it. We can identify an emotional benefit by the presence of these words and, as we observe from the Reach example, "confidence" among others. The prescription brand Fosamax, which is used in the treatment of osteoporosis, puts the *focus of sale* in their earlier direct-to-consumer (DTC) print advertising on an emotional benefit. The first of a three-page spread ran the copy, "Since I found out about my osteoporosis, I've been afraid to walk to my mailbox when it rains." Imagine, the targeted consumer–patient is afraid to perform a simple, everyday task. Undoubtedly, for good reason. If you are familiar with osteoporosis you know that bones can break easily.

In this case, the consumer–patient is probably elderly and fears not just a broken bone but, perhaps, an irretrievable decline in health that such an accident can bring to one who is unable to mend quickly or completely. At the extreme this decline raises the fear of death. The Fosamax advertising urges the target consumer to "Fight Your Fear." While the copy carried by the ad spells out both product and customer benefits, the focus of sale is clearly an emotional benefit. Fosamax promises not only a way to rebuild bone and bone strength (*product benefit*) so the consumer can do what she wants and likes to do (*customer benefit*) but, more important, restores the consumer's confidence to overcome fear (*emotional benefit*).

Emotional versus Functional Benefits

The benefit can be functional (product or customer) or emotional. Regardless, the benefit should provide the product or service you market with a competitive advantage in the marketplace. It must give the customer a reason for choosing your brand in preference to someone else's product or brand, or, nurture loyalty and/or immunize the customer against the lure of competitive pricing promotions.

When a functional benefit is shared by a competitor, regardless of whether it is a product or customer benefit, the brand's emotional benefit may provide the compelling *point of difference* that wins the customer and creates brand loyalty. We refer to emotional benefits as "higher-order" benefits.

If you think back to your basic college psychology course, you may recall the teachings of the eminent clinical psychologist, Dr. Abraham Maslow. Accordingly to Dr. Maslow we encounter a *hierarchy of needs*. At the lowest rung of the ladder is the need for survival. Said another way, give me food. Give me clothing. Give me shelter. When needs on the lowest rung are satisfied we move up the ladder to the next rung. At the top of the metaphorical ladder is self-actualization. This is a state whereby an individual is at peace with herself, and gives herself the permission to pursue interests free from the control of the value judgments of others. Progression up the ladder to this lofty, theoretically attainable position requires the satisfaction of needs on lower rungs. In other words, we do not climb to the next rung until the previous rung has been attained! Stated another way, reaching a given rung assumes attainment of lower levels.

Consistent with Maslow's theory, the emotional benefits are higher-order benefits. What's more, attainment of an emotional benefit may suggest realization of lower-level product and customer benefits. Always Sanitary Protection Pads promise to keep women *feeling cleaner and drier*. If it makes one "feel" cleaner and drier, it is natural to assume that it provides better protection (which may or may not be true).

Mariner, the outboard motor company, ran a campaign that promised a compelling emotional benefit. One print ad shows some poor sap in a fishing boat with the headcover off his outboard motor. The boat is tied up to the dock while he goes through a vain attempt to start the outboard motor. Obviously, he does not have a Mariner outboard. In the background we see a procession of men with their boats on an adjacent ramp impatient to begin launching into the water. On the dock, we see the buddy of the erstwhile fisherman, arms folded over his gut with foot tapping, anxious for the motor to catch and the boat to push off. We are given insights into what might be going through the fisherman's mind ("Shouldddda, shouldda, couldda, couldada . . . shoulddda boughttta Mariner"). The ad creates the impression that we can be confident that Mariner engines will save us from incredible embarrassment (*emotional benefit*). Additionally, the emotional benefit *leads us to believe* Mariner engines are dependable (*product benefit*) and will give the owner many more hours on the water to enable him to enjoy his water activities (*customer benefit*).

Actually, the experienced brand builder and advertiser can play these benefit types as easily as a professional musician plays a scale. If one has a meaningful product benefit that competition can't match . . . play the product benefit for as long as growth remains strong. When competition is able to deliver a comparable product benefit . . . move up the scale to play the customer benefit. You guessed it. Lead your competition to capture an emotional benefit, to ensure that you remain ahead of the growth curve and at least one step ahead of competition in the minds of your customers.

The key here is the perception we want to create in the minds and hearts of potential customers. It is the feeling the customer gets about your product or service that differentiates it in a meaningful way from competitive products. This is the positioning benefit. The benefit played in the advertising merely stimulates the take-away intended in the positioning as well as serves in the achievement of an important marketing objective.

As it relates back to advertising, really great advertising plays all three benefit types in the same spot or print ad, like the Mariner ad, to create an impression of superiority. Master Lock used to air one TV spot per year—during the Super Bowl! At more than a million dollars per 30-second pop, it had better be good! A few Super Bowls ago they ran a spot that showed various toughs attempting to break into areas secured by a Master Lock of one type or another. Classical music is played in the background as a counterpoint to the mean-spirited action. The ad communicates the three benefit types: the Master Lock branded products hold up to the various attacks (*product benefit*); it keeps our belongings and property safe (*customer benefit*); and it makes us feel secure and protected from what may lurk in the dark, mean streets of Anytown USA (*emotional benefit*).

Benefit Linkage and Relationships

In selecting a benefit, there are a few linkages of which you need to be aware. While they are self-evident, our experience working with client advertisers and their agency counterparts suggest they are worth mentioning.

1. The benefit must be consistent with the physical attributes of the product or service. The Swiss Army Knife is a good case in point. Even if we haven't owned one, we are familiar with their versatility. What makes the Swiss Army Knife so versatile (product benefit) and for us so resourceful (customer benefit)? It's the product's physical attributes. Each Swiss Army Knife incorporates a wide variety of tools. There's a ruler, small scissors, a corkscrew, and much, much more. The benefit flows from the product's physical attributes.

Unfortunately, one of our clients failed to understand this vital relationship between product attributes and the benefit. The client was attempting to re-launch a sports beverage that failed to achieve their expectations.

Unlike the market leader, Gatorade, our client's product contained carbonation, albeit a low level (i.e., lower than soft drinks). However, sports enthusiasts do not want carbonation because they can't slam the beverage down to quickly relieve thirst and replenish essential elements lost from sweating. Also, carbonation is gas. Who wants or needs gas when you are involved in strenuous physical activity? Despite our advice that they eliminate the carbonation or pursue a different target customer, the client chose to go head-to-head with Gatorade. Consequently, they have not been able to establish a meaningful or enduring franchise on a broadscale basis. Recently, they brought the level of carbonation yet lower in an attempt to achieve some success!

2. The benefit will change depending upon the competitive framework. The benefit and competitive framework in the Brand Positioning Statement are also interrelated. If we go back to the often used, classic Jell-O example

The (Competitive Framework)	That (Alternate Benefits)	The (Competitive Framework)	That (Alternate Benefits)
Brand of Gelatin	• Is highest quality • Is preferred	Dessert	• Is fruity • Is inexpensive • Is light • Is refreshing • Is non-filling • Is for kids • Is for old people
Packaged Dessert Mix	• Is fruity • Is refreshing		
Light Dessert	• Is fruity • Is inexpensive • Is versatile		• Is fun
		Way to end the meal	• Is light • Leaves a good taste in mouth • Is non-filling • Is sensible • Makes you feel good

we find that the benefits will be different if we put it into a dessert competitive framework (i.e., it's light, non-filling, fruity, etc.) versus a gelatin (i.e., is preferred, etc.).

So it is important to define a competitive framework against which we can deliver a meaningful point of difference to establish a competitive advantage. Certainly, the customer must be accepting of the competitive framework that you offer if you are to plumb its potential corresponding benefits. If the customer is not, then he will throw out your entire proposition and reject your product.

3. The benefit and target customer group are also interrelated. A benefit that translates to a meaningful point of difference may be established with a certain kind of person. Excedrin, "The Headache Medicine," features and calls out to people who claim to have severe headaches—The kind of headaches that other pain relievers just can't remedy. What does this target group lead us to believe about Excedrin? We think it suggests that Excedrin is a strong, powerful pain reliever made especially for headaches. Not a bad take-away for Excedrin. Evian has used health- and fitness-conscious young adults to build its franchise and create an impression that its water is pure, natural, and good for you.

Establishing a benefit through the use of a specific target customer group may be used to:

- Differentiate your brand from competitive products (who uses your product tells something about it)
- Create emotional customer identification (yes, I want to be perceived as one of those people)
- Insulate the brand versus competition (you may have the same product attributes, but I have "badged" a select group of customers)

Single versus Multiple Benefits

Imagine, you are now the category manager for oral hygiene products. Your company has entries in mouthwash, toothbrushes and dental floss. But it lacks a presence in the large toothpaste category. Your product research and development manager informs you her team has developed a multiple-benefit toothpaste to give you a formidable entry into this category. The new toothpaste eliminates plaque, contains fluoride to help prevent cavities, has a special ingredient to guard against periodontal disease, contains a whitener to keep teeth white, and on top of it all it is less abrasive than competitive brands of toothpaste. Now what benefit, or benefits are you going to select for your Brand Positioning Statement? Choose one from the following multiple-choice selection:

a. The one most important to consumers
b. The one my brand can win versus competition
c. The top two or three
d. No more than three
e. All of them or
f. Depends upon what I learn from market research

This question is becoming more frequent. The response varies based upon the conventional wisdom of the participant's organization. Thinking ahead to the advertising, some will say, "I'll select the one benefit the customer will most appreciate." Others state they will find the one benefit that gives them a point of difference. Yet others will submit to picking the top two, but no more than three, benefits. Who's right? Who's wrong? We are about to tackle the issue of the ages: single versus multiple benefits.

Before we address the issue, however, let's pause to consider the wisdom of introducing a product with multiple benefits and not building them into the positioning and/or communicating them. If you are only going to establish your brand on one product benefit then why build additional benefits into the product? After all, we can expect that these additional benefits will add to the cost of goods or services. And, what if you gain your competitive advantage from the additional benefits? Would we not squander a unique opportunity to gain an advantage versus competition in creating brand loyalty?

What we have here is a dilemma brought about by communication concerns. As for the communications, this is a probability game. A single benefit improves the likelihood of *successful communication*. From the early days of television many advertisers have measured the success of their advertising based upon memorability of benefits as evidenced by the day-after recall score. The more benefits you shoehorn into a spot, the less the probability that the customer will remember what you want her to recall. Stated another way, the probability for a successful communication (i.e., one that achieves a recall score equal to or better than the norm) falls as we add additional benefits. From this simple fact came the maxim to stick with a simple, single-minded message which was further translated to "stick with a single benefit." The maxim is reasonable but the translation is a perversion.

On the other hand, there is *effective communication*. Effective communication persuades, motivates customers to think about your product and take the action you desire. This perception will in some way be one that leads to brand loyalty. The action could be to switch to your product, use more of it or use it more often, or pay a premium price. If your advantage resides within the multiple benefits you could be abdicating the opportunity for effective branding and communications in an effort to achieve successful communication (i.e., recall score).

In today's increasingly more competitive marketplace we may very well need multiple benefits to profitably win and maintain customers. What good is a memorable message (i.e., successful communication) if it fails to win customers (i.e., effective communication)? We need a positioning that will put us ahead of the competition. We need communications that are both successful and effective.

Additionally, in some categories that are heavily regulated (such as over-the-counter, OTC, medications), the marketer is required to establish her or his product as possessing and, therefore, communicating, multiple benefits (where multiple compounds or actions exist). For example, Tylenol PM is a combination analgesic and sleep-aid. It cannot be one thing to one target and another to a different target. It must talk about pain relief and its ability to induce sleep. Why? The FDA (Food and Drug Administration) does not want people who have pain to take a combination product unless they also have a sleeping problem. They rightfully do not want people overmedicating. So in this instance, like it or not, the marketer must communicate multiple indications which are the product's benefits.

Improving the Likelihood of Successful and Effective Communication of Multiple Benefits

Linking this to advertising, we may improve, and should strive to improve, the likelihood of both successful and effective communication of multiple benefits by: a) utilizing a single-minded proposition; b) broadening the competitive framework; and c) employing multiple executions.

Single-Minded Proposition—This entails the alignment of benefits under the umbrella of a single-minded proposition. The single-minded proposition reflects the spirit of the maxim to be single-minded and keep it simple without enslaving the advertiser to a single benefit. The single-minded proposition increases the likelihood that the customer will remember, understand, and act upon the message. The single-minded proposition is communicated in the Campaign Idea. The Campaign Idea is discussed in detail in Chapter 14.

Returning to the new toothpaste entry with multiple benefits we may observe that this is a real case. The brand is Rembrandt toothpaste. They employed the single-minded proposition "The new standard in oral hygiene." One may legitimately argue the power of this particular single-minded proposition (which we think is generally weak and unimaginative). However, we do believe it sets the brand apart from other entries as being better. The reason it is better is the multiple benefits it claims to deliver. More recently Colgate introduced Colgate Total. Now this brand trademark does a better job, in our judgment, to communicate multiple benefits than the collection of key copy words employed by Rembrandt.

A fine example is NyQuil. This brand has run the same advertising campaign for about 20 years. It was launched by what was then Richardson-Vicks and has been fueled by its current parent Procter & Gamble. The campaign is anchored by a single-minded proposition that communicates the brand's benefits: providing multi-symptom cold relief and, at the same time, enabling cold sufferers to get to sleep so they can rest (and function like normal the next day). The single-minded proposition goes like this: "NyQuil. The nighttime sniffling, sneezing, coughing, aching, stuffy head, fever, so you can rest and have a good morning medicine."

As for the litany of benefits, we do not believe it is important that the customer remember each and every one. We certainly don't! Instead, we are more concerned that customers come away with the impression that NyQuil is the best medicine for relieving all the cold symptoms and enabling a person to get to sleep. In this case, as in most, the general impression that reinforces the positioning is more important than the specifics.

Building Upon the Competitive Framework—Everyone knows what an antiseptic does, or is supposed to do. It kills germs to prevent infection of wounds. We also know that antiseptics burn when applied to a freshly opened wound. Ouch!!! The burning sensation is even more intense for children. (At least that is how it appears based upon the strong reaction that the mere mention or sight of an antiseptic medicine brings to a child with a fresh surface skin wound.) The mention of the designator "antiseptic" communicates the product's benefit of killing germs.

Johnson & Johnson Brazil introduced a combination antiseptic and anesthetic medicine for the treatment of wounds. The introductory spot shows a boy who is about to have his wound treated with an antiseptic medicine by his mother. The room in which he sits turns into a scene from a horror movie. We see lights blinking on and off, hear the tearful child scream "no" to his mother, and see her emerge from the dark with distorted, and rather monstrous, features. But, the product is Johnson & Johnson antiseptic with anesthetic medicine. Now, the scene grows calm. The mother is shown to be nurturing and tender. The boy grows docile and is thankful for the relief. What we have here is a broadening of the competitive framework. This is the antiseptic with an anesthetic. It's the antiseptic medicine that doesn't hurt. Two benefits made more memorable and compelling by broadening the competitive framework.

Multiple Executions—We used to believe this was a luxury for those advertisers with deep pockets (i.e., loads of money to spend on advertising). But we have learned better. Even marketers with relatively small budgets may make use of this practice to improve the likelihood of successful and effective communications.

In this practice, each benefit is communicated in a separate execution. It works if the benefits are aligned and can be captured with a single-minded proposition. In this way, the spots are not disparate but linked to build the intended brand positioning.

For years Lexus has successfully employed multiple executions in their campaign "The Relentless Pursuit of Perfection." Each spot and print ad focuses on a specific benefit of their automobiles. In one spot we witness a world-class guitarist actually recording his music in the back seat of a Lexus speeding down a highway. The message is that Lexus gives you the quietest ride possible. The execution borrows from the single-minded proposition while at the same time it strengthens it. But then, Lexus has deep pockets. They can afford multiple executions.

Enter Orthoxical from Australia. Orthoxical is an OTC medicine for the relief of multi-symptoms from colds and flu. The brand is supported with 15-second TV spots. Each spot features a specific symptom (such as runny nose as depicted by a leaky faucet) and ends with the single-minded proposition "Take Orthoxical and take control." The spots are not costly to produce. The airtime allows them to run many more messages than they could if the commercial length was 30 seconds. The single-minded message links the spectrum of symptoms to educate customers of the multi-symptom relief promised by Orthoxical.

So, if you need to define your positioning with multiple benefits to establish a competitive advantage, don't shy away from the task at hand. The single-minded proposition, broadening of the competitive framework, and use of multiple executions can serve to improve the likelihood of your successfully and effectively seeding multiple benefits and an impression of superiority. It's not easy. It will be a challenge for your agency. But look around in the world and you'll find the marketplace is replete with brands that have successfully employed these practices. As you watch television and read magazines take note of the number of brands that are able to successfully communicate multiple benefits. The successful ones do it effortlessly.

Benefit Laddering Tool

Now it is time to put what we have learned to use. The Benefit Laddering Tool, shown below for Tide laundry detergent, enables us to identify potential product, customer, and emotional benefits for our brand of products

Benefit Laddering Tool

Tide Example	Your Brand
1. **Target:** *Demo:* Moms with active children and husbands who get clothes really dirty *Usage Behavior:* Frequent/heavy detergent usage; tend to buy specialized products and/or on promotion *Need:* Get clothes their cleanest without undue wearing or overspending	**Target:** *Demo:* *Usage Behavior:* *Need:*
2. **Product Benefit:** • Cleans clothes • Gets out dirt • Removes stains	**Product Benefit:**
3. **Customer Benefit:** • Keeps clothes cleaner longer • Colors look brighter • Clothes are softer/more comfortable • Need fewer washings • Look good	**Customer Benefit:**
4. **Emotional Benefit:** • Feel sharper/more together • Confident making good/best presentation • Reflects well on me	**Emotional Benefit:**

and services. It is easy to use. Try it for your brand using the directions provided below.

1. We start by reprising the ideal target customer group definition using demographics, usage behavior, and that meaningful need which our product satisfies best. It is important that we keep the target customer foremost in our collective mind. Perhaps, you might even want to name him or her.

2. Fill in the potential product benefit(s). What does your product or service do (e.g., cleans clothes, removes dirt and stains, etc.)? Think about the product's attributes. Think too about alternate competitive frameworks. Where does it lead you?

3. Next identify customer benefits resulting from the preceding product benefits. So Tide cleans clothes. Now what does that mean to you a customer of the category or brand? Perhaps it helps your clothes stay fresh or cleaner longer. Or maybe it makes your clothes feel more comfortable. Or it means your personal presentation is at its best. Go figure it out! Don't hesitate to inquire of your customers, prospective customers and or even those of your competitors as to why the product benefits are important to them. In other words, what does it mean to you, Ms. or Mr. Customer?

4. Now we are going to translate customer benefits into emotional benefits. In the case of Tide laundry detergent the customer benefits may lead you to emotional benefits of feeling sharper or more presentable. Or, it could be that you feel you are taking better care of your clothes. What is going on in the minds of customers as it relates to their feelings and belief structure when the customer benefits are probed for higher-order emotional benefits? Think about this, and apply it to your brand.

You should have a large number and wide variety of benefits. It's decision time. Which do you believe are most meaningful to your target customers? Which can you deliver against, given your product's attributes? Which can you use to differentiate you versus the competition? Which can you own? Don't stop here! Check these conclusions out with customers. Find out what they can do to make your brand more competitive and more compelling in the marketplace.

KEY PRINCIPLES
Summary

✔ The benefit is the payoff for the customer. It provides her with the basis for choosing your brand of product or service. Therefore it must be meaningful to the customer, competitive, and ownable.

✔ Keep in mind that the three benefit types are *product, customer* (functional), and *emotional.* The *product* benefit gets at what the product does. The *customer* benefit addresses the rewards of the product benefit to the customer. The *emotional* benefit characterizes customer feelings and beliefs that grow from the *customer* benefit.

✔ *Emotional* benefits are higher-order benefits. Successful planting of an *emotional* benefit may suggest realization of lower-level *product* and *customer* benefits.

✔ If you have a meaningful *product* benefit that competition cannot match, then play the *product* benefit. If competition is able to deliver a comparable *product* benefit, move up to a *customer* benefit. When competition is able to neutralize your *customer* benefit, consider playing an important *emotional* benefit. We want to stay ahead of our competition and avoid a slowdown in the growth curve.

✔ Really great advertising plays all three benefits in the same TV spot or print ad.

✔ The benefit needs to be linked to product attributes, target customer group, and competitive framework. Certainly, product attributes allow the benefit as we witness with many brands. The target group may be utilized to establish a point of difference, as Pepsi-Cola has been able to achieve versus Coca-Cola. The potential set of benefits, and importance of each to customers, will change with the competitive framework.

✔ A single benefit improves the likelihood of *successful communication* (i.e., one that achieves a recall score equal to or better than the norm).

✔ *Effective communication* is measured by motivating customers to perceive your brand as superior, and to take an action that you desire (such as bolster brand loyalty, stimulate trial purchases, etc.). In today's competitive marketplace we may very well need to communicate multiple benefits in order to create brand loyalty.

✔ Proven practices to improve the likelihood of both successful and effective communication of multiple benefits are: a) utilize the single-minded proposition; b) broaden the competitive framework; and c) employ multiple executions.

✔ Employ the Benefit Laddering Tool to display potential benefits and identify those that are competitive, meaningful, and ownable.

CHAPTER 7

Engineering Benefit–Credibility With the Reason-Why

*"Just give me one good **reason why** I should buy your brand instead of someone else's."*

Your next new customer

Reason-Why and the Brand Positioning

If it can be rightly said that the **benefit** (or **point-of-difference**) part of the brand positioning is where the sale is pitched, then it is also true that the **reason-why** (or support) part is where the sale is closed. Think about it. What does it take to close a sale–any sale? A compelling benefit, to be sure, but most prospective customers want something more . . . they want a reassurance that they're making a wise decision.

In other words, they're seeking a kind of reinforcement for their beliefs. The flip side of that coin for the manufacturer-seller is to **be credible**. In engineering a solid reason-why into the brand positioning, you have the opportunity to fundamentally establish your brand's credibility. More specifically, you can anchor the believability of your brand's primary benefit–by providing your prospects with "sell," not just "tell," and by giving them permission to believe in your promise of benefit.

Which leads to an important distinction among **credibility** devices for the brand positioning: the "fine line" difference between conventional **reasons-why** and **permission to believe.** The former are typically *intrinsic* to the product itself (either design/formulation-driven or process/manufacturing-driven). The latter, on the other hand, are typically *extrinsic* to the product— but clearly consistent with its usage (endorsements, challenges, "acid tests"). To illustrate the distinction, look at what Gatorade does:

Main benefit:	*Unsurpassed thirst-refreshment and replenishment*
Reason-why:	*Special isotonic formula*
Permission to believe:	*Endorsement by National Basketball Association, Major League Baseball, National Hockey League, and National Football League*

Gatorade's inferred brand positioning incorporates both a formula-driven credibility aid and the endorsement of all four of America's major professional sports leagues—intrinsic and extrinsic devices. Such a double-barreled approach not only helps close another Gatorade sale, but it also makes would-be competitors work all the harder to gain their *own* credibility.

This is not to suggest that every brand positioning requires both kinds of credibility. In fact, there are some brands (even categories) in which conventional reasons-why seem ineffective. Brands whose sales are predominantly driven by *badging* and *distinctive imagery*—such as perfumes, fashion clothing, jewelry—don't seem to require the same level of credibility for closing sales as do the more rationally pitched brands (household products, health and beauty aids, food products). But a good rule of thumb when constructing or examining your brand positioning is this: *If I elect not to include a reason-why and/or permission-to-believe, do I have a good reason-why?*

Some Other Tips

When you are committed to bolstering the credibility of your brand positioning via a compelling reason-why, here are some important "design features" you'll want to include:

Make Sure the Reason-Why Dovetails Precisely with Your Main Benefit—What Coors has historically done, emphasizing "their water," may have first seemed a little odd in an industry where *real beer taste* is king. After all, highlighting the water in your formulation would seem to create all the wrong impressions: watered-down taste, weak, even (perhaps) less alcohol. But Original Coors is the only major beer brewed entirely with Rocky Mountain Spring Water . . . a very, refreshingly appealing kind of water. Even more to the point, the Coors taste and texture has consistently been described as more water-like "easier drinking" and more refreshing—a real dovetailing of main benefit and reason-why credibility.

That's connecting a benefit with a *formula-driven* reason-why. But look at what some of Coors' competitors have done over the years with *process-driven* reasons-why: Bud's beechwood aging, Stroh's fire brewing, Miller Genuine Draft's cold filtering. In each case the attempt is to add reassurance to the customer's beliefs about the brand's appetite appeal and real beer flavor.

Make Sure Your Reason-Why Is Spoken in Customer Language—Some manufacturers are masters at this. Procter & Gamble, in particular, consistently crafts the key reason-why words almost as if they were to become "sub-brands" in their own right. Take the Always brand of sanitary protection. The base product has a unique design feature that protects against leakage by pulling wetness away from the skin (a similar design to that in Pampers, in fact). But rather than letting the engineers name this feature something like "capillary wicking," P&G managers elected to go with the friendlier (and much more memorable) "Dri-Weave" protection.

In the much less technical coffee business, P&G also supports the rich flavor of its Folger's brand with the simple (process-driven) "Mountain

Grown." What makes this reason-why all the more compelling is that, effectively, all commercially available coffee brands are made with beans that are mountain grown; it's just that P&G is the only brand that can lay claim to that wonderful set of words—they trademarked them.

Do Whatever Is Necessary to Own Your Credibility Support—As in the foregoing example, it's especially helpful toward building equity, ownership, and (ultimately) a competitive edge if you can trademark your specific reason-why or permission-to-believe. "Dri-Weave," by the way, is also trademarked. And P&G has gone that effort one better: they have selected print advertising that focuses on "Dri-Weave." In other words, they *are* treating it as if it were a "second mark" or "sub-brand" of Always; they're also investing in the long-term equity potential of the reason-why itself.

There are other ways to gain ownership besides these. Look at how cleverly the Coca-Cola Company has established ownership of Sprite's reason-why—"Lymon." In the first place, they own it because they created it—literally. It's a fact that Sprite's formulation has a different lemon and lime oil ratio than, say, that of 7-UP. But soft drink customers (particularly teenagers) could care less about the ratio of oils. So, enter the mythological fruit, the "Lymon," to give credibility to Sprite's point-of-difference taste.

One other example of a creative approach to reason-why ownership can be seen in what Advil has done—out of necessity. The brand's main ingredient, ibuprofen, is not something exclusive to Advil; any number of private label brands also use it. So, how to imply ownership of a reason-why? "Advanced Medicine for Pain" becomes Advil's standing customer language for ibuprofen; even better, it alliterates beautifully with the brand name: Advil/Advanced Medicine.

One final way, perhaps the best of all, to guarantee ownership of your brand's credibility is by *creating your own authority*. Of course, once you go to this trouble, you also have to keep investing in that authority (via advertising mentions, direct mail pieces, sponsorships, PR efforts, and the like); otherwise, what you've created never gathers sufficient equity to *be* credible. We've already seen (in the Competitive Framework chapter) how Excedrin has staked its claim as "The Headache Medicine." While there have been clinical studies done to support the brand's headache relief efficacy, the brand has not been content to rely on those for its sole support. Rather, they've created something they call the Headache Resource Center, a tangible "place" where, presumably, experts are working hard to make headaches less frequent and easier to deal with (maybe even a thing of the past!). Whether there really is an institute or center location where this hard work goes on is pretty much irrelevant. What is relevant is that Excedrin is producing separate advertising and direct mail newsletters for the Headache Resource Center, thereby delivering on what many customers would rightly expect of a brand that calls itself "The Headache Medicine."

Avoid Talking to Yourself—Either Going Intrinsic or Extrinsic—

Going back to the sanitary protection reason-why example, while Always was building the equity of "Dri-Weave," one of its competitors (in Australia)—Stayfree—was getting caught up in their own internal successes. They launched a product upgrade that contained a superior absorbency material called sphagnum. Unfortunately, they used this odd and unappealing term in their launch advertising as their reason-why. "Sphagnum" may protect better than "Dri-Weave," but try convincing customers of that! (After the launch, Stayfree elected to make a change; they now call sphagnum "Nature Sorb.")

Something else to watch out for in this same vein is the last-ditch "cite-our-leading-sales-position" approach. This typically results when brand business teams get desperate for some kind of credibility (and when they believe there are no other substantive or creative ways to instill credibility). Not long ago, the Trojan condom brand resorted to something like this in their print campaign: "America's Number 1 Selling Condom." As support for a protection benefit, such information is pure telling, and no selling. If anything, in these days of customer skepticism, being Number 1 is grounds in itself for suspicion! Besides, Americans always prefer the underdog. In cases like these where there are no compelling intrinsic or extrinsic support points, no reason-why is probably in the brand's best interest.

Sometimes You Have to Borrow Interest—No brand likes to admit it, but there are times when citing another brand or product in the company's portfolio—or even going outside the company for another mark—is the right way to gain maximum credibility for the brand's main benefit. The introduction of the hugely successful Swiss Army Watch was supported by nothing less than the world-famous "corporate mark," the Swiss Army Knife. Advertising simply showcased the new watch visually and reassured the sale by the statement: *"Built Like Our Swiss Army Knife."*

Look at what Hallmark Greeting Cards has done in their highly unconventional print campaign: the simple but elegant *"Hallmark"* logo centered on a white page is the gist of the advertising. In other words, *"What makes Hallmark special is that it's Hallmark."* Not many brands could plausibly carry off such an assumptive stance. But because so many greeting card customers *do*, in fact, check for the Hallmark insignia when they shop for (or receive) a greeting card, it works. The "interest" that Hallmark is borrowing comes straight from their "trademark equity bank."

There are also an increasing number of brands and line extensions that are leveraging **co-branding** for added credibility. Haagen Dazs has tried to bolster its position this way in the high-growth, frozen novelties segment—more specifically, the ice cream sandwich segment. One might assume that the brand name alone would be sufficient to give that current customer "one good reason-why" he or she should try Haagen Dazs; but the company isn't assuming that. Rather, they have teamed up with Pepperidge Farm in their ice cream sandwiches to give added interest (and indulgent taste reassurance) to the customer. The result: a co-branded, intrinsic reason-why.

Finally, in some categories the best interest you can borrow is *where it's from.* We all appreciate something of quality—even more so when that quality derives from a unique place: the Alps (Evian), Tennessee Mountains (Jack Daniels), Belgium (Godiva). But such "lifestyle" brands are not the only ones that can build in more credibility or authenticity via a special location. Wal*Mart continues to tout its "all-American" made products (even after they were found to have overstated that claim!). And Land's End often features their products in the context of their appealing, special sources—such as their Shetland Sweaters (which they assert "shouldn't come from Brooklyn").

Synopsis of Reason-Why/Permission-to-Believe Approaches

By way of summary, here are some further examples of credibility devices in a brand's positioning:

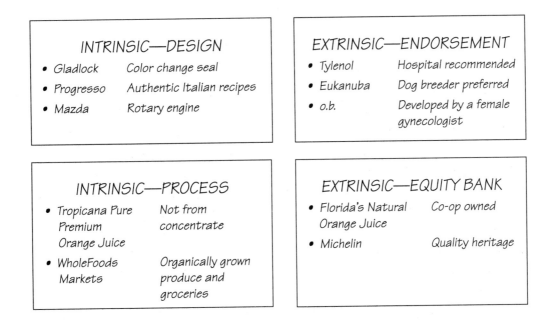

INTRINSIC—DESIGN	
• Gladlock	Color change seal
• Progresso	Authentic Italian recipes
• Mazda	Rotary engine

EXTRINSIC—ENDORSEMENT	
• Tylenol	Hospital recommended
• Eukanuba	Dog breeder preferred
• o.b.	Developed by a female gynecologist

INTRINSIC—PROCESS	
• Tropicana Pure Premium Orange Juice	Not from concentrate
• WholeFoods Markets	Organically grown produce and groceries

EXTRINSIC—EQUITY BANK	
• Florida's Natural Orange Juice	Co-op owned
• Michelin	Quality heritage

Multiple Reasons-Why

As with multiple benefits, there are times when it makes good competitive sense to have more than one reason-why. And, as with multiple benefits, when that happens it's critical that all reasons-why be in alignment, that they come together in an articulated, single-minded proposition. A good example of this is what Reach toothbrush did upon introduction. The product had a number of features that supported the benefit of cavity prevention. But these all found common expression in the notion of "like a dental instrument" (i.e., "angled neck," "higher and lower bristles," and "compact head"). That simple-minded notion is what customers remembered. And, as a multiple-intrinsic reason-why, it brought powerful credibility to the new brand.

Reason-Why and the Benefit(s): Constructing the Mechanics

We've already noted the importance of "dovetailing" the reason-why with the benefit. The two are so closely related that they form the linchpin of the Brand Positioning Statement. When you are thinking through the construction of this linchpin, keep in mind that there are two basic approaches available to you: *the classic approach* and *the default approach.*

The classic approach truly distinguishes legitimate reason-why material (design features, formulae, proprietary processes) from "benefit material." Whereas the default approach actually uses "benefit material" for support—more specifically, employing a "lower-order" benefit (such as a product benefit) to provide the reason-why for a "higher order" one (such as a customer/functional benefit). To make this clearer, here are some examples of each:

Approach	Positioning Benefit	Positioning Reason-Why
Classic	1. Gladlock keeps your food fresher (customer benefit) 2. Tums fights osteoporosis (product benefit)	1. Support: Gladlock's patented green color change seal (design feature) 2. Support: Tums calcium-rich formula (formula)
Default	1. Goodyear Tires reassure you that your family will be protected from danger (emotional benefit) 2. Fosamax helps you fight fear of osteoporosis (emotional benefit)	1. Support: Tires grip the road (product benefit) and you maintain expert road-handling (customer benefit) 2. Support: It builds bones and gets you moving (product and customer benefit)

Of the two, the classic approach inherently has more appeal because it adds specific, ownable brand traits or "properties" to the brand positioning. It also avoids the most likely pitfall of the default approach: building a benefit-upon-benefit "house of cards" that fails to close the sale.

Reason-Why Checklist Exercise

Much like the competitive framework exercise, here is a handy checklist you might want to use to identify a good starter list of credibility material for your Brand Positioning Statement. Keep in mind that we are talking about engineering the credibility into that strategic document. There are many other ways to build credibility into the total brand proposition, such as using testimonials or challenges in your advertising execution. But these kinds of "executional credibility" can come and go; what's built into the positioning should last.

Reason-Why Checklist

BENEFIT(S): _____

_____

REASON-WHY OPTIONS:

Design: _____

_____

Formula/Ingredient: _____

_____

Endorsement: _____

_____

Claim Research: _____

_____

Source: _____

_____

Other: _____

_____

KEY PRINCIPLES

Summary

✔ Reason-why and permission-to-believe are two sides of the same coin—both are means of instilling *legitimate credibility* into your brand positioning—mainly against the main benefit. The former tends to be intrinsic; the latter, extrinsic. If used in combination, the effect can be powerful.

✔ Not every brand has to have the added credibility of a reason-why or permission-to-believe. But when a brand elects to forgo these, it's a good idea to ask, "Are we missing a competitive-edge opportunity here?"

✔ Reasons-why should dovetail with the product's main benefit(s). They also need to be couched in customer-memorable language, not high-tech jargon.

✔ The biggest danger toward losing the credibility you seek is in *manufacturer-speak* . . . or talking to yourself. Sticking with customer language will help you avoid this.

✔ Whenever possible, attempt to own your reasons-why—by using them consistently, trademarking them if possible, and supporting them with advertising investment.

✔ Don't be reluctant to go with multiple reasons-why in your brand positioning, particularly if you're offering multiple benefits or you're driving for a competitive edge. The key is to align the "bundle" of reasons-why into a single-minded "credibility proposition." Be sure to list them in rank-order of importance in your positioning statement, so that it's clear which ones are to work the hardest.

CHAPTER 8

Developing a Winning Personality
Through Brand Character

"Image is everything."
Andre Agassi

Now we come to the sixth and final element of sound brand positioning: brand character. And while it is the final element, it is in no way to be interpreted as the least important. It is, perhaps, the most influential element of brand image. As the quote above suggests, taken from a Canon camera commercial aired years ago in which Andre Agassi appears, image is exceedingly important.

What It Is

As you have learned from an earlier chapter, *competitive framework* deals with **what** your brand is as a category or classification of products. Is your Ricoh a fax machine or multi-tasking small business tool that contains fax, copier, and printer all in one? Is Jell-O the brand of gelatin or the light dessert?

Brand character, on the other hand, addresses **who** your brand is as a personage. It reflects the very personality you create for your specific brand. It represents the complexion, temperament, and spirit of the brand. As such, it is a strategic element of positioning and of the brand.

What It Isn't

Brand character should not be confused with "tone," which is a frequent mistake made by client advertisers and agency people who should know better. Tone denotes mood, style, or manner of expression for a given execution. Tone is an executional element, not a strategic one.

Stated another way, brand character gets to the very values of the brand's personality, whereas tone captures a particular mood. As an example, one may be a very serious-minded individual who engages in a bit of whimsy from time to time. The personality is serious-minded. The specific mood at a given point of time is one of whimsy. Brand character is part of the personality make-up of the individual, whereas tone reflects an episodic mood.

Keep in mind that if all the advertising for your product reflects the same tonality, your current and potential customers will come to perceive that tonality as the brand's personality. A campaign for an OTC product that is executed with humor may tag it with a personality customers perceive as humorous and, perhaps, ineffective. So, it is very important to define the personality you want to establish for a brand in its positioning and to review executional submissions to ensure they are in sync with that personality. Otherwise, the marketer risks having execution define personality, which is a case of the proverbial "tail wagging the dog."

Importance of Brand Character

Brand character is an important strategic weapon. It serves to:

Differentiate Brands with Common Features and Benefits—Take the two soft drink giants, Coke and Pepsi, for example. During the 1970s Coke battled with an image (personality or brand character) it perpetuated which consumers perceived as conservative, stodgy, republican, old, and such.

Needless to say, this image is not very attractive to the youth of America, who have the highest per-capita consumption of soft drinks. Pepsi, on the other hand, enjoyed an image of youthful, fun, active, and adventuresome, among other personality traits. Think about it. If you were to engineer a brand character for a soft drink, which would you choose? Coke of the 1970s? Hardly. If you know anything about soft drinks and the consuming core you would choose Pepsi. So did America's youth!

The brand character of Coke came about as a function of its position in the marketplace and campaign executions whose tonality was baseball, apple pie and Chevrolet—a piece of Americana. Pepsi's brand character was crafted to set itself apart from Coca-Cola in a way that would: be positive with heavy soft drink consumers; make a weakness of Coke's ubiquity and resultant imagery; and be difficult, if not impossible, for Coke to occupy. Basically, it came down to creating a brand character Pepsi could own, and making it the focus of sale.

No one TV spot captured these differences in brand character better than Pepsi's *Shady Acres*. This spot serves to use brand character to differentiate Pepsi from Coke. It starts off with a party of septuagenarians and octogenarians dancing to rock 'n' roll music. We also view old people tossing Frisbees and roller-blading. They are drinking Pepsi as they party. The location is Shady Acres, a retirement community that portrays its residents as being young at heart.

The commercial cuts to two route salesmen who are off-loading cases of Coca-Cola. One says to the other, "Wait, I thought Shady Acres was to get the Coke and the frat house was to get the Pepsi." The other responds, "Coke, Pepsi, what's the difference?" with a shrug of his shoulders.

The spot then cuts to the frat house where a very stuffy young man calls out a number, "I-24," for a game of bingo while he sips Coke through a straw. The music is classical . . . and boring. We hear snores coming from his frat brothers who are asleep in deep, stuffy chairs.

Once again, the spot cuts back to Shady Acres as a young-minded octogenarian man dances, holding a can of Pepsi, to rock 'n' roll music with a fiery septuagenarian woman.

The difference is clear; the imagery portrayed for Coke is old-fashioned, stuffy, conservative, everything a young person does not want to be identified with. On the other hand, the Pepsi character is active, fun, young at heart, outrageous, or everything a young person would aspire to be—personality-wise! The difference is not only clear but also meaningful. The difference is not what is in the can (i.e., the liquid) but the brand character. And what a difference it is!

Give Customers an Additional Reason to Choose Your Brand—We like buying from people we like. When you establish your brand as likable (i.e., reflecting a personality or set of values that you appreciate) you encourage customer affiliation and a potential positive relationship. In making the brand more attractive and appealing in character to the target, the marketer invites customers to join the brand. After seeing Shady Acres, who would want to join Coke? On the other hand, all party-loving teens would certainly want to be affiliated with Pepsi and the brand character it represents. It comes down to 'what do you stand for' and 'who will you attract' with that stance.

Perhaps one of the most successful trademarks to be built upon brand character is Nike. Nike epitomizes the positive values of sports—marketing its products by lauding the exploits and personalities of alpha athletes such as the former NBA great Michael Jordan. Who doesn't want to be like Mike? He's not just a winner but a hero! He is competitive, a leader, a positive role model, numero uno, genuine in a world of phonies, a gentleman, articulate, and not just likable, but lovable. (But then what would you expect me to say about Michael? I'm from Chicago and a loyal Chicago Bulls fan who bemoans his retirement!)

This brand character is one with which every sports-minded individual would like to affiliate, regardless if you are a fan of the Seattle Supersonics or the Chicago Bulls, or a youth from America or Lebanon. Nike has successfully established an enduring brand character to differentiate its products from its competition. Yes, Nike may enjoy some technological product advantages, but the majority of its consumers are either unaware of the value of the technology or, believe it or not, don't even use the product for its intended sport.

The Pepsi and Nike brand characters are not fortuitous. They didn't just happen. They were engineered. Both Pepsi and Nike just did it!

Importantly, the brand character is not just a collection of words whose sounds and meanings are created to please senior management. Instead, they are words that articulate an enduring personality, one envisioned and embraced by senior management to embody the brand. What's more, the brand character is reflected in product design, benefits, and all elements of the brand's bundle (i.e., marketing mix elements such as package design, promotion, and so on). In fact, Michael Jordan got involved in the actual design and testing of products bearing his endorsement for Nike.

Understanding Brand Character—A Tale of Two Campaigns

When we introduced Reach toothbrush, while I was its product director at the Johnson & Johnson Company, we articulated a brand character we hoped to establish for the emerging brand. In 1977 we were among the first marketers to recognize the importance of brand character and employ it in competitively positioning a product. It is evident in the introductory TV commercial for the brand, "The Inventor." In this spot, we see a male presenter who is in his mid-fifties, dressed in a white shirt and bow tie. The presenter (the inventor) looks the camera (or viewer) in the eyes while he holds up a standard toothbrush and asks, "They invented fluoride toothpaste to help fight cavities, why hasn't someone invented a better toothbrush?" Then he proceeds to ask questions about design (such as "What if they angled it like a dental instrument so it could clean hard-to-reach back teeth?") as he transforms a standard toothbrush into a Reach toothbrush. When we ask marketers to define the brand character from a review of the TV spot, they respond "professional, advanced, efficacious, scientific, credible," etc. Now for the next question: if this is the brand character and you are leading product research and development, what would you work on? Your answers are probably similar to theirs, which consistently register:

- advanced designs
- clinical studies demonstrating superior cleaning and/or cavity fighting efficacy
- endorsement from the American Dental Association
- new products directed at specific dental care problems (e.g., brush for people with orthodontics)
- a youth version of the adult brush

The introductory spot ran for several years (it worked!). It was replaced by a campaign referred to as "Mr. Reach." The campaign features an animated character, Mr. Reach, who has a flip-top head (to demonstrate the brush and way it cleans). Voice-over is used to establish the situation for Mr. Reach. The announcer voice-over is distinctly British, but lighthearted. When marketers are shown a spot from this campaign and asked to define the brand character, they respond with "approachable, fun, whimsical, lighthearted," etc. Now, let's ask the same question we raised with "The Inventor" spot. "If this is the brand character and you are leading product research and development, what would you work on?" The answers to this question are predictable:

- fun shapes and designs
- character endorsements and icons on the handles (such as Disney or Looney Tunes)
- neon colors

These activities do not reinforce the brand's superior efficacy and advanced imagery. Yet those were the kind of actions taken. The company introduced neon, glow-in-the-dark colors. In effect, they undermined the superior efficacy imagery of the Reach toothbrush. Why? Your guess is as good as ours, but we believe it was probably because a revolving-door marketing team didn't fully appreciate the value of brand character and allowed a creative idea (albeit a very engaging one) to supersede strategic direction.

Through all these examples, we hope we have made it clear that brand character is a strategic element of sound, strategic brand positioning.

Getting at Brand Character

In defining a brand's character or personality the marketer needs to use words that describe someone's personality. After all, in defining a brand's character we are really describing its personality. The words one uses must be words you would use in talking about a friend's, family member's or even your own personality. We use words such as approachable, charismatic, friendly, authoritative, intelligent, enthusiastic, knowledgeable, discriminating, and such. Any time you come across a word to describe brand character that does not identify a personality trait or value, throw it out! It doesn't belong in the brand character statement.

Exercise #1—Identifying Brand Character

Let's put what we have learned about brand character to work. Pick a category—cars, perfumes, notebook computers—whatever. Look through a few magazines (e.g., *Newsweek, Good Housekeeping, Men's Fitness, Money*) and pull out ads for brands in the category you have selected. Select two brands and define the brand character for each.

Word choice is extremely important. Not only is it important to ensure that each word identifies a personality trait but also to ensure that all the personality traits are in harmony. Once again, we are in search of integrity of character. In the few cases where clients have defined a brand character, we often find that the words used are contradictory. For example, we often see the words "caring" and "authoritative" together in the same brand character description. Perhaps they can coexist, but we believe they can be found together because those attempting to sell a specific brand character

> ## Remember:
>
> *The words one uses must be words you would use in talking about a friend's, family member's, or even your own personality. Any time you come across a word to describe brand character that does not identify a personality trait or value, throw it out! Replace it with an alternate word that you would clearly use to describe someone's personality.*

are catering to the biases of their management. In other words, the specific word choice is being influenced by what the authors of the brand character believe their management wants to see. Sometimes, words like these are just picked up from an existing brand character statement (i.e., use what has been there).

Developing Brand Character

Identifying an existing brand character is not a difficult task. On the other hand, developing a brand character for one's own brand is typically more problematic. Marketers find it difficult to create a brand character and, when that task is complete, to gain agreement on that identity from diverse groups of people (such as the advertising agency, internal support groups, senior management, etc.).

We have found it helpful to start with the concrete. Here is one way to do it.

Identify a Celebrity Who Best Characterizes Your Brand—One of the most productive techniques is to identify a celebrity who you believe best characterizes your brand. We are not referring to a spokesperson or endorser. Instead, we are asking you to address the following question: *If your brand were a person, who would it be?* This could be any person. But any person may not be known to those with whom you want to co-create a brand character, or to convince that it is the right one for your brand. If we suggest in this first step that our brand is Arthur Goldberg you are very likely to ask, "Who is Arthur Goldberg?" However, if we were to say our brand is Mel Gibson, we start on common footing because you know who he is. You may disagree with our choice, but we have established common ground for our dialogue and creation of a brand character. So we start by asking, *"If your brand were a celebrity, who would it be?"* In this way, we are taking the task from the abstract to the concrete so that everyone involved may participate and understand.

Define the Personality Characteristics of the Chosen Celebrity—If you were to agree that the brand character is best exemplified by Mel Gibson, we are ready to go to the next step, which is to define which of his personality characteristics match the brand. We might agree that it is not Mel Gibson as we think we know him but Mel Gibson in a specific role such as William Wallace in *Braveheart*. We then use this concrete example to identify personality characteristics to define the brand's character.

What do we do if there is not general agreement on Mel Gibson overall or on his role as William Wallace in *Braveheart?* Simple. Throw out another celebrity. Find out where the disagreement lies. It won't be in the celebrity but in the personality characteristics. So it leads to contrasts, new word choices, and alternate celebrities. Through this dialoguing process the team of creators shouldn't have too much difficulty agreeing on a celebrity and a set of personality characteristics.

Identify Personality Characteristics You Wish to Establish for Your Brand Consistent with the Product Features and Brand Bundle— This is not a process of wishful thinking. Please don't choose a celebrity because you would like to be like him or her. Instead choose a celebrity because the personality characteristics resemble those of your brand. If we are marketing something that is fine, such as Fendi silk scarves, Mel Gibson will not be appropriate. Instead, we might choose Audrey Hepburn or Isabella Rossellini. Their personality characteristics of elegance, class, sophistication, luxury, etc., more closely match the product, its features, benefits, and imagery. If the personality characteristics do not match the intended brand bundle then you need to find a celebrity whose characteristics do match. Also, everyone has a multitude of personality characteristics, so the marketer's challenge is to select those few that best match up and create the brand character you wish to establish.

There are other ways to approach development of brand character besides the use of a celebrity. Some marketers have had success by selecting an animal and defining its personality characteristics and values. We have experienced significant success with using magazines. This is particularly helpful in selling others because it allows for visual contrasts. Another technique is to borrow from well-known, established brands in other categories. In borrowing from other brands we start by identifying the brand whose brand character we believe we share. We then go on to identify those characteristics of that brand which we believe are applicable to our brand. Yet another technique is to identify a specific role in society that is familiar to all (such as the babysitter from next door).

The key to all these techniques is to start from the concrete, someone or something everyone knows. In this way, the marketer will be able to establish common ground and begin a meaningful dialogue to enhance the development of brand character. Celebrities, animals, magazines, other established brands, societal roles—choose the one that works for you!

Exercise #2—Developing Brand Character

Try using the celebrity technique to create a brand character for your brand.

Celebrity:

Personality Characteristics

-
-
-
-

Toward More Meaningful Communication

A young, highly creative product director with whom we worked believed that the focus of sale for his brand should be brand character. He found his brand in a similar situation to that of Coke in the 1970s. His brand had a very old-fashioned image. It was a brand one's father or mother used but not oneself. While his advertising agency agreed the brand character needed to be updated, the agency was not able to come to a common understanding of what that brand character should be.

Frustrated by numerous attempts to co-create a brand character or gain agreement to a proposed character, the creative product director had a three-minute film developed to **illustrate** the brand character he believed should define the brand. The film was made up of clips from TV ads (from a multitude of brands from diverse categories), supers of words, and provocative music. Everything he used in the film was taken from existing material. He created nothing new but the resultant pieced-together film.

Coming onto the scene well after the product director had been faced with the challenge and developed the film, we were very impressed by this example of defining and communicating a brand character. We were impressed with his initiative, creativity, and use of available materials to make his words come alive, to make them concrete. We were particularly impressed with his use of music. Think about it. Music is yet another way to express brand character, personality. Thinking back to our days in the soft drink business, new campaign development was marked by a selling idea, key visual, and music (which went beyond tune to include words).

You may not have to go as far as this talented and creative product director did. You have enough techniques with those we gave you. But add music to a magazine cover or stills from magazines and you will find a more compelling way to define, communicate, and make understandable the desired brand character you wish to establish.

One Final Note

Established brands such as the one managed by our product director client typically have a more difficult time in establishing a brand character. The reason is that through years of marketing, or mis-marketing, they already have a brand character. The further one departs from the existing brand character, the more likely the attempt will fail. So what do you do when your brand is at point B and you need to get to point Z?

First, you need to **recognize** where you want to get to . . . point Z. You are the architect of the brand and one of your roles, as we have mentioned, is to create the strategic vision and platform for the brand. If you need, want, or aspire to get to point Z, then recognize it.

Second, **chart** and **manage** your way to point Z *over time!* Do not try to do it in one leap. It takes time to wean potential customers off their perception of your brand. If you move too quickly, if the change is too radical, they will not believe you. At best you confuse the customer. At worst they outright reject this new notion and your brand.

Making significant changes to brand character will require you to know where you are going, identify and manage your way there, and allow the time needed for potential customers to get comfortable with the changes. It will also take commitment and constancy of effort. Finally, the emerging new brand character will be communicated via each element of the marketing mix—not just advertising. As such, it may require formulation changes, new packaging architecture and/or graphics, trademark modification, endorsements, line extensions, addition of new services, and so on. Brand character comes from more than what you say. Potential customers perceive it by everything that you do.

KEY PRINCIPLES

Summary

✔ Brand character is a strategic element of brand positioning and strongly influences imagery.

✔ Brand character deals with **who** your brand is as a personage. It defines and reflects the personality of the brand.

✔ It should not be confused with tone, which denotes mood or style of expression. Tone is an executional element.

✔ Keep in mind that if all the product's advertising reflects the same tonality, current and potential customers will come to perceive that tonality as the brand's personality.

✔ Brand character may be used to differentiate products with common features and benefits.

✔ It may also provide customers with an additional, important reason to choose your product. It encourages customer affiliation and a potential positive relationship.

✔ Successful brand characters are engineered.

✔ The successful brand character is reflected not just in words but in all elements of the marketing mix. It gains meaning from everything you do—from product formulation, to packaging, to servicing, and so on.

✔ Moreover, brand character influences everything you do. Marketing mix elements such as product development and design, line extensions, and such, will be influenced by the brand character.

✔ In defining a brand character, use words that you would use in talking about a friend's, family member's, or even your own personality.

✔ Any time you come across a word to describe brand character that does not identify a personality trait or value, throw it out! It does not belong there.

✔ Not only is it important to ensure that each word identifies a personality trait but also to ensure that all the personality traits are in harmony.

✔ In developing a brand character, start with the concrete.

✔ One of the most productive techniques is to identify a celebrity who you believe best characterizes your product and intended brand bundle. We start by asking, *"If your brand were a celebrity, who would it be?"*

✔ Next, define the personality characteristics of the chosen celebrity.

✔ Then, identify personality characteristics you wish to establish for your brand that are consistent with the product features and brand bundle. Everyone has a multitude of personality characteristics. The marketer's challenge is to select those few that best match up and create the brand character you wish to establish.

✔ Other techniques that may be used to go from the abstract to the concrete in developing brand character include the use of animals, magazines, other brands, and societal roles.

✔ Remember to link specific personality characteristics with product attributes, features and/or benefits. The brand characteristics are more than wishful thinking.

✔ Add music to a magazine cover or stills from magazines and you will find a more compelling way to define, communicate, and make understandable the desired brand character you wish to establish.

✔ Making significant changes to brand character will require you to know where you are going. Identify and manage your way there, and allow the time needed for potential customers to get comfortable with the change.

✔ The emerging new brand character must be communicated via each element of the marketing mix—not just advertising.

✔ Brand character comes from more than what you say. Potential as well as current customers perceive it by everything that you do.

CHAPTER 9

Bullet-Proofing Your Positioning

"Wax-on, Wax-off; Brush-up, Brush-down"

Now it's time to pull together a Brand Positioning Statement for your brand.

Wax-On, Wax-Off

In the movie *The Karate Kid* a gang of thugs is terrorizing Daniel, a teenager new to their high school. Unfortunately, his tormentors are dedicated students and enthusiastic practitioners of karate, which means Daniel takes a lot of abuse. Physical abuse! In an effort to put an end to his torment, or just survive for the moment, he challenges one of his assailants to a match at a future karate tournament. His only salvation is to learn karate and learn it fast.

Mr. Miyagi, an elderly Okinawan who has befriended Daniel, offers to teach him the empty-hand way of self-defense. Mr. Miyagi takes Daniel to his home where he puts the rather nervous and frightened teen to work reconditioning his deck and wooden fence. He instructs Daniel in the techniques of wax-on and wax-off to recondition the deck. He shows Daniel how to brush-up and brush-down to paint the fence. After a few days of this backbreaking, muscle aching work the frustrated Daniel rebels and confronts Miyagi. He tells Miyagi he is tired of being his personal slave. He needs Mr. Miyagi to teach him karate, not to take advantage of his availability and work him to exhaustion.

Mr. Miyagi responds by demanding that Daniel show him the technique used to wax-on and wax-off. The boy goes through it half-heartedly. Mr. Miyagi demonstrates and has Daniel imitate the technique with focus and precision. He also barks out an order for Daniel to show him the technique he taught him to brush-up and brush-down when painting the fence. Once again Daniel makes scant effort to execute the technique properly. Mr. Miyagi shouts for the boy to focus. When Miyagi gets the response he is looking for he throws a flurry of quick punches and kicks at young Daniel who deftly blocks each one with the wax-on and wax-off, brush-up and brush-down techniques he has been taught and applied over the preceding days in his labors.

Up to now, with each exercise we have undertaken, we have been engaged in waxing-on and waxing-off, brushing-up and brushing-down. Unto themselves, the exercises are highly productive but of limited importance. Put the results together and one could have the start of something big. We have everything we need to pull it all together into a competitive Brand Positioning Statement.

Brand Positioning Statement

To _____, _____
          (Target Customer Group-Need)   *(Brand)*

Is the brand of _____
                              (Competitive Framework)

That _____
                              (Benefit)

Because _____
                              (Reason-Why)

The *(Brand Character)* is _____

If you have been diligent in participating in the exercises, using the tools presented in the previous chapters, you can easily piece together a draft Brand Positioning Statement. Use the format provided on page 110 to create a Brand Positioning Statement for the product or service you are responsible for marketing. One piece of advice: write in pencil. It makes the editing process easier!

Technically Speaking

With your Brand Positioning Statement completed we are ready to bullet-proof it. We start with an audit of those technical aspects of the statement. In other words, did we follow the principles espoused in earlier chapters? Ask yourself these questions:

1. Is the **target customer group** specified by demographics? Usage behavior? An important need we can uniquely satisfy and/or own with our brand? Remember we want to capture all three in our quest for the ideal target definition. Go back and incorporate them all. Also make sure you have identified a need your product can uniquely satisfy; or one that is important but has been ignored by the competition. Remember this need serves as a trap by which we will entice our target. The benefit that pays off this need will ensnare the target customer group and make it ours.

2. Is the **competitive framework** too broad? This essential element identifies where your product will source its volume. Or it may be used to provide customers with a new frame-of-reference from which to springboard a meaningful benefit. If the competitive framework is too broad customers will not take the product or your claims about it seriously. On the other hand, we also need to check and ensure that the competitive framework is not too narrow. If it is, we are going to miss important volume growth and benefit claim opportunities. How do we tell if we have the competitive framework just right? This is an important question; one that needs to be answered by the target customer group.

3. What is the **intended customer take-away?** Is it obvious from reading the benefit statement? The most common problems stem from imprecise

language in the benefit statement. For example, the benefit may be stated as "efficacious" in remedying whatever malady the product treats. But the word efficacious may be interpreted in many different ways. Should it mean fastest, most complete, longest lasting, fool-proof, etc.? Make certain that the statement is incapable of being misunderstood.

Another underlying problem is the employment of a litany of benefits that are not aligned in an expected and/or memorable manner. Yes, we said that the Brand Positioning Statement is written using strategic, not customer, language. We are not changing our position. Instead, we are emphasizing that the benefit should be clear to all constituencies. This includes the customer, members of the marketing team, agency partners, and even senior management. The benefit is the payoff for the customer, so it needs to be crystal clear. A good test is to share the Brand Positioning Statement and have that individual playback the benefit. If s/he is unable to do so, then you know your benefit statement is not clear. We don't want to confuse the marketing team, agency partner, or customers!

4. Does the benefit deliver a **meaningful point-of-difference** to the target customer group versus the competition? We want customers to choose our product, *prefer it*, based upon their perception that it better meets their important needs. Check to ensure you have not just laid out a category benefit that fails to distinguish your product from, or make it more appealing than, the competition. We are about creating brand loyalty and it takes, among other things, a benefit that meaningfully differentiates your product from the competition.

5. Is the **reason-why** aligned with the benefit? Clear? Meaningful? The reason for the reason-why is to support the benefit and perception you want to create in the minds of your customers. Its purpose is to make the benefit believable and put your positioning on rock-solid footing with customers. First and foremost, the reason-why must be aligned with the benefit. If your benefit is fastest relief, then the reason-why must support this benefit. You may have a compelling reason-why for long-lasting relief, but if it is not your benefit then it is misguided to use it alone.

The reason-why must be clear to all. By clear we mean it must evoke a head-nod of understanding from your intended target customer as it relates to the benefit. It must also be readily understandable so that your target, not just company insiders and experts, appreciates how it works. And yes, it must be meaningful. This relates to two factors. One, look for intrinsic elements. Specifically, the product design, attributes, etc., provide strong potential support for the benefit. A good example to keep in mind is Always sanitary protection brand with Dri-Weave. The Dri-Weave design is part of the intrinsic design of the Always products and is used to make more meaningful the superior benefit of best protection versus competitive sanitary protection products. Two, reason-why needs to further differentiate your product in such a way that it contributes to the kind of loyalty enjoyed by brands (as opposed to products). In other words, it needs to be convincing and add credibility. Try to include an extrinsic element to add credibility. In this instance you might want to keep Gatorade in mind in terms of their securing endorsement from the major sports leagues (e.g., National Basketball Association) in America and alpha athletes such as Michael Jordan in his heydey playing professional basketball.

6. Does your **brand character** statement reflect an image and personality you want to establish for your brand in the marketplace? The brand character statement has strategic implications, which we pointed out in the Reach toothbrush example. Accordingly, this question should address two points. The first deals with meaningfulness, the strategic imperative. Do you know what it will take to drive your brand and encourage customer affiliation with it? The second is about clarity, nothing more than ensuring that the brand character statement captures the intended personality and image you intend.

The words you use for the brand character should be personality characteristics and values. The words chosen must be the way you would refer to another person. Along this line, try to identify a celebrity who embodies the personality and image you are trying to establish. Do you have a celebrity? Did the listing of personality characteristics flow from the celebrity? Including the name of this celebrity in the brand character statement should serve to make more readily understandable the image you plan to establish. Additionally, inclusion of the celebrity's name gives the brand character statement a dimension often lacking with a listing of mere personality characteristics.

It is a good idea to convert the listing of personality characteristics into a narrative descriptor of the intended brand character. We find this latter approach is a more rich way of communicating the brand character in a Brand Positioning Statement, even though it is a more difficult practice to master.

The Audit Tool

You might find it helpful to use the bullet-proofing audit tool provided to strengthen your Brand Positioning Statement from a technical standpoint. Use a 10-point rating scale with "10" representing excellent and "1" indicating it is poor. This will help objectify your subjective judgment. But we are going for more than rating scores. The purpose is to identify areas of the Brand Positioning Statement that need improvement with an opportunity to identify the direction needed to strengthen the statement. Give it a try, and then go back and edit your Brand Positioning Statement so it is technically perfect!

The Big Strategic Picture

We have bullet-proofed your Brand Positioning Statement using the audit tool. But piecing together technically correct parts does not mean that we have created a positioning to drive brand loyalty. It only means that we have done an admirable job in optimizing the strategic positioning we have chosen.

What we need to do now is step back and ensure that our Brand Positioning Statement is strategically sound. In other words, this is about separating the forest from the trees—seeing the big strategic picture. Strategy serves a higher purpose and order. Strategy is about winning in the marketplace by getting customers to think and behave in a way that contributes to creating brand loyalty.

So let's move on to the next chapter to learn how to get the big strategic picture through the use of the Positioning Matrix. This practice and tool will help you display your strategic positioning versus your competitors. Additionally, this tool can be used to display alternate strategic positioning options for your brand.

AUDIT TOOL
Brand Positioning Statement

Target Customer Group-Need	Rating	Needed Adjustments
• Demographics • Usage behavior • Ownable need • All 3-dimensions	_____ _____ _____ _____	

Competitive Framework	Rating	Needed Adjustments
• Too broad/restrictive • Meaningful frame-of-reference	_____ _____	

Benefit	Rating	Needed Adjustments
• Clear customer take-away • Meaningful point-of-difference	_____ _____	

Reason-Why	Rating	Needed Adjustments
• Aligned with benefit • Intrinsics consistent with product • Utilizes extrinsic credibility aid • Easily understood/appreciated by target	_____ _____ _____ _____	

Brand Character	Rating	Needed Adjustments
• Identifies celebrity • Contains personality characteristics/values meaningful and consistent with brand bundle and desired image • Clearly communicates brand character	_____ _____ _____	

CHAPTER 10

Getting the Big Picture with the Positioning Matrix

If developing your brand positioning is "job number one," then understanding your competitors' brand positionings has got to be "job number two."

Getting to a Competitive Positioning

As we have seen so far, crafting a unique brand positioning requires deep "spade work" within each of the six elements of a positioning statement. But being unique doesn't necessarily mean being competitive, which is the ultimate goal for any brand positioning. How can you know, really, how competitive your positioning is without "cross-checking" the *inferred positionings* of your key competitors?

This notion of "cross-checking" (what good pilots do with their various aircraft instruments, to keep the plane headed in the right direction) should be taken literally . . . because the best way to size up the competitiveness of *your* brand's positioning is to lay it out right next to those of your competition. As you'll see in the following chart, this laying out of positionings is nothing more than a build on the basic structure of a Brand Positioning Statement—a "format twist" to *displaying your thinking*—you know, that

116

mental and written activity that answers the question, "How do I really know what I think, until I see what I say?":

Positioning Matrix

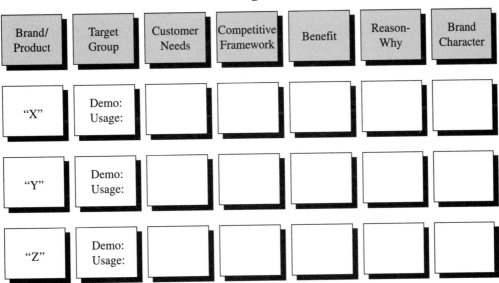

Brand/Product	Target Group	Customer Needs	Competitive Framework	Benefit	Reason-Why	Brand Character
"X"	Demo: Usage:					
"Y"	Demo: Usage:					
"Z"	Demo: Usage:					

The simplicity of this matrix tool is evident, but once each "square" is filled in, the matrix becomes a highly analytical tool as well. Of course, the value of any analysis you do with the matrix is directly proportional to the validity of the "square inputs." Completing the matrix squares for your brand should be the easy part—assuming you've already built your own brand positioning. Here are some pointers for the more difficult part—inferring the brand positionings for each of your key competitors:

Inferring Competitive Positionings

- Assemble a varied team of colleagues whose opinions you trust (from your agency, other category brands in your company, market research, etc.)

(continued ...)

- Assemble the current *packaging, advertising campaign, promotional materials* and any other relevant competitive information that's publicly available (such as pricing) for each of your competitors

- Have each team member complete her/his own matrix using "bullet points" while viewing the current ad campaign (*all spots possible*)

- After sharing everyone's matrix, build a "consensus" matrix

Once you have "consensus positionings" for your competitors, it's a good idea to put them aside for a few days, and then look at them with fresh eyes (and maybe even with those of a couple of other colleagues, who didn't take part in the consensus build-up). Now you're ready to do the analytical work—to try to objectively assess which brand in the category has the most competitive positioning platform.

This assessment requires at least two phases: the *judgment phase* and the *check-out phase*. In the judgment phase, you're still relying on intuition (as well as on any inside knowledge you may have regarding the strengths and weaknesses of your category). In the check-out phase you're confirming and amending the collective judgments by hearing from category users—preferably heavy users (who typically have the best knowledge of the current positionings of category brands).

Competitive Positioning Assessment—Judgment Phase

Perhaps the most challenging aspect in *objectively* assessing your competitors' brand positionings is in laying aside your natural biases. Somehow we can always see the errors of our enemies' ways, but we have a much tougher time with any of our own shortcomings. In working with the positioning matrix, it's a good idea to assume—if only for the sake of argument—that your positioning is *not* the best, strongest, or most competitive (a kind of devil's advocate posture).

Once you've done this, there are a number of "tricks" you can use in quickly getting into the matrix and deciphering its points of strength and weakness:

1. Start by looking across each brand's positioning—how well do the six parts hang together? Is there a continuity to the statement? (This is also a good time to use the positioning audit tool we looked at earlier.)

2. Recognize that, within any positioning statement, there are *natural pairs*, elements that reflect off one another, or that act as two sides of the same coin. Among these natural pairs are: **customer needs and benefit; target customer group and brand character; and benefit and reason-why.** There should be a tight linkage between each of these pairs, to the extent that they often include some similar language. Take a look at a recent advanced toothbrush category matrix:

Check out how well you think some of these natural pairs hang together. Colgate Precision's stated customer needs include both a **physical or rational need** (prevent gum disease) and a **psychological or emotional need** (peace of mind). One naturally expects the brand's main benefits to address these needs, but only the rational benefit appears to be covered in the "Benefit Box." An oversight? Whatever the case, the positioning statement already has a linkage issue; even worse, the brand would appear to be missing an opportunity to pay off a key need (kind of like leaving money on the table).

Try another set of pairs. Colgate's target group includes young adults who are not only actively concerned about their oral hygiene and health, but who also seem better informed about these things. The brand's stated character (young, contemporary, smart, in control) looks to be an accurate reflection of such a target, so it should have a good chance of "reeling them in."

3. Once you and your colleagues have checked out these pair relationships, scan the columns to judge which brand appears to have the most compelling position. You can't go wrong focusing on the benefit column to start; as the heart of each brand's positioning, this plank alone can reveal a great deal. In our toothbrush category example, you can see that each brand of Advanced Toothbrush offers a different benefit (but all of them are physical

Positioning Matrix—Advanced Toothbrush Category

Brand/ Product	Target Group	Customer Needs	Competitive Framework	Benefit	Reason-Why	Brand Character
Colgate Precision	Young, contemporary, educated adults who are concerned about oral hygiene/ health	1. Prevent/ avoid gum disease 2. Peace of mind	Leading toothbrushes	(Only one to) fight gum disease	Bristles to reach all parts of teeth and fight plaque more effectively	Young, contemporary, sincere, friendly, smart, in control
Reach Advanced Design	Adults (who are more concerned with the cleanliness of their teeth)	Clean(er) teeth	All other toothbrushes	"Maximum clean in minimum effort" (best cleaning without all the work)	"Advanced Design" • Angled neck • Rubberized handle • Streamlined head • 3500 bristles	Whimsical, fun, light-hearted, approachable
Butler Gum	Moms who are concerned with their family's long term oral health care	Healthy teeth (and keep them that way)	All other toothbrushes	Healthier teeth that last	Tapered bristles clean below the gumline	Quasi-scientific, educational, helpful, friendly, down to earth

or rational ones). Each one insinuates a *superiority*: Colgate Precision is the "only" one; Reach is the "maximum;" and Butler promises "healthier teeth." So, which brand has the most competitive offering? The honest answer is that only advanced toothbrush users know for sure, so on to the check-out phase.

Competitive Positioning Assessment: Check-Out Phase

There are many research methods available—from qualitative to quantitative—to learn from category users: (1) what the current brand positionings are, (2) which ones have the most appeal, and (3) what manufacturers might do to strengthen them. But the trick always comes down to this: how to get normal, everyday customers to respond to "a positioning"? After all, customers don't typically think in terms of brand positionings. You can show them "white-card concept statements," but these often fall short, especially in communicating viscerally (either the emotional benefit or the brand character).

A better idea may be to show them some advertising—the *same* advertising you and your colleagues studied to come up with the inferred category positionings. See if heavy category users (including regular users of each brand in question) play back the same kinds of needs, intended targets, competitive frameworks, benefits, and so on.

But there is still another form of "stimulus" that seems to work well in getting normal customers to articulate what they take as a brand's positioning—a short-form print ad. This particular stimulus consists of only a benefit-headline, a benefit or reason-why sub-head, and a target-group–brand-character key frame visual. These are typically put together by one or more creative teams, usually via stock art and computerized graphics—much like the two examples here (for single-serve pastry products). To get to these, the creative teams literally used the inferred positioning statements as blueprints.

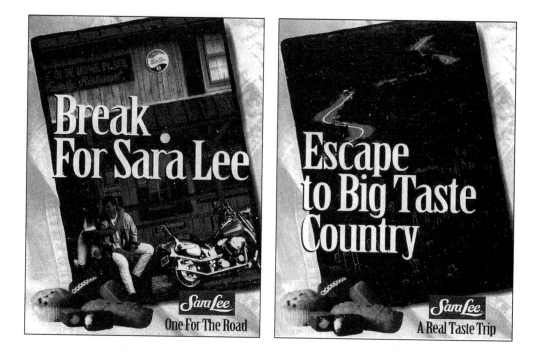

These kinds of minimal print ads actually make it easy for customers to "take a quick read;" they invariably evoke both rational and emotional responses as well. From these responses, you get the answers you're looking for, especially about which brand positioning in the category hits the most hot-buttons, has the most appeal, is the most competitive.

Other Creative Uses for the Matrix

While we've used the positioning matrix to mainly understand the competitive picture, the analytical tool is by no means limited to this use alone, nor should it be thought of as a "set format." Some categories are better understood by mapping out their range of customer needs (for example, from emotional to rational), and then aligning the various brands where they best fall along the continuum. For example, here's how the positioning matrix for the single-serve pastry category might lay out on this basis:

Inferred Pastry Brand Positionings: Current Marketplace

More Emotional _____ More Rational

Customer Needs	Self-Indulgence	Care-Giving	Sharing	Hunger Satisfaction		BFY Hunger Satisfaction
Brand	Entenmann's	Sara Lee	Little Debbie	Dolly Madison	Hostess (Base)	Hostess Lite
Target						
Competitive Framework						
Benefit (Functional)						
Benefit (Emotional)						
Reason(s)-Why						
Brand Character						

You can see in this creative twist on the matrix format that each brand in the category tends to occupy some customer needs turf—at least more so than its competitors. Such a display can be most helpful for someone wishing to enter this category for the first time: *Where will I center my new entry? What kind of positioning innovation should I develop to push aside current entries?*

In working with the Positioning Matrix you should experiment with format twists that meet your needs best. You should also consider using the matrix (or some variation thereof) for these kinds of situations or analyses:

- Prior to new campaign development, review the *historical advertising* for the brand and "track" the brand's positioning evolution through these historical snapshots.

(continued ...)

- When developing a positioning for a new product, use the matrix format to create a wide range of potential positionings—from close-in to far-out.

- When seeking to update or "push the boundaries" of a well-worn positioning (established brand), use the matrix to position companies/brands you admire and apply what they do well to your brand.

- Use the matrix as a diagnostic tool to evaluate your advertising campaigns.

The Matrix and the Big Picture

In this chapter's title, we referred to "Getting the Big Picture." Laying out your competitors' inferred brand positionings is one way of getting a broader perspective—namely, on your marketplace and where your brand fits within that marketplace. But this notion of a big picture goes beyond this "fit" perspective. It has to do with putting forth the honest, analytical effort to judge just how strong—in the absolute and relative to other brands—your brand positioning really is.

As we have taken apart each of the six positioning elements, we have focused more on how to craft a *technically sound* brand positioning, one that adheres to rock-solid principles that, if followed, will lead to a written positioning statement that is crystalline in its clarity. But just as being technically accurate doesn't guarantee a piece of historical fiction will read as a great story, neither does crafting a technically correct positioning guarantee great sales. To get the sales, you also need a *strategically sound* positioning.

Be hard-nosed in your judgments once you've laid out your positioning matrix. For each of the six blocks ask yourself some questions like these:

- What, specifically, is my point-of-difference in this element of my positioning?
- How solid is my footing here? Could my differentiation be neutralized, even obsoleted? How?

- What if I *did* place one of these other category brand names into my positioning—would it work for them too?

Using the matrix tool like this will not only give you the real big picture, it will also set you up for the logical next step: transforming your positioning into a power positioning.

KEY PRINCIPLES
Summary

✔ Once you're satisfied that you have a viable brand positioning, put it to the acid test by comparing it to your competitors' inferred positionings. Collect competitive advertising, packaging, and other materials and get some colleagues to take a shot at inferring these positioning statements with you.

✔ Assess your brand positioning by cross-checking with your colleagues and then among heavy users.

✔ Look for the *natural pair elements* within each positioning: customer needs + benefits; target + brand character; benefits + reasons-why. These pairs should link together in an almost seamless way.

✔ When checking out positioning alternatives among heavy users, use *short-form print ads* which can be very effective at eliciting ready responses (as well as assessing the relative strengths/appeal of the alternatives).

✔ Tailor the Positioning Matrix for your specific needs. Play with the layout to make it your own.

✔ Make it a regular practice within your strategic planning cycle to re-visit and update your matrices.

✔ Use the matrix to literally check off how your positioning fares versus the others in your brand's category. Ask hard questions about each element of the positioning to see beyond the *technical* merits of your statement all the way to the *strategic* merits. As an ultimate challenge, see if your brand's name, and *only* your brand's name, works in your Brand Positioning Statement.

CHAPTER 11

Going Beyond Words to Establish Power Positioning

"What you do tells me more about who you are than what you say."

We have painstakingly put together a technically correct and strategically appropriate Brand Positioning Statement. In doing so, we have served to transform our product (or service) into a brand. Our brand positioning work is complete, right? Wrong! The creation of brand loyalty and, consequently, our professional lives should be so easy. Our work has just begun in establishing this notion of a brand.

Power Positioning

An insightful young marketer participating in one of our Strategic Positioning & Ad Colleges came up with this statement about brand positioning: "It is uniquely tied to your brand. If any other brand tried to use the same positioning it would be false." Inherent in this statement is the notion of an ownable, competitive positioning. What we have, with our technically correct and strategically appropriate Brand Positioning Statement, is merely a blueprint for the origins and development of the brand.

Now we need to convert this blueprint into the real article. We need to develop "Power Positioning." Power Positioning is a competitive, enduring, and ownable brand positioning. Power Positioning is reflected in all marketing mix elements and is adapted, over time, to reflect changes in the marketplace. In that way, we are able to create brand loyalty. In Power Positioning the brand's positioning becomes the source of the marketing strategy and initiatives. At the same time, the brand positioning becomes a product of the marketing strategy and initiatives.

It's What You Do

In order to own a competitive brand positioning in the marketplace, it must be reflected in everything you do, not just what you say within the confines of your organization, or in the business press, or in advertising. An ownable and competitive brand positioning, Power Positioning, is established through your actions. It grows from your product (i.e., tangible and intangible factors), the competitive landscape, customer needs, and the capabilities of your company to execute with quality and precision against the brand positioning. It is the unique relationship you establish with customers through what you do.

It is reflected in all the marketing mix elements. This includes product design, pricing, advertising, promotion, and so on. We refer to these marketing mix elements as the "positioning planks" for the brand. The ownable brand positioning is built plank by plank. The sum of these planks comprises the whole of customers' perceptions regarding your brand positioning and their relationship with it.

The execution against each positioning plank, and their integration, will have a profound effect on how competitive and ownable your brand positioning is with customers. Here are some thoughts you might want to consider, with just a few planks, in being able to develop Power Positioning:

Product—The most important positioning plank is the product itself. Marketers need to know their products, *really* know them from the perspective of the customer and within the context of competitors' offerings. We need to overcome corporate myopia. An important way to do this is to actually see the product through the eyes of customers. Some questions you should ask include: What are the key features and benefits to customers? How meaningful are those features and benefits perceived by customers (not the manufacturer)? What are the advantages and disadvantages versus competition?

An existing product needs to be evolved to maintain and/or grow a brand positioning in a changing marketplace. The marketplace changes can be brought about by demographic, regulatory, or competitive dynamics—to name just a few. A product as mundane as laundry detergent has become a powerhouse brand through Tide's instituting something like 55 product changes in the first 30 years following its introduction alone. These changes Tide laundry detergent are, importantly, more likely a function of a leadership mindset and practices. The Tide brand group has proactively sought to harness available technology to deliver superior performance to consumers versus competition.

A new product needs to be engineered to create meaningful differentiation. Lever 2000 was the first deodorant bar soap that contained moisturizer. As such, the product was appropriate for all bodies and body parts. The combination soap captured significant market share from competitors, such as Dial soap, who were slow to introduce combination deodorant and moisturizer line extensions that would enable them to neutralize the Lever 2000 advantage.

Intangibles—Intangibles add value beyond the mere physical dimensions of your product. While intangibles are non-material to the product, they are anything but immaterial in their contribution to establishing an ownable and competitive brand positioning. Intangibles provide us with the opportunity to meaningfully differentiate our products and services from competition.

The introduction and marketing of NutraSweet illustrates the importance of intangibles. NutraSweet is the brand name for aspartame, a white powder that is 20 times sweeter than sugar. But when customers such as Coca-Cola and General Foods purchased NutraSweet they received much more than its physical qualities. They purchased something akin to a seal of approval, a positive halo that served to encourage trial and repeat purchase.

Consider this, that consumers are exposed to two cans of diet Coke. Both have the same formulations. Both are formulated with NutraSweet. The only difference is that one can has the NutraSweet logo on it, with its identifiable red swirl, the other can of diet Coke does not. Consumers are asked to taste product from each can and rate their preference. Guess what? Consumers overwhelmingly prefer the taste from the can of diet Coke with the NutraSweet trademark and logo on it—even though both formulations are identical. An intangible value, this branding of NutraSweet had tangible results.

At the time, the NutraSweet Company went beyond branding to provide their customers with additional "non-material" value. They provided a strong and meaningful "scientific base" in people and experience. This translated to assisting customers in the development of new product and/or improved product formulations.

Intel is another company that has increased the value perception of Windows-compatible computers using a similar strategy to NutraSweet. The familiar "Intel Inside" message serves to reassure customers that they are getting the most advanced, reliable, and best performance from their computers. An intangible, this branding of Intel has a very tangible impact on customer perceptions and business results for those computer manufacturers building with Intel microprocessors.

Intangibles may take the form of servicing, warranties, terms, branding, and special relationships, to name a few.

Distribution—This is usually treated as a given as opposed to an important component of marketing and brand positioning. The Coca-Cola Company employed it prudently in its more than 100-year history in growing the soft drink category with its strategy and practice of making Coca-Cola available "just around the corner from everywhere." The company moved beyond the pharmacy via a unique (at the time) complex and highly effective bottling distribution system to make the brand available in grocery, stores vending machines, hotels, offices and factories, ballparks, and wherever people in need of refreshment congregate. The Coca-Cola Company also set up a separate distribution system to aggressively go after fast-food outlets capturing the lion's share of this business. Moreover, the company went well beyond the confines of U.S. borders to establish Coca-Cola as a global brand.

Starbucks is another interesting example. As the purveyor of fine coffee beverages and European experiences moved eastward, it carefully picked cities and locales to get started in new geographies. But the really interesting distribution strategy was to precede establishment of its own retail outlets with venues within Barnes & Nobles Booksellers stores. This enabled Starbucks to be discovered by prime prospects, seed demand, and create a positive halo for its stand-alone retail outlets to follow.

AMAZON.com is another interesting example. Its business is built upon a new distribution network, the internet. Its distribution system is integral to its competitive positioning in the market and its value. According to the August 1998 issue of *FAST COMPANY* magazine, AMAZON.com is the biggest virtual bookseller. Founded in 1995, the company has zero square feet of retail space with a market cap of $4 billion. The biggest physical bookseller, the aforementioned Barnes & Noble, founded in 1873, has 11-million square feet of retail space and a market cap of $2.4 billion. As brand builders we need to think through how and where we distribute in establishing an ownable and competitive brand positioning.

Authority Opinions—A legendary talk-show host of late-night television announces one night to his millions of loyal viewers that there is a shortage of toilet paper. The next morning masses of viewers flock to retail stores to stockpile toilet paper. The net result is short-term out-of-stocks at retail and a shortage of toilet paper.

An accomplished singer, who is also an acclaimed actress, producer, and director vocalizes her support for a political candidate for the U.S. Senate. People listen and cast their votes in 1992 to elect Carol Mosley Braun as senator from the state of Illinois.

This is the power of perceived authorities—key influencers. Want to know if a car is reliable? Check it out with J. D. Powers. Need to know what washing machine is the most reliable? Look it up in *Consumer Reports*. If you have difficulty appreciating the impact of authority opinions, of which celebrities, journalists, and newscasters may be included, just talk with Coca-Cola executives who were with the company during the ill-fated introduction of New Coke. Customer marketing is critically important. There is no denying it! But it is also important to market to (perceived) authorities when establishing a competitive and ownable brand positioning.

Reputation—This is a critically important plank in establishing and/or reinforcing a brand positioning. The executives at Johnson & Johnson know it well. They identify themselves as "A Company that Cares." When product tampering was an issue for the Tylenol brand, Johnson & Johnson did all the right things for its legion of customers (retail trade, hospitals, and consumers), which turned out to be the right thing for its reputation and business health. You can "trust" Tylenol and Johnson & Johnson. They proved they care!

As customers we like to do business with people we like, people who like and respect us. It takes years to build the reputation of a company. Yet, this same reputation can be destroyed with just one wrong action. It is important to state the values of the company or brand, to provide a credo, which will clearly define the relationship with customers and guide all future behavior. Johnson & Johnson has such a credo. The company's chairman at the time, James Burke, followed the guidelines in the credo (which, undoubtedly, were also imprinted in his heart and soul) to deal with the Tylenol situation.

It is also important to be meaningful. False bravado is not meaningful. You may be familiar with what we are talking about. A company introduces a new product that is, for all practical purposes, the same as existing competitors' offerings. When asked, "What is/are the anticipated factor(s) for success?" the management responds the "company trademark." So a company like Starter believes it can trade on its name in athletic apparel to enter the sports beverage market and beat out rivals Gatorade (Quaker Oats Company),

Powerade (Coca-Cola Company) and All Sport (PepsiCola USA). The land-scape is littered with failures from this kind of corporate hubris. Reputations are earned by deeds. In other words, speak with action!

Credit Card Case History

Chances are you have a wallet full of credit cards. They are invaluable. Credit cards enable us to purchase services and goods in lieu of using cash. Moreover, they provide the opportunity to leverage rather finite financial re-sources. Credit cards are generally made from the same material, are the same dimensions and basically work the same way. Yet many people will pay a premium for the privilege of using a particular credit card. Namely, American Express Platinum. Now why would anyone want to do that?

As shown on page 133, the American Express Platinum card has created a competitive and ownable brand positioning that sets it apart from Master-card in a meaningful way. This is accomplished through execution and inte-gration of each of a host of positioning planks. For American Express the brand positioning is truly both a source and product of its marketing intia-tives. It is a Power Positioning.

For the American Express Platinum Card all the positioning planks come together in an integrated whole. Each follows from, and contributes to, the development of a Power (brand) Positioning. This establishes the integrity of the brand positioning and basis for Power Positioning.

Evolve or Perish

Despite rather frequent and significant changes in positionings as new man-agers take responsibility for a brand, the conventional wisdom is that brand positioning should not change. It should be like the Ten Commandments, carved in stone. However, if we refuse to change our brand positionings we are preparing to allow our brands to become obsolete to new, or more in-novative, competitors. Instead, change is good. In fact, it is essential, pro-viding the change is geared toward realizing the brands' full potential

	American Express Platinum	**Master Card**
Product:	Credit Card	Credit Card
Pricing:	$300 per year	Free
Distribution:	Select media and locations	Everywhere and anywhere
	• Upscale	• Mass
Target Consumer:	Professional white-collar with stringent minimum income	Everyone with a good credit rating
Imagery:	Successful/Achiever	Utilitarian
Authority Opinions:	Carried by successful individuals	None
Intangibles:	• 30-day terms • "Platinum" • "Member" • "Additional features" —Innovator/Leader • "Prestigious • Cooperate with key accounts • Detailed expense printouts	Revolving credit Cardholder additional features —Follower
Corporate Reputation:	• "American" • Goes everywhere • Service	Diluted by local bank issuance

and/or managing against important changes in the marketplace. Also, change needs to go beyond what we say to include what we do, as the Tide laundry detergent brand evidenced with their many significant formulation changes.

Basically, what we are talking about is adaptive recreation, over time. Evolution is the acceptable mode of adaptive recreation. Revolutionary changes are unacceptable, except in dire circumstances. Imagine your brand has been supported with $10 million dollars in advertising for each of 10 years. At this point in time, you have invested $100 million dollars to advance a specific brand positioning. If a revolutionary change in positioning were to be introduced it would negate the positioning you had previously seeded. You would be undermining the investment you had made in the brand. You would be walking away from, as opposed to expanding, the turf you occupied in your customers' minds. Furthermore, this could be expected to lead to customer confusion and loss of identity. If it sounds schizophrenic, it is that and more.

On the other hand, it is wise to evolve the brand's positioning. It is all part of our concept of Power Positioning. Importantly, the evolution should be confined to select elements. Among some of the many reasons to consider evolution include those discussed here:

Demographic Changes—The marketing people at Kellogg's recognized that the core of their franchise was abandoning Kellogg's Frosted Flakes cereal as the core grew into adults. These customers were migrating to what they perceived to be more "adult" cereals. Research indicated that while these lapsed customers purchased it for their children, they eschewed the brand for less sweet, health-oriented cereals. This action was taken despite liking of, and preference for, Kellogg's Frosted Flakes cereal. So marketing broadened their target customer base to include adults and embarked on the development of a flanker advertising campaign directed at these adults. You're probably familiar with the flanker campaign that ran for some 15 years that shows adults who have grown up on the great taste of Kellogg's Frosted Flakes cereal confessing their love affair with, and indulgence in, the brand.

(See Chapter 1 for more on this campaign.) The result was strong growth in recapturing more breakfast occasions among lapsed users.

New Products in the Marketplace, Especially Those That Resegment the Category–How the customer perceives our brand is made up not just from our positioning but from what competitive brands do to position us in the marketplace. The rise of the portable computer has given way to the laptop computer . . . has given way to the notebook computer . . . has given way to the sub-notebook computer . . . has given way to the electronic organizer . . . has given way to . . . . Certainly, many of these moves require product improvements and innovations. This is consistent with our concept that a brand positioning should be a vision, providing meaningful direction for the evolution of the brand to achieve its full potential.

Product Improvements/News–You add a fragrance to your soap and guess what? You are not longer just a "body cleanser" but a "body refresher" or "body enhancer" or some other dimension of customer need fulfillment. Or take the aspirin segment of the analgesic category. Studies show that taking aspirin on a regular basis can significantly lower the risk of a heart attack and stroke. It's news! Now, the Bayer aspirin brand is no longer just a pain reliever but a potential lifesaver or life extender. Whatever it is that your brand is, it is certainly more than it had been. It justifies evolution of the brand's positioning.

Desire for New Growth–Arm & Hammer baking soda brand realized new growth through the evolution of its positioning. It demonstrated use-occasions to consumers that the consumer may not have been familiar with or hadn't taken to heart. The brand positioning reflected the versatility of the product. The result was new growth for Arm & Hammer baking soda. The change in positioning also spawned the development of new products for specific functions (such as toothpaste for teeth whitening) carrying the Arm & Hammer trademark.

Swiss Army has expanded its business beyond knives to include articles such as watches. Basically, the company is seeking to sell additional merchandise to their franchise base of Swiss Army Knife customers. In this case, they are deliberately growing the equity value of the trademark to sell a wider variety of merchandise. They are engaged in evolving the positioning of their "umbrella trademark."

Power Positioning is the way to developing great brands. These are brands with competitive, enduring, and ownable positionings. This may be accomplished by reflecting the brand's positioning in all its positioning planks. In this way, positioning is truly the source of the marketing strategy and initiatives. At the same time, the brand positioning is a product of these same marketing strategies and initiatives! It is also accomplished through evolution of the brand positioning and marketing mix elements consistent with the dynamics of the future marketplace to keep the brand fresh and healthy.

KEY PRINCIPLES

Summary

✔ The creation of brand loyalty requires more than a technically correct and strategically appropriate Brand Positioning Statement. We need to establish Power Positioning.

✔ Power Positioning is a competitive, enduring, and ownable brand positioning. It is reflected in all marketing mix elements and is evolved, over time, to adapt to changes in the marketplace and the realization of the vision for the brand.

✔ In order to own a competitive brand positioning in the marketplace, it must be reflected in every marketing mix element, the positioning planks, and not just what you say within the confines of your organization, the business press, or in advertising.

✔ The sum of the positioning planks comprises the whole of customer perceptions regarding your brand positioning and relationship with it.

✔ The most important positioning plank is the product itself. Marketers need to know their products, really know them from the perspective of the customer and within the context of the competitors' offerings. An existing product needs to be evolved to maintain and/or grow a brand positioning in a changing marketplace. A new product needs to be engineered to create meaningful differentiation.

✔ Intangibles are anything but immaterial to their contribution in establishing an ownable and competitive brand positioning. Intangibles provide us with the opportunity to meaningfully differentiate our products and services from competition.

✔ Distribution is another component of marketing and brand positioning. As brand builders, we need to think through how and where we distribute in establishing an ownable and competitive brand positioning.

✔ Company and brand reputation are critically important planks in establishing and/or reinforcing a brand positioning. As customers, we all like to do business with people we like, people who like and respect us. It takes years of diligent effort to build the reputation of a company and/or brand.

✔ All the positioning planks need to come together as an integrated whole. This establishes the integrity of the brand positioning and basis for Power Positioning.

✔ It is wise to evolve the brand positioning. The evolution should be confined to select positioning elements.

✔ Some of the reasons to consider evolution include:
—demographic changes
—new products in the marketplace
—product improvement and/or news
—desire for new growth

PART THREE

Managing Really Great Advertising

CHAPTER 12

Defining What Makes Advertising Really Great

"If the most popular ads in America result in a decline in sales, what message about the effectiveness of advertising does that send to corporate chieftains?"

Rance Crain
Advertising Age, January 22, 1996

When you talk about advertising, there are probably no two words that get as much play as "great advertising." A neighbor who knows that you work in marketing tells you about an ad she saw last night that was "so funny . . . really great." Or, your colleagues gather at lunch after the Super Bowl to compare notes on which brands' advertisements were most clever, entertaining, or great (and to argue about the day-after *USA Today* Super Bowl ad rankings).

From everyday conversations like these, it seems that we tend to differentiate the great from the not-so-great in our advertising mainly on the basis of *humor, entertainment value,* and *popularity.* This is certainly what *Advertising Age* editor Rance Crain was talking about when he cited the current Budweiser campaign, which has featured animated anteaters, ants, frogs, and lately lizards—a campaign that through much of the mid-to-late 1990s has

141

ranked #1 in likability and memorability polls. But is this campaign "really great advertising"? Crain doesn't appear to think so, for one glaring reason: after the campaign had been running for nearly two years, it still hadn't been linked to any significant sales growth.

What gives? When the most popular and memorable advertising campaign in the country doesn't lead to a brand's growth, what does this say about the odds of developing great advertising for any brand? Well, it says several things:

1. Regardless of humor, cleverness, or entertainment value, a brand's advertising—like any other business investment—has to meet key objectives to be considered merely *adequate*, much less *great*.

2. Among advertising campaigns that *do* meet their objectives, there will always be a range of performers—from those that meet them (adequate, effective) to the few that far exceed them (great).

3. Using only one or two yardsticks to judge a campaign's greatness are insufficient. There are too many critical variables that underpin a great ad campaign (and *likability* or *popularity* is usually well down the list).

Getting Great Advertising: The Underpinnings

The quest to achieve great advertising is really no different than that to achieve any other worthwhile business objective. Accordingly, it should start with an open-minded and far-reaching consideration of *what the assembled business team currently finds most important*. Such a consideration would automatically include looking at things such as recent volume trends, competitive moves, shifts in customer attitudes and behaviors, and longer-term corporate direction.

These kinds of "data points" form a broad framework within which to consider the more specific criteria that will be used to judge the effectiveness (or "greatness") of the ensuing advertising. Unfortunately, too often it seems that these more specific criteria are never laid out upon the table. Make no mistake about it: your odds of achieving something beyond *average* or *adequate* advertising can only go up if you take the time at the outset of work to set specific criteria that define what you and your colleagues mean by great advertising effectively, how you will all recognize great advertising when you see it.

While there are several specific criteria that come to mind when thinking about yardsticks for advertising effectiveness, these same criteria tend to fall into three general groupings: **Essential, Critical,** and **Lucky Strike Extras.**

When you step back from a criteria list such as this, great advertising can suddenly seem even more daunting. That's why it's so important to have the assembled business team—the ones taking on the challenge of delivering the advertising—make some conscious decisions about **which specific criteria** are most germane to the job at hand and therefore will be used along the way. Once that is decided, it becomes a matter of determining what methods to use for tracking and measuring the results against each criterion.

Essential Criteria

- ***Builds Volume and Profit***—Such a criterion would seem to go without saying, but no advertising can be great unless it's associated with tangible growth—in numbers

- ***Delivers the Positioning***—More than any other element of the marketing mix, the advertising must be the mirror reflection of what the brand stands for in the customer's mind

- ***Is Competitive***—There is no reason to assume you'll successfully source volume from other brands unless you play to win

- ***Has Endurability***—The number that counts most (after the volume and profit growth) is how many years the advertising runs successfully

---

Critical Criteria

- **Relevant**—The central message of the advertising strikes a response in the intended target (ideally, both a head and heart response)

- **Believable**—The message is one of integrity "beyond the shadow of a doubt"

- **Ownable**—The advertising (message and approach) are linked directly with your brand; any other brand would have a very difficult time copying it

- **Memorable**—The linkage made in the advertising between your brand and its key message is stored in customers' minds and recalled easily

Lucky Strike Extra Criteria

- **Impactful**—Presumably, advertising that gets noticed is also remembered

- **Evocative**—If you're going to sell to the heart as well as the head, evoke the right emotions in your advertising

- **Involving**—Prospects for your brand need to be brought in, whether your category is a "high involvement" one or not (99 percent aren't)

- **Insightful**—Advertising that leverages a "key insight" is one thing; but advertising that gives your customers some new insight (or way of seeing things) is yet another

- **Informative**—In this age of information, how can you argue against the value of relevant information?

- **Likable**—Popularity alone won't win the day; but it often does make selling easier

Help Is On Its Way—A Story

Lest you *do* become overwhelmed (or even a little discouraged) in your quest for really great advertising, at least wait until you've read on with us. Throughout this part of the book you'll find all kinds of practical help in your quest, sometimes where you least suspect it, much as in the following story:

Once there was an elderly man named Joe who lived for many years alongside a big river. Joe was a most religious man who firmly believed his God would always look after him.

One year, the river threatened to flood. As water trickled to Joe's doorstep, his evacuating neighbors called to him: "Come with us in our rowboats, Joe. We'll get you out of here." But Joe refused, stating flatly: "The Lord will not let anything bad happen to me."

A few hours later, the water had risen to Joe's second-story bedroom window. He looked out as a police motorboat approached and urged him to swim to a life preserver they would toss. But again Joe refused, saying, "The Lord will not let anything bad happen to me."

At midnight, Joe found himself on the roof clinging to his chimney as the water rose around. From up above, a Coast Guard helicopter circled, dropped a rope ladder, and announced over their foghorn: "This is your last chance. Please grab ahold and we'll save you." But Joe remained intractable: "I've been a believer all my life and I'm certain the Lord won't let anything bad happen to me."

Sorry to say, Joe drowned. Upon arriving in the afterlife, Joe was hopping mad and spitting many an angry word as he faced the pearly gates. He realized that something bad *had* happened to him—he had died! When he at last ran out of words, he received this humble, heavenly reply: "But Joe, we sent you two boats and a helicopter . . . what more could you have wanted?"

Keep your eyes peeled for the "boats and helicopters" we send your way. You'll be surprised at how many big and not-so-big things you'll discover—all to improve your odds of achieving really great advertising.

KEY PRINCIPLES
Summary

Great advertising has little to do with luck and almost everything to do with hard work. There are some things you can do, however, to make the work go a little more easily:

✔ Have an honest, up-front discussion with the advertising development team—you, your agency account and creative teams, and your management—about what constitutes great advertising. Ask these colleagues to show examples.

✔ Set *measurable* criteria for the effort; benchmark against other successful company campaigns, if desired.

✔ Set a big stake in the ground that will drive the development team beyond normal boundaries—for example, ask them to create a campaign that is so powerful it has a book written about it (like Absolut Vodka).

Finally, should you have difficulty in narrowing down the quintessential criteria for great advertising, you'll never go wrong with these Top Five:

1. **Execute a *competitive* brand positioning**—In today's "age of sameness," this alone can make all the difference.

2. **Achieve *stretch* business and marketing objectives**—That is, goals that go well beyond what you and your management would consider "required"; goals that boldly double or triple volume and share over a period of time.

3. **Endure as a campaign**—For example, delivering a Ten-Year campaign—one that would outlast almost that many marketing teams!

4. **Incorporate a unique, provocative, and memorable idea**—Develop an idea that no one else has done before (and if they tried it, it probably wouldn't work for them).

5. **Be recognized by your peers**—This carries a couple of important side benefits for fueling the campaign's success: attracts the best and brightest creatives to work on the business; excites management and *incites* them to spend more behind the campaign than they might without all the "buzz."

CHAPTER 13

The Surefooted Way to Setting Ad Direction

"If you don't know where you are going any road will take you there."
Yogi Berra

Getting really great advertising, or even effective advertising, is extremely difficult. It is fraught with major pitfalls and challenges. Ask anyone who has tried it. Often you will hear comments that the positioning appeared to be strategically sound but, in the final analysis, the creative just did not deliver and achieve the desired results in the marketplace. What's the issue? One of the key factors is the absence of a strategically appropriate and meaningful **advertising strategy** (that is appreciated by and has the commitment of the agency–client team), which is the basic subject of this chapter. Included are discussions of the customer insight (without which the ad strategy might be ineffective) and the agency brief, which complete the picture for ensuring surefooted ad direction.

Importance of the Advertising Strategy

The advertising strategy defines the intent of the advertising in capitalizing on a key customer insight to address the marketing objective or a specific brand issue. The objective might be to: stimulate category growth; drive customer compliance or frequency of usage; motivate brand switching; immunize your customers against the lure of competitive price promotions or new entries in the marketplace; reassure customers; and the like. You need to identify the marketing objective following a careful situation analysis of the business and understanding of customer attitudes and behavior. The ad strategy serves us in at least these three important ways:

1. *The advertising strategy* (abbreviated as **ad strategy**) *paves the way for the realization of the marketing objective.* It puts into play the specific belief and behavior needed to realize the brand's marketing objective. It addresses issues such as exploitable opportunities and barriers which need to be removed.

2. *The advertising strategy provides direction for the development of the brand's advertising.* It drives the agency brief and, ultimately, the creative brief, which is prepared and used by advertising agencies. The agency's creative brief is its vehicle to manage and, in turn, drive the creative campaign development. (Since this is initiated by the agency, with each having its own way to handle it, we have chosen not to include a discussion of it in this book.) Having no ad strategy means that the client and agency have not agreed upon direction. This is a major pothole on the road to effective advertising. More likely it is a manhole that will disable subsequent creative efforts, draining precious agency resources and wrecking havoc on its morale. The opportunity loss to the brand, of which one may count delayed ad schedules, lost sales, and, worse yet, contribution to the growth of competitive sales due to miscues, can be huge.

Without the ad strategy the creative output is at best a "hit or miss" proposition with the emphasis on "miss." The creative that is selected, and the advertising that subsequently runs, become a function of what the client and agency like about the execution, as opposed to something that the target customer group would find important. In other words, the more important element of what the relevant message is (i.e., the substance) falls prey to how anything is said (the execution). This is a no-no! We need substance and execution. But first we have to get the substance.

3. *The ad strategy provides a common thread for the assessment of the advertising agency's creative submissions.* This ensures the style or mode of execution is in

keeping with the substance. This also serves to simplify matters as it relates to reviewing creative options. Randall Rothenberg, in his fascinating account of the advertising business, *Where the Suckers Moon*, chronicles a creative presentation by Wieden & Kennedy, the famed advertising agency for NIKE, and its client Subaru. As he tells the story, Wieden & Kennedy is convinced, after about two years of working with the client, that it has the creative talent that will reverse Subaru's declining sales and establish positive momentum for the company. At the presentation are various client factions (such as corporate marketing, field marketing, and franchise management, among others), each with their own perspective of the marketplace and, as such, agenda. During the presentation an argument grows among the alternate factions. The basis of the argument is the differing opinions regarding the primary benefit of Subaru to the consumer. Imagine, two years of work, meetings, endless discussions, miscues, aborted creative efforts and, assuredly, deep frustrations. Yet the client and its agency have not reached a mutually agreed upon decision regarding the brand's benefit (which is certainly substantive). But this isn't just about client and agency. The various factions within the client body were unable to agree on the benefit!

As strange as it may seem, this is not uncommon. Ad agencies are often directed to begin creative development without clear strategic direction. In these cases, the agency must take it upon themselves to articulate the creative direction (via their creative brief), often without the client's real appreciation of or agreement about the fundamental strategy upon which the advertising will hinge. This makes for a sad story and a "no win" situation for all.

The ad strategy should result in a more efficient utilization of agency creative resources and time since it identifies the basic decisions regarding target, benefit, and support. Therefore, neither agency nor client needs to rethink these decisions with each new creative effort and presentation. Instead, it enables the team to focus upon capturing the strategic intent in compelling customer and executional terms. In other words, it then enables the agency creatives to focus on *how* to deliver a strategically important message versus *what* the message is.

Ad Strategy versus Brand Positioning

Occasionally a client advertiser will ask, "If I have a Brand Positioning Statement why do I need this thing you call an advertising strategy? Aren't they the same?"

In a word, No! The brand positioning and ad strategy are two distinctly different entities. *Whereas* the brand positioning provides the strategic foundation for all the brand's efforts, the ad strategy deals with the advertising element of the marketing mix. *Whereas* the brand positioning defines the way we want customers to think and feel about our brand versus competition, the ad strategy identifies the specific opportunity, presented by a meaningful customer insight, to exploit. *Whereas* brand positioning states the very reason for the brand's existence, the ad strategy articulates the intended message to effect customer attitudes, and ultimately behavior, in a predetermined manner to pay off the marketing objective for the brand. *Whereas* the brand positioning precedes the development of all sub-strategies for each of the marketing mix elements, the ad strategy is consistent with and reflects the brand's positioning. *Whereas* the brand positioning evolves consistent with long-term developments in the marketplace, the ad strategy capitalizes on immediate needs and the current situation.

Keep in mind that the ad strategy directs the development of the brand's advertising campaign to pay off a specific marketing objective. On page 151, are some examples of differing intents between the brand positioning and ad strategy. Note how the ad strategy is linked with the marketing objective we have inferred for each brand (in reviewing its advertising).

The Customer Perspective

Our need is to link our marketing objective with the customer perspective in arriving at the ad strategy. To gain a customer perspective that will assist us in developing a message of substance we need to do some detective work for insights into the customer. The customer insight is a critically important element in the development of a strategically competitive ad strategy. But

Ad Strategy versus Brand Positioning
(Examples)

BRAND	POSITIONING	MARKETING OBJECTIVE	AD STRATEGY
Jell-O Gelatin	Light, refreshing dessert the whole family will enjoy	Increase usage occasions	Lighter and more satisfying than Snackwell's cookies, etc.
Advil Pain Reliever	Most advanced and effective pain reliever	Convert competitive brand users	More effective than any 2 Tylenol
Michelin Tires	Safest, most reliable tires	Increase share of household requirements	Family (not just head of household) deserves the safety of Michelin tires
Always Sanitary Protection	Best protection	Choose versus competitive brands (in category where failure rates are high)	Dri-Weave (Reason-Why)
Scope Mouth Wash	Superior breath cleaner	Stimulate brand switching	Fights morning breath (torture test)

talking about the customer insight is easier (and even this is not what we would call "easy") than uncovering one. According to *Webster's Seventh New Collegiate Dictionary* insight is defined as: **insight (n): 1) The power or act of seeing into a situation: Penetration; 2) the act of apprehending the inner nature of things or of seeing intuitively.**

Insight requires discrimination, depth of discernment, judgment, imagination, knowledge, interpretation, and intuition. These are not the kind of words we use in the tough-minded, analytical business world of hard and cold facts. Imagine telling your boss that the action you are recommending, which may cost many millions of dollars, is based upon your intuition. Now imagine the look you get. Incredulity would likely be too mild a word to describe that look, and the feelings that lie beneath it. (My intuition tells me you are not long for this company!)

These words "imagination, discernment, intuition, interpretation . . ." suggest that the same set of facts may be perceived differently by two or more people. Think about a piece of evidence in the hands of a master detective like Sherlock Holmes. Now put this same evidence in the hands of an amateur. We are not likely to get the same result. The same piece of data can lead to very different hypotheses and conclusions when investigated by different managers. In fact, one manager may totally overlook a piece of data that may seem significant to the other.

So we need to find a tool, or tools, to help us the way the magnifying glass served as an indispensable aid to Mr. Holmes. This tool needs to help us gain a handle on customer beliefs and attitudes, and consequent brand purchase and usage behavior, since they lie at the heart of the customer insight.

Customer Insight—What You Need

In order to be successful in identifying meaningful customer insights you will have to satisfy a number of key needs. Specifically, you will need:

- *An understanding of purchasing dynamics for category customers by segment and, in particular, your target customer group*—Knowledge of purchasing dynamics would include information such as what products they are purchasing, frequency of purchase, compliance factors, how and when used, among others.
- *A thoughtful review and analysis of available customer research to piece together potential hypotheses concerning customer motivations*—This would include qualitative as well as quantitative research, syndicated as well as custom research. (Yes, we did say "qualitative" research. We like

to feel the fabric of the customer's soul.) Your market research manager can help you identify the key issues and pull together all research conducted for, or relating to, the brand. We find it works best when you are able to piece together diverse pieces of research to create a mosaic to enhance your understanding of customer behavior and the motivations that lead up to it. One of our initial steps in working on an ad development assignment for a client and its agency is to conduct a research review with the client and agency. Also, we make it a practice to get into the marketplace and talk with customers face to face, which includes the use of focus groups. You can explore key purchaser segments such as: exclusive customers; those who purchase your brand most frequently; those who purchase both your brand and those of competitors equally; those who purchase competitive brands most frequently; and those who purchase competitive brands exclusively. Talking with these various kinds of customers, and/or those identified by alternate designs, should provide you with important insights into attitudes and subsequent purchase behavior. Importantly, it should provide a context for reviewing quantitative research and be a source for yet additional hypotheses.

- ***Development of customized customer research to resolve unanswered key issues*** —In many cases new research is needed to get at the specific, important issues you have identified. If needed, you should undertake additional research. However, we are loath to spend money that could be used to fuel brand growth if the research is not needed. A good practice is to identify the actions you will take and the potential impact on the brand from alternate outcomes. Unless the impact is substantial or a high level of risk is involved, we would not conduct additional research.

- ***Intangibles such as experience, intuition, and imagination, among others, with a willingness to experiment through trial and error*** —If you are lacking any of these intangibles, utilize your team resources. Even if you possess all of these invaluable intangibles, utilize your team resources anyway. Stick your neck out and go beyond the conventional wisdom of the organization to explore breakthrough possibilities.

Customer Insight Thought Process

We employ a thought process to aid the development of customer insights. While there is no guarantee it will result in a pivotal customer insight, like all of the tools we have presented throughout this book, it can improve the probability that you will do so. Importantly, it provides a pathway to guide your thinking and approach discovery of customer insights. The Customer Insight Thought Process involves six steps:

1. Identify the **target customer group.** Who is it that you need to tap into to achieve the brand's marketing objective. Current users who are in some way lagging in purchases of the product? Competitive brand users who are not aware of the meaningful point-of-difference inherent in your product? Who? This is a critically important first step. The target customer group you select may unto itself represent an important customer insight.

2. Identify the prevailing **current belief** among this target customer group as it relates to competitive products, your brand, or the category that influences current, undesired purchase behavior or usage. When we refer to "undesired purchase behavior or usage" we mean that customers are not behaving in a way that is consistent with your objective. Perhaps they are favoring competitive brands. Or they might not even have your brand in their evoked set (i.e., under consideration for purchase). These are just a few from a number of avenues to explore.

3. Identify **current (undesired) purchase behavior** dynamics that result from this prevailing current belief. This will in some way be adverse to your brand and the achievement of its goals.

4. Define what **future purchase or usage behavior** you desire from the target customer group in the future. This needs to be consistent with the marketing objective, putting you in a position to achieve it.

5. Uncover the **customer insight** that enables you to understand and exploit the thinking of the target customer group, leading to a compelling future belief.

6. Explore alternate **compelling future beliefs** you must establish in order to capitalize on the key customer insight and achieve the desired

future purchase or usage behavior that will favor your brand (and lead to the achievement of the marketing objective).

You will undoubtedly note that we hearken back to the marketing objective. If you have not yet established one based upon a sound situation review and vision of what you want the brand to achieve, you will need to create one.

We use a simple tool, the **Customer Insight Thought Process,** for getting a fix on the customer insight that has been inspired by a model utilized by the Leo Burnett Company for creating what they call the "consumer proposition." See the chart on the next page.

Let's walk through the Customer Insight Thought Process tool using the former Tide advertising campaign "If it has to be clean it has to be Tide" to get a feel for the thought process in uncovering a key customer insight.

First, we need to identify the **target customer group.** In this case, we will choose, "*Cost-conscious moms of large blue-collar families with active children (particularly boys), who wash so frequently they wear out their families' clothes and, as such, do not (frequently) purchase Tide because they don't believe it gets clothes significantly cleaner than price-promoted heavy-duty detergents.*"

Next comes the **current belief.** We have articulated this in part in the identification of the target customer group. Here we might crystallize the belief as, "*All heavy-duty detergents get clothes clean. But frequent washing with them can also damage fabrics.*"

We then proceed to identify the purchase behavior of the target customer group, that is, their **current behavior.** Given that they are cost-conscious, eager to make their hard-earned dollars stretch, and believe all heavy duty detergents clean at parity, their purchase behavior is at the same time predictable and evidenced by market research. For **current behavior** we have, "*Purchase heavy-duty detergent brands within their evoked set based upon available store price promotions and/or consumer incentives (e.g., couponing, refunds, etc.).*"

Now comes **desired future behavior** for our target customer group. This must be in sync with the brand's marketing objective, which might be to grow penetration and frequency of purchase by immunizing consumers against the lure of competitive pricing incentives. We have inferred the

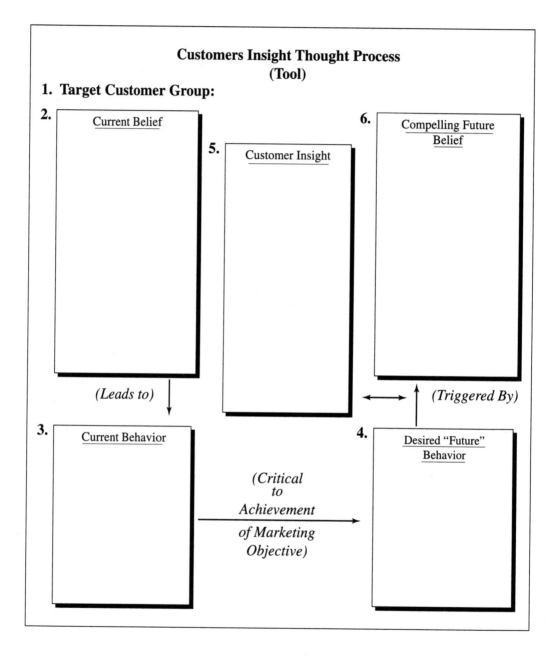

Customers Insight Thought Process
(Tool)

1. Target Customer Group:

2. Current Belief

(Leads to)

3. Current Behavior

5. Customer Insight

(Critical to Achievement of Marketing Objective)

6. Compelling Future Belief

(Triggered By)

4. Desired "Future" Behavior

following for **desired future behavior:** *"Purchase Tide for all laundry care needs regardless of competitive incentives."*

It is very important that you identify the **desired future (purchase) behavior** for the target customer group before you proceed to the **customer insight** or **compelling future belief.** In our practice we have observed clients who want to jump to the **customer insight** and/or the **compelling future belief** before they have identified the **desired future behavior** for their target customer group. This short-circuits the process and leads to client rationalization of the conventional wisdom. The resultant advertising strategy neither reflects a meaningful customer insight nor is tied to achieving the marketing objective.

Once we have completed what we want the target customer group to do in the future we are ready to sleuth for a **customer insight** that will lead to the **compelling future belief.** This is not an easy task. But it is what clients get paid big bucks to do. And if you don't have a meaningful customer insight, you are undermining your ability to develop a competitive advertising strategy, no less on a consistent basis.

As per **customer insight** we uncover through qualitative research a basic belief expressed by the customer as, *"The kids really get their clothes dirty. I have to wash so often I actually wear their clothes out. So I can't afford to buy new clothes all the time or pay for a detergent that basically doesn't clean any better than less costly brands."* Note that we have taken pains to express the **customer insight** in the customer's language. This serves to encourage empathy and, more important, to represent the customer versus the client's point-of-view.

So following the process and springing from the **customer insight** we utilize our practical judgment to identify the **compelling future belief** to be, *"Tide gets clothes their cleanest and keeps them looking new."* Since we take our word choice seriously (as we advertisers must) we should ensure that the future belief is truly compelling. Your marketing research resource manager can help you: a) get a quantitative fix on the **customer insight;** and b) distinguish from potential alternative **compelling future beliefs.** The Customer Insight Thought Process for Tide using the tool is illustrated on page 158.

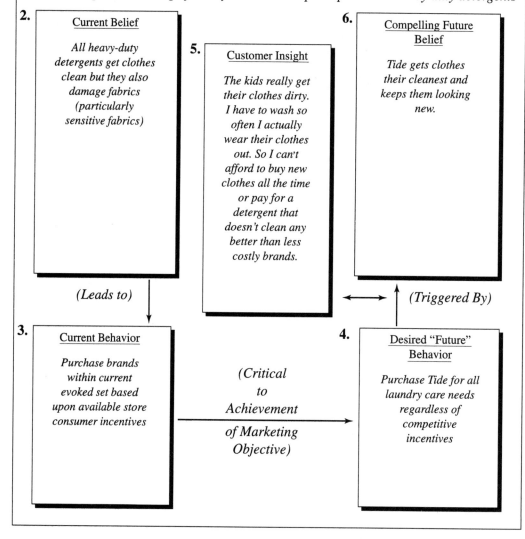

**Customer Insight Thought Process
(Tool)**

1. Target Customer Group: *"Cost-conscious moms of large blue collar families with active children (particularly boys), who wash so frequently they wear out their families clothes and, as such, do not (frequently) purchase Tide because they don't believe it gets clothes significantly cleaner than price promoted heavy duty detergents"*

2.
Current Belief

All heavy-duty detergents get clothes clean but they also damage fabrics (particularly sensitive fabrics)

5.
Customer Insight

The kids really get their clothes dirty. I have to wash so often I actually wear their clothes out. So I can't afford to buy new clothes all the time or pay for a detergent that doesn't clean any better than less costly brands.

6.
Compelling Future Belief

Tide gets clothes their cleanest and keeps them looking new.

(Leads to)

(Triggered By)

3.
Current Behavior

Purchase brands within current evoked set based upon available store consumer incentives

(Critical to Achievement of Marketing Objective)

4.
Desired "Future" Behavior

Purchase Tide for all laundry care needs regardless of competitive incentives

Customer Insights That Work

As we stated earlier, it bears repeating, the value of the customer insight rests in **effecting a change in customer attitudes and behavior** that benefits the client's brand, leading to the achievement of the marketing objective. The customer insight must be exploited via a benefit or belief system that establishes a perceived meaningful point-of-difference that the brand can deliver. The benefit, that meaningful point-of-difference, or desired belief, is at the heart of the advertising strategy. Reviewing the Tide laundry detergent example evidences the linkage of opportunity, customer insight and benefit:

Tide Example

Opportunity	Customer Insight	Benefit
Barrier to over-come among cost-conscious consumers that a premium-priced detergent brand (Tide) is not substantially better at cleaning clothes (to warrant premium pricing).	The kids really get their clothes dirty. I have to wash so often I actually wear their clothes out. So I can't afford to buy new clothes all the time or pay for a detergent that doesn't clean any better than less costly brands.	Tide gets out the toughest dirt while keeping clothes from fading or fraying from washing. So clothes don't just look cleaner, they stay newer looking longer wash after wash.

Try applying the Customer Insight Thought Process tool found on page 160 to your product or service.

As mentioned earlier, the famed Sherlock Holmes put every piece of potential evidence under his magnifying glass. Likewise we have created a few different filters for the magnifying glass of your mind's eye. These will help you determine if you are onto a meaningful insight. But remember, the

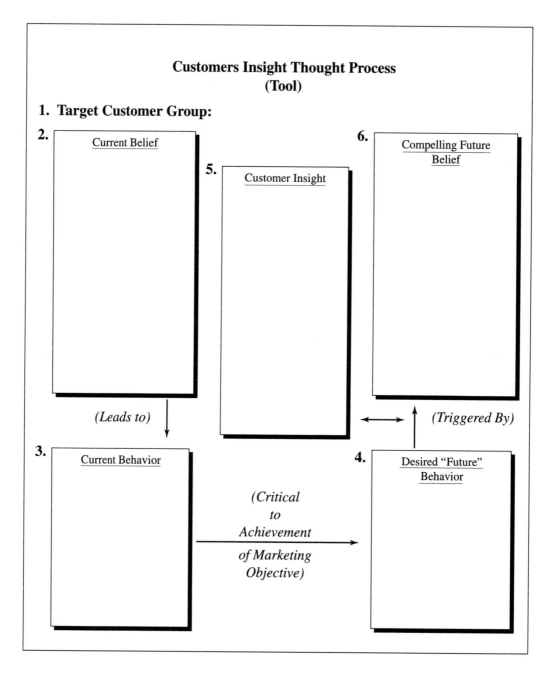

Customers Insight Thought Process
(Tool)

1. **Target Customer Group:**

2. Current Belief

5. Customer Insight

6. Compelling Future Belief

(Leads to)

(Triggered By)

3. Current Behavior

4. Desired "Future" Behavior

(Critical to Achievement of Marketing Objective)

customer insight needs to be paid off by a point-of-difference benefit. The filters for your consideration are:

- Customer-perceived or real weakness to be exploited of competitive product performance, image, or value;
- Attitudinal or perceived barrier to overcome in the minds of customers regarding your brand or, perhaps, the category; or
- Untapped compelling belief which, if tapped into, would lead customers to choose your brand.

Key Components of the Advertising Strategy

With the customer insight we are ready to proceed to developing the Ad Strategy Statement. We have everything in hand. The ad strategy consists of three major components:

1. The Who—This refers to the target customer group. We met this requirement when we defined the target customer group for the Customer Insight Thought Process tool. Keep in mind that the target customer group should be defined as precisely as possible (similar to what we did for brand positioning) through the use of demographics, usage behavior and, importantly, attitudes and needs. The target customer group is not necessarily a carbon copy of that used in the positioning statement. However, it cannot lie outside the positioning target but, must at least be a subset. An example of when a client advertiser may want to use a subset of the positioning target is to call out and reach a key influencing segment of the larger target customer group population.

2. The What—This refers to the specific belief about the brand that the advertiser must establish to get the target customer group to favor it in achieving the marketing objective. It needs to emphasize a benefit that will satisfy the target customer group's need. The benefit could be product, customer, or emotional. It could be a function of one of the key positioning elements such as brand character that translates into a meaningful benefit to the customer. For Pepsi-Cola, the brand character badges those that choose it versus other soft drinks as hip, cool, and popular. This benefit must capitalize on the customer insight to establish a meaningful point-of-difference that motivates customers to act in a predetermined way to achieve the marketing objective.

3. **The Why**—This is the specific support for the belief, making it more credible. It is the permission to believe that is essential to closing the sale. Not all brands have a "why." Thinking back to the Pepsi-Cola *Shady Acres* example we find that there is no real "why" as we defined it in Chapter 8 (dealing with reason-why). Execution is used to drive the brand character. But you may be missing an important opportunity if you do not have a reason-why or some other credibility aid.

The Advertising Strategy Statement

Now we are ready to complete the development of the Ad Strategy Statement. We have: 1) reviewed available research to gain a fact-based understanding of brand performance, customer attitudes, and purchase behavior; 2) articulated the marketing objective; and 3) undertaken the Customer Insight Thought Process using the tool provided to arrive at the future compelling belief.

The advertising strategy statement is a brief statement focused against *"Who"* (the target customer group we want to convince); *"What"* (the benefit or belief that creates a meaningful point-of-difference); and *"Why"* (the support that makes the benefit credible to the target customer group). We frame these outputs with:

Convince:	"Who"	(Target Customer Group)
That:	"What"	(Compelling Future Belief)
Because:	"Why"	(Credibility Aid)

Again, "*Why*" aids credibility to "*What*," the compelling future belief. It is the reason-why support for the point-of-difference. In the case of Tide, the "*Why*" is both intrinsic to the product (i.e., improved formulation) and extrinsic (i.e., expert endorsements). For more information, return to the chapter on reason-why.

Continuing with the Tide example, we express the Advertising Strategy Statement as:

Tide
Advertising Strategy Statement
(Example)

Convince (Who—Target): *Cost-conscious moms of large blue-collar families with active children (particularly boys), who wash so frequently they wear out their families' clothes and, as such, do not (frequently) purchase Tide because they don't believe it gets clothes significantly cleaner than price promoted heavy-duty detergents.*

That (What—Benefit/Belief): *Tide gets clothes their cleanest and keeps them looking new.*

Because (Why—Reason-Why/Support): *a) "Improved" Tide formulation powers out stains while keeping clothes from fading or fraying; and b) Trusted and endorsed by the Cotton Association.*

Keep in mind that this is one strategic option. There could very well be others because the Customer Insight Thought Process may lead different managers to different insights and future compelling beliefs. This is okay. In fact, we like options. Remember that your marketing research team member can assist you in finding ways to choose from among alternate customer insights, compelling future beliefs, and the Ad Strategy Statements to which they lead.

Characteristics of a Sound Ad Strategy Statement

The Tide example reflects the characteristics of a sound Advertising Strategy Statement.

1. *It's directed toward the realization of the marketing objective*—A sound Ad Strategy Statement needs to effect customer attitudes and behavior that is favorable to the achievement of the brand's marketing objective.

2. *It's clear*—The belief structure upon which the consumer is being asked to think and act upon our brand in preference to others (in the context of the marketing objective) should be clear to everyone involved. It should be incapable of being misunderstood by anyone on your marketing team (from both the client company and agency).

3. *It's simple*—The number of ideas in the advertising must be kept to a minimum to avoid confusion or dilution of the intended message.

4. *It's succinctly written*—We need to edit, edit and edit, then edit some more! Cut out extraneous words and ideas and make clear those words and ideas you employ. It seams that whenever we have difficulty articulating a point we choose to employ more words. Instead of clarifying our point, more words tend to obfuscate it. Moreover, it could lead the agency to make the choice for us, which we might not want.

5. *It's free of executional direction*—The advertising strategy identifies the substance, that is, *what* benefits we are to present to customers. It does not contain executional direction. Execution deals with *how* these benefits are to be presented to customers. The *how* is the responsibility and expertise of the agency.

6. *It's competitive*—The Ad Strategy Statement should suggest a meaningful point-of-difference that will lead your target customer to adopt the attitude and purchase/usage behavior called for in the marketing objective. It should, if properly executed, lead the customer to assert, "Ah, *this is why I should buy/use your product rather than the one(s) I am currently buying.*"

Commitment—The Name of the Game

There is one element missing that needs to be addressed before we may consider our Ad Strategy Statement to be a meaningful guide to creative development. It's commitment. Are you committed to achieving the Ad Strategy Statement? If not, the Ad Strategy Statement may lack meaning and, as such, you should not move forward to creative development. Not only should you be prepared to accept the commitment to the Ad Strategy Statement but so should your advertising agency and senior client management. Remember the lesson from the unfortunate Wieden & Kennedy situation with Subaru. If you don't have full commitment, you are sending the agency off on a torturous and dangerous trip into unknown territory without a map. Chances are they will not reach the landing site everyone has in mind. When the agency presents creative work, the client management will be mulling strategic issues. Disagreements will surface. Further misdirection will be likely. Timelines will be extended. Frustration, resentment, and mistrust will be fueled. You will have a mess on your hands.

So commit and gain commitment. The best way we know how to gain commitment is to involve key managers in the actual development of the Ad Strategy Statement. Don't sell them. Let them build and buy into it, creatives included. Also utilize research, as needed, to assist your judgment in dealing with multiple options, or as a disaster-check for the proposed direction. Do whatever it takes to gain commitment before moving on to creative development.

Agency Brief

Whew! The strategic work is now behind us. It has been a lot of hard work, and it will be worth every moment of time. We have established the platform for a successful creative development process.

Next comes the communication of the strategic direction we want to pursue with the agency. This is about the agency brief for new campaign development. There are many differing opinions regarding the purpose and conduct of the agency brief. As you might imagine, we have some thoughts on this subject that we want to share with you. We leave it to you to adopt what you like, modify as you wish to make it fit better with your situation, and drop what you think will not work for you.

First, the agency brief is more of a rallying point to us. It is a final review before actual creative development work begins. It is the time to seek clarification and reassert understandings.

Second, in many respects the actual presentation of material should be nothing more than a formality since the client and agency team should have co-created each and every piece that comprises the brief. There should be no one attending the briefing who has not participated in the development of its components. But if there is, s/he should be able to grasp it all, without a hint of confusion, from reading the brief.

Some managers believe this is the time to inspire the creatives. This suggests a dog and pony show or perhaps poetry of words. A dog and pony show is a waste of effort, and if you can make poetry of words, then perhaps you might want to consider making your fortunes as a copywriter. If there is to be any inspiring, it should come from your knowledge and dedication to the business, collaborative style, openness to new ideas and the opinions of others, leadership, and unswerving support for good ideas, among others. On the other hand, you would be wise to utilize the tools and practices that we have discussed throughout the book. For example, when discussing the target customer group, here's an opportunity to review the video that the agency created of a day in the life of your bull's-eye target customer. When it comes to brand character, bring out the collage and music that the team pulled together to bring it to life. These are not to impress or inspire but merely to add context and ensure shared understanding.

The core components of the agency brief used to launch new campaign development are the: marketing objective; assignment; customer insight; Ad Strategy Statement; brand character; and mandatories. These are exhibited in the Agency Brief tool on page 167.

Throughout the book we have been working with each of the components mentioned in Agency Brief, with the exception of the "assignment" and "legal/ regulatory" mandatories. The assignment component is rather

---

Agency Brief

Marketing Objective:

Assignment:

Customer Insight:

Ad Strategy Statement:

- **Convince**—Who (Target)

- **That**—What (Benefit)

- **Because**—Why (Support)

Brand Character:

Legal/Regulatory Mandatories:

-

-

-

-

---

simple. It identifies the key deliverables. It deals with the medium and timing. As for mandatories, we are hesitant and apprehensive about including this element because its very presence invites managers to find new ways to shackle creative development by imposing needless limitations. But we have included this component because client companies are likely to demand it. However, we advise, urge, and plead with you to stick only to legal and regulatory mandatories. Please, absolutely no executional mandatories should be included. Executional mandatories should only be tolerated once you have a winning campaign and want to ensure all pool-outs contain the key executional elements that contribute to driving the campaign. These then become part of a pool plan, which is an entirely different document. A guideline for each component comprising the agency brief follows:

Agency Brief

Marketing Objective:

What is it that the brand needs to accomplish? Increase penetration? Build loyalty? Increase frequency of usage? What?

Assignment:

Television? Print? Outdoor? Other . . .
What is the timing (i.e., when do you need to air/publish it)?

Customer Insight:

What insight do you have into customer attitudes and behavior that can effect a change in attitudes and/or behavior that favor the brand in the achievement of the marketing objective?
- Perceived or real weakness to be exploited
- Barrier to overcome
- Untapped compelling belief

Ad Strategy Statement:

- *Convince*—Who (Target)—Include demographics, usage behavior, and need to be exploited.
- *That*—What (Benefit)—What will lead customers to choose your brand?
- *Because*—Why (Support)—Reason-why/credibility aid for the benefit.

Brand Character:

Taken from the Brand Positioning Statement.

Legal/Regulatory Mandatories:

- Challenge them all
- Keep to an absolute minimum
- Make sure they are real
- Should not be executional

Now let's see how this works. Here is what we get when we apply the agency brief to Tide Laundry Detergent.

Agency Brief
Tide Detergent Example

Marketing Objective:

Profitably grow marketshare by:

- Increasing share of laundry product requirements per consumer
- Immunizing consumers against the lure of competitive price promotions

Assignment:

Develop integrated campaign for all Tide products that will cut across all mass media (i.e., television, print and radio). The new campaign needs to be aired/published in September.

Customer Insight:

The kids really get their clothes dirty. I have to wash so often I actually wear their clothes out. So I can't afford to buy new clothes all the time or pay for a detergent that doesn't clean any better than less costly brands.

Ad Strategy Statement:

Convince Cost-conscious moms of large blue-collar families with active children (particularly boys), who wash so frequently they wear out their families' clothes and, as such, do not (frequently) purchase Tide because they don't believe it gets clothes significantly cleaner than price-promoted heavy-duty detergents.

That Tide gets clothes their cleanest and keeps them looking new

Because a) "Improved" Tide formulation powers out stains while keeping clothes from fading or fraying; and

b) Trusted and endorsed by the Cotton Association.

Brand Character:

Strong ("a rock"), traditional, dependable, practical, a leader, and frugal . . . Harrison Ford.

Mandatories:

None

Armed with the customer insight, Ad Strategy Statement, and agency brief document, you now have a surefooted way to setting ad direction for successful creative development. Let's get on to creative development of really great advertising.

KEY PRINCIPLES

Summary

✔ The advertising strategy defines the intent of the advertising in capitalizing on a key customer insight to address the marketing objective or a specific brand issue.

✔ The ad strategy provides the direction for the development of the brand's advertising. Additionally, it provides a common thread upon which to assess the advertising agency's creative submissions.

✔ Without the ad strategy the creative output is at best a "hit or miss" proposition with the emphasis on "miss."

✔ The Ad Strategy Statement is different from the Brand Positioning Statement. Whereas the brand positioning provides the strategic foundation for all of the brand's efforts, the ad strategy deals with the advertising element of the marketing mix.

✔ The customer insight is a critically important element in the development of a competitive ad strategy.

✔ In order to be successful in identifying meaningful customer insights you will have to satisfy the following needs:

  • An understanding of purchasing dynamics and attitudes for category customers by segment and, in particular, your target customer group;
  • A thoughtful review and analysis of available customer research to piece together potential hypotheses concerning customer motivations;
  • Development of customized customer research to resolve unanswered key issues; and

- Intangibles such as experience, intuition, and imagination, among others, and a willingness to experiment with trial and error.

✔ The Consumer Insight Thought Process tool provides an important pathway to direct your thinking and approach discovery of customer insights.

✔ The Consumer Insight Thought Process calls for the identification of: the **target customer group;** their **current belief;** what they **currently do** (that we wish to change) as a result of their belief; **desired future (purchasing or usage) behavior;** the **customer insight;** and, finally, the **compelling future belief** that will get the target to adopt the desired future behavior and realize the marketing objective for the brand.

✔ The customer insight is expressed in the words of the customer. This encourages empathy and, more important, represents the customer's versus client's point-of-view.

✔ Remember, the value of the customer insight rests in effecting change in customer attitudes and behavior that benefit your brand, leading to the achievement of the marketing objective. So it must be linked to a meaningful benefit or belief.

✔ Filters used to determine if you have a meaningful customer insight are:

- Customer perceived or real weakness of competitive product performance, image or value to be exploited;
- Attitudinal or perceived barrier to overcome in customers' minds regarding your brand or, perhaps, the category; and
- Untapped compelling belief which, if tapped into, would lead customers to choose your brand.

✔ The Advertising Strategy Statement contains and delivers the following outputs:

Convince: *"Who"*–Target Customer Group;

That: *"What"*–Benefit or Belief;

Because: *"Why"*–Support for the belief.

✔ A good Advertising Strategy Statement is: directed toward the achievement of the marketing objective; clear; simple; succinct; free of executional direction; and competitive.

✔ Make certain that you, the agency, and your senior management are prepared to accept the commitment to achieve the advertising strategy before you proceed to direct the agency to undertake creative development.

✔ The purpose of the agency brief for new campaign development is to communicate the relevant strategic direction we want to pursue. It is a rallying point. The information in the briefing should be a mere formality because everyone should have been involved in its development.

✔ The core components of the agency brief are the: marketing objective; assignment specs; customer insight; Ad Strategy Statement; brand character; and legal/regulatory mandatories.

CHAPTER 14

Creating Campaign Ideas for More Compelling Communications

"Tell me short and show me true, or else, my dear, to hell with you."
—old Irish saying

In the long and challenging "process of exchange" that client-advertisers and their agency partners pursue towards getting great advertising, the **Campaign Idea** truly serves as the ideal currency of exchange. Why? Its focus on a single, big idea makes it the perfect medium for **provocatively expressing the brand's benefit(s) in customer language.** It is the Campaign Idea that finally translates our hard-won strategic language into customer language. And this translation must go beyond words to include a *dramatization*. In more technical terms, the Campaign Idea is creative work comprising: (1) a set of key copy words and (2) a core dramatization. Together these two elements communicate the brand's benefit(s).

Who can forget the classic Lite Beer from Miller All Star campaign? Across hundreds of spots the Campaign Idea remained anchored on its key copy words and core dramatization: "Tastes Great, Less Filling" (key copy words) being chanted back and forth by unlikely pairs of athlete "celebrities" arguing in a bar (core dramatization). And heavy beer consumers never failed to take away the key twin product benefits.

173

A Campaign Idea with this kind of communicative power does even more than drive home the strategic benefits, however. It serves as the "main thread" in the long-term evolution of a great campaign. It's literally what drives people—marketers and consumers alike—to readily recall detailed aspects of the Miller Lite All Stars Campaign years after it has ended. Such an effect certainly lives up to the advice expressed in the old Irish saying.

Key Copy Words

Sometimes you'll hear people refer to the key copy words of a Campaign Idea as the *tag line*—those words on the screen at the close of a television commercial or underneath the brand name in a print ad. Often, the tag line and key copy words are one in the same; but sometimes they're not. For years a character named Mr. Whipple admonished shoppers with the tag, "Please don't squeeze the Charmin." But this set of words did not represent the real key copy words. They were more specific about the benefit and were said elsewhere in the advertising: "Only Charmin is so squeezably soft it's irresistible." So, regardless of where they occur in advertising, the key copy words are the ones that sell the benefit.

Make no mistake about it, when it comes to selling your distinct benefit, there's nothing like the power of words to force the issue. We're not talking about trite, overused, flat words like "best" or "better," but words that spark the imagination and strike a responsive chord (words that "demand a response"). If you're at all skeptical about the selling power of key copy words, take a quick look at the list below, which compiles just a handful of current and classic selling lines. See how well you remember the brand that each is distinctly linked to on page 175.

Each of these classic and current key copy words incisively cuts to the fundamental strategic benefit—whether rational or emotional (or both) in nature. But because in most cases the brand name is so readily recalled, each also does a masterful job at linking that benefit to the brand. This linkage is

Classic Key Copy Words

- Bet you can't eat just one.

- The taste you hate, twice a day.

- _____spells relief.

- Look Ma, no cavities!

- You can be sure if it's _____.

- We're number 2. We try harder.

- L.S.M.F.T.

- It's the Real Thing!

- Like a rock.

- _____cleans ring around the collar

(Lays, Listerine, Rolaids, Crest, Westinghouse, Avis, Lucky Strike, Chevrolet, Coke, Whisk)

Current Successful Key Copy Words

- _____. What a surprise!

- _____. It's everywhere you want to be.

- Creating a higher standard.

- A diamond is forever.

- A lifetime of beautiful skin.

- _____. Because so much is riding on your tires.

- _____. Australian for beer.

- _____. Eat what you like.

- Be all that you can be.

- _____. Solutions for a small planet.

(Milk, Visa, Cadillac, DeBeers, Oil of Olay, Michelin, Foster's, Healthy Choice, Army, IBM) what drives ownability, along with a commitment from the advertiser and the agency to keep the key copy words relevant and fresh.

There's probably no better example of such a commitment than in what the Tide detergent brand has done over a period of many years. As the schematic below shows, during the many years when the Tide brand positioning was anchored in the "best against dirt" benefit, the advertising development teams changed the key copy words (to freshen it up or to launch a product improvement). But in so doing, they never gave up the rhythmic magic of the line. (And notice, too, how consistently the brand name is central to the way the line rolls off the tongue.)

Even when the positioning main benefit evolved beyond dirt—to "clean"— the key copy words ring true to their heritage. Now that's a commitment to selling. It helps explain why Tide is America's runaway laundry detergent leader—with reported sales of roughly $1.6 billion in 1997 (versus the number two brand, Cheer, with reported sales of less than $400 million).

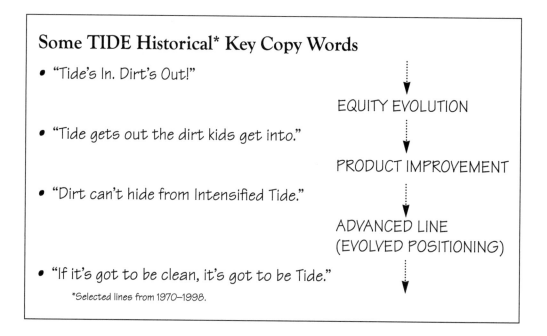

Some TIDE Historical* Key Copy Words

- "Tide's In. Dirt's Out!"

  EQUITY EVOLUTION

- "Tide gets out the dirt kids get into."

  PRODUCT IMPROVEMENT

- "Dirt can't hide from Intensified Tide."

  ADVANCED LINE
  (EVOLVED POSITIONING)

- "If it's got to be clean, it's got to be Tide."

  *Selected lines from 1970–1998.

Core Dramatization

Because television and print are visual media, once you have a provocative, compelling set of key copy words for your campaign, you would also like a *central visualization* to bring the words to life. This is the *core dramatization.* And it can happen in any number of ways: **a unique demonstration** (when Tide key copy words evolved to "Dirt can't hide from Intensified Tide," the advertising introduced a now-famous dirty-sock-hidden-in-the-pants demo); **a nifty plot or situation; a dramatic product "switch"; a product reaction shot;** or even **ownable iconography**.

Probably no other brand in recent years has consistently done as fine a job in crafting the switch or "choice" situation as Pepsi-Cola has. Time and again, over a period of 10–15 years, their core dramatization (in support of the key copy words, "The Choice of a New Generation") was a clever demonstration of people's choice of Pepsi over Coke. It was a demonstration rooted *not* in some rational product benefit, but in the higher-order, emotional benefits. ("*my* kind of soft drink").

Or how about the way Michelin has taken a very simple visual device—the baby in the tire shot—and turned it into a bull's-eye delivery of their emotional benefit: "Because so much is riding on your tires." For them, what started out as an almost overly literal association of their product and its most precious passengers has turned into their ownable icon.

Speaking of hard-working icons, there is probably none more widely recognized than that of Marlboro's yellow-slickered cowboy—the man from Marlboro Country. His image, seen around the world, conjures up all the rugged individualism and strong-taste benefits that Marlboro stands for. In many ways, it's this core dramatization that drives the Campaign Idea on Marlboro. Here are some other examples—from effective current campaigns—of dramatizations that drive a Campaign Idea on page 178.

In some of these examples, you'll probably recall that there is more to the dramatization than the visual. The music track for Coca-Cola's "Always" campaign is as integral part of the Campaign Idea as the visualization of Coke icons that have been contemporized. And, while the Energizer bunny is a visual itself, it is also a kind of "spokes-character" for the brand. A good many brands

---

Core Dramatizations

- (Cheer) Cocktail shaker and ice demo

- (Coke) Contour bottle and "button emblem" icons

- (Energizer) Pink bunny with drum

- (Absolut) Bottle shape customized to geography and venues

- (Nike) Swoosh icon and alpha athletes

- (Master Lock) Torture test attempts to break the lock

---

have successfully created their own characters, which in turn have become additional key components of the long-term Campaign Ideas (from Tony the Tiger of Kellogg's Frosted Flakes cereal to Chester Cheetah of Cheetos).

KEY PRINCIPLES

Summary

✔ A great Campaign Idea is at the heart of any great advertising campaign. It consists of two essential components: *key copy words* and a *core dramatization.*

✔ A Campaign Idea serves the advertiser in a number of ways:

—**Translates** dull, strategic language into compelling customer language (that should be instantly memorable)

—**Serves** as a "main thread" in the continuity of a long-term campaign;

—**Promotes** the brand character.

✔ More than anything else, the Campaign Idea must communicate the brand's main benefit(s) to the consumer. In doing so, it should visualize

Campaign Idea Assessment

A Campaign Idea is the provocative expression of a brand's benefit(s) in customer language. It uses key copy words and a core dramatization to communicate the benefit(s).

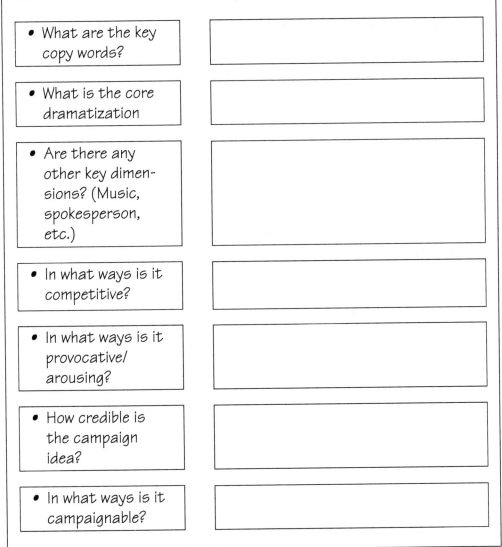

• What are the key copy words?	
• What is the core dramatization	
• Are there any other key dimensions? (Music, spokesperson, etc.)	
• In what ways is it competitive?	
• In what ways is it provocative/ arousing?	
• How credible is the campaign idea?	
• In what ways is it campaignable?	

the benefit in a compelling, ownable manner. It should also link the brand name and the benefit together distinctively.

✔ The key copy words and core dramatization sometimes gain added leverage from an original piece of music or from an on-going character. Both can become "creative equities" for a brand and contribute to building its character.

✔ Finally, when assessing Campaign Ideas, refer to the checklist on page 179. Use it to logically sequence your thoughts.

Making the Campaign Idea More "Selling"

What we said in Chapter 2 ("Positioning—The Foundation for the Brand") about this being the age of sameness is well worth recalling when developing—no, *creating!*—Campaign Ideas. Regardless of our brand's technical performance versus its competition (superiority, or more likely nowadays, parity), we and our agencies have the responsibility to engender a perceived, credible advantage for the brand among the intended target customers. In plain English, we have the responsibility to sell our brand at the expense of someone else's.

Sometimes you'll hear agency people urge caution—that it might be too risky forcing "hard sell" into a finely crafted, well-wordsmithed, customer-friendly Campaign Idea. But such admonitions, even when well-intended, miss the point. There is a world of difference between "creative sell" and "hard sell." In fact, there are a fistful of ways the determined, clever, and competitive agency creative team can engineer perceived, credible advantages into your brand's Campaign Ideas (without resorting to breast-beating, brow-beating, or any other kind of hard-sell turn-off!)

Nine Sure-Fire Ways to Build in "Sell"

Here's a handy checklist of methods one can use to bolster the Campaign Idea's credibility, competitiveness, and selling power:

- Visualization of the benefit
- Visualization of the reason-why
- Demonstration
- Torture test
- Endorsement—expert, celebrity

- Testimonial
- Challenge
- "Halo"
- Guarantee

Let's take a look at each of these methods (via some specific print and broadcast examples) in more detail.

Visualization of the Benefit—You might think, given the tried and true advertising adage, "If it's not in the pictures, it's just not there" that every Campaign Idea—by definition—must include a visualization of the main benefit. Our definition at the start of this chapter did, in fact, require a Campaign Idea to "dramatize the brand's advertising objective and strategy—particularly its consumer benefit." But when it comes to making the Campaign Idea sell better, merely including some kind of benefit visualization is usually not enough. What's needed is a particularly provocative, maybe even unexpected, visualization that gets the target's attention and forces him or her to perceive your brand in a new, better way visually that grabs and holds so tight it insists, "I'm better than the others."

For some telling examples, consider what a couple of high-tech manufacturers (Minolta—copiers; Sony—sound speakers) have done in recent years to visualize their respective main benefits, in a most unexpected manner. Both promise incredibly lifelike, natural images/sounds; but neither seems to have the proprietary technology to claim an outright advantage against their myriad competitors. Parity. And yet, each Campaign Idea—using a live-interaction between an animal and product—clearly suggests that Minolta's color copier and Sony's The Box speakers have more natural color and sound than other options.

Minolta cleverly engages a hungry, bug-hunting lizard who is so fooled by the color-copied image of a fly that it attempts to snag it. Similarly, Sony confronts a long-legged, heron-like bird with pre-recorded sounds of its mate—and nearly causes a mating of bird and Box in the process! You might expect that more technical brands such as these (who may even be managed by engineers) would visualize their benefit in terms of dpi registration or tweeters and woofers. But, quite unexpectedly, they defy convention and demonstrate their unsurpassed imaging/sound quality in a simple "you-can't-fool-Mother-Nature" approach. And the intended customer is left with no other impression than that these are cut-above products.

Or take another example—this time in print—of a Campaign Idea for Eastpak backpacks. How do you visualize a benefit of lifelong durability? You be the judge of the effectiveness of this approach. The mind-arresting visual (of a human skeleton wearing only an Eastpak stranded in the desert) can pretty much communicate the benefit on its own: "Guaranteed for Life. Maybe Longer." These are the key copy words. Combined, they effectively make Eastpak look like a better kind of pack.

One last thing to keep in mind when trying to gain perceived superiority via benefit visualization: No matter how *effective* you (or the agency) believes a particular approach is, a competitor can probably find a way to go you one better. Take, for example, the case of the push-up bra—as advertised by two respected competitors: Victoria's Secret and Wonderbra.

The client for Victoria's Secret would be hard-pressed to challenge the breast-enhancing benefit in their agency's creative, which features a striking and well-endowed young woman, smiling ever-so-suggestively in her Victoria's Secret bra. But only a glance at the creative from Wonderbra's agency team quickly illustrates how their approach—against the same categoric benefit—creates an impression of an even more effective brand. Part of this impression no doubt derives from the more provocative (even vixenish) pose by the Wonderbra model. But part also comes from the most unusual key copy numbers—"34-22-36" becoming "36-22-36"—which tell virtually any target prospect what she most wants to hear. The lesson in this mini-case is this: never stand pat with a visualization that you find merely effective; rather, with your agency partners, continue to push the boundaries for that mind- and heart-grabbing *drama* that plainly says your brand's better.

Visualization of the Reason-Why—Although a step removed from the all-important benefit, as we noted in Chapter 6, employing a reason-why (or permission to believe) can go a long way toward *closing the sale*. It does this mainly by bringing added credibility to the party. So, it only makes sense that visualizing a reason-why—as part of the Campaign Idea—can provide yet another angle toward a perceived advantage for your brand.

The same principles apply to this kind of visualization as they did for the benefit: aim for the provocative, the unexpected; aim for a visualization that is so crystal clear that it stands on its own; and never settle for a visual that just "gets the job done." These days it seems to have become almost formulaic to plug in a reason-why "middle" halfway through many television spots—especially for health- and beauty-related categories (analgesics, antacids/acid blockers, shampoos). More often than not, these "middles" are computer-animated, high-tech-type bar charts, body scans, and various other squiggles that are supposed to visualize a process or ingredient point-of-difference. However, many of these add little or nothing toward: (1) establishing a perceived advantage in the consumer's mind, or (2) closing the sale.

Once again, the secret to success is in how you and your agency choose to visualize your reasons-why. Consider the bottled water category. It would be hard to find a category with as many "name brands" fighting it out—all with essentially the exact same product. Some say that in a parity-commodity-locked category such as this it takes distinctive imagery to gain a preference. Perhaps. But any and all imagery in bottled water ties back to *the source*, which is nothing more than the reason-why (Evian is healthful because its "factory" is the Alps, Ozarka is purer because it comes from the Ozark Mountains, and so on).

In this kind of competitive framework, brands face an especially tough challenge when attempting to visualize a compelling reason-why point-of-difference. One brand, Echo de los Andes, launched in Argentina within the past few years, has found a particularly compelling way to visualize its source, the Andes. Using computer-generated facsimiles of the Andes range, the television spots literally move the mountains (and all their crystalline water flow) into the heart of Buenos Aires to the beat of some stirring new-age music. The consumer take-away is simple—a cleaner, crisper, (even revered) and therefore better source of bottled water (or, as the copy puts it, *"una agua superior."*)

Demonstrations—When you get down to it, nothing beats a clever, honest demonstration of a brand's efficacy for adding sell to a Campaign Idea. You may not have personally witnessed the early days of live television, but anyone who has will eagerly recall the live, real-people demonstrations that characterized much of television advertising in the 1950s and 1960s. Whether it involved the tension-building efforts of a ten-year-old girl attempting to start a Sears lawnmower for the six-hundredth-straight time, or something as simple as watching a beagle to see if it could "pick its favorite dogfood" (Alpo), these kinds of "proof positive" tests gave consumers instant permission to believe. They also closed many a sale right on the spot.

With the loss of live television, there has also been some loss of instant credibility. The advertising hall of fame is loaded, nonetheless, with winning campaigns that are demonstration-driven (recall the famous "Dirt Can't Hide from Intensified *Tide*" campaign and its sock-inside-the-sock demo mentioned earlier.)

More recently, the Dove Bar Soap brand has driven dramatic growth thanks to a most unconventional 30-second television demonstration: the litmus test. Just about everyone who took high school chemistry has seen a litmus test done. But Dove is a beauty bar; what has that got to do with high school chemistry? Well, that's part of the provocativeness of the demonstration. What would happen if you put a number of brands to the mildness test (based on pH)? How would Dove fare? It turns out, in fact, that on the basis of pH *only* Dove is as mild as distilled water. Or, as their key copy words put it, "Dove is mildest. Bar none." So convinced of the campaign's impact to sell were the advertisers that they ignored age-old beauty care "mandatories" such as, "You must show beautiful skin." In a further show of their convictions, they also direct-mailed mini-litmus test to U.S. households, so even skeptical consumers could prove the efficacy for themselves.

Dove made the most of its superiority performance with this dramatic, extended demonstration spot. But, so compelling can a well-crafted demo be that it's able to make even a *parity-performing* brand seem superior, particularly when it becomes the heart of a campaign. Take the case of Cheer laundry detergent. In what has to be the longest-running "demo campaign" currently on-air, Cheer (and its well-recognized mustachioed demonstrator) has literally turned its parity claim—*"Nobody's Better in Cold"*—into one of perceived superiority. Acting in a wide range of clever situations, the demonstrator performs his convincing cocktail-shaker washing demonstration (that is, stain removal "on ice"). And in every case the resulting fabric comes clean, white, and bright! Nothing beats the sell of a credible, dramatic demonstration.

While demonstrations are by definition dramatic, this doesn't mean they only work in broadcast media. In fact, print demos can also be highly effective (and durable). For several years now Noxzema Shave Cream has demonstrated its richer, thicker lather via the "pencil test," showing how its ultra-thick lather indeed supports a pencil standing on its end. The success of a demo such as this depends on two things: (1) it's instantly understood upon first glance; and (2) the demonstrated product attribute of *richness* translates almost as instantly to *better skin protection* in the intended target customer group's mind.

As one of the nine "sure-fire" ways to build more sell into your Campaign Ideas, demonstrations are hard to beat. If you don't currently use a demonstration in your advertising, you would be well-served to conduct a special "exploratory" with your agency and business team (including research and development, often a wonderful source for demo ideas). Push the agency to craft a demo-centered campaign and, at a minimum, get some demo copy into test. In the age of sameness, a distinctive, credible demo can make a real point-of-difference.

Torture Test—Who hasn't, at one time or another, referred to a particular personal ordeal as being like "water torture"? Well, while not exactly the same term, the notion of a "torture test" is more of an *ordeal* among demonstrations, which is to say that a torture test is really a demonstration taken to the extreme. As such, it typically allows for some "suspension of disbelief" and may even make use of exaggerated humor for effect. But whatever the specific executional approach, the torture test aims to accomplish what any good demo does: to convince someone in a memorable way that your product performs better than the competition.

Probably the most famous torture test in the annals of advertising was the long-running American Tourister Luggage campaign that featured gorillas in a zoo-cage manhandling the product by banging it against the cage, slamming it from the ceiling, and tossing it end-to-end (in other words, in a parody of consumers' perceptions about how airline baggage handlers really treat their luggage behind the scenes). Not only did this campaign strike a real-life chord with consumers, but it demonstrated that, no matter how brutal the handling, American Tourister stood up to it all and still came out looking about like new.

Yet another famous torture test came from outside the United States (from France, originally) during the introduction of Super Glue 3. In an amazing "single take" 30-second sequence, an announcer (turned upside-down) has a mere dab of Super Glue 3 applied to each of his shoes and is promptly hoisted, feet-first, to the ceiling of the room where, naturally, he bonds—shoes and body—instantly. Left hanging by his feet, he continues to point out that the product works just as well on rubber, plastic, china, and other materials.

If you choose to engage in torture testing, keep in mind that you are still, fundamentally, selling via demonstration. So the same rules-for-effectiveness apply: keep it clear; make it compelling; and make sure it's credible. If, on top of all this, the "torture" adds an engaging element of humor or fun, so much the better.

Endorsements—Back in our discussion about the reason-why, we looked at the necessity of giving customers "something more than a compelling benefit" to close a sale. That something more is a reassurance that they're making a wise decision. This is precisely what endorsements are all about; they *sanction* a sale for the prospective customer. Such sanctions may come from a range of endorsers (or endorsing "bodies"): experts in a field; celebrities from sports, entertainment, government; inspection boards and publications such as *Consumer Reports*. But whatever the source of the endorsement, just as with demonstrations, the force of the effectiveness depends upon its "ring of truth" . . . or, relevance and credibility.

Endorsements from "experts and expert bodies" seem to be most commonplace among higher-end, higher-performance kinds of products. Where would the automobile industry be without the coveted J.D. Power & Associates endorsements? Such a simple endorsement for, say, GM Cars (even executed in a written-by-hand style, for added legitimacy) might well be that last piece of "reassurance" a prospective new car buyer needs to make a GM purchase.

And, while it has lost some of its relevance today, the Good Housekeeping Seal has long been a looked-for endorsement across numerous "performance product" categories. (In some ways, the GH Seal has probably been obsoleted by specialized endorsements, such as the Baldrige Awards for quality.)

Celebrity endorsements seem to have become the more popular form of sanctioning, across all advertised brands and categories. No doubt much of their popular appeal derives from our culture's deep-seated interest in the lives of known personalities. The trick, though, in attempting to leverage a known personality for a sale is all in selecting the right one to fit with your brand. Who could better represent Jell-O brand over the years than Bill Cosby—particularly given his (until very recently) pure family image and expertise in interacting with children? A celebrity endorser simply must convey trust—to give the customer that added reassurance in making the purchase.

Clearly, the best-known endorser in the United States today (and maybe even the world) is Michael Jordan. And why not? His heroic accomplishments, his unmistakable smile, and his proven "purchase pull" are nearly unheard of. *The Chicago Tribune* ran an article not long ago that tracked his formidable purchase pull; they cited something called the "Jordan Factor," which is the sizable increase in TV viewership (as in ratings) that came with Jordan's presence in a televised game—typically a 66 percent increase over games without him. That's something to think about when looking for an endorser "point-of-difference."

Of course there are some celebrities who might be in a league with Michael Jordan, but they refuse to endorse as a matter of principle. Take Paul Newman, for instance. If Jordan has the world's most recognizable smile, Newman surely has the most recognizable eyes. Newman has been approached many times with endorsement offers (excluding, of course, his

Newman's Own products); but he has tenaciously refused them. So, there's an end to it, right? Wrong!

With tenaciousness of your own—alongside some creative manipulation of what constitutes an endorsement—you might well convince a "won't do" celebrity like Paul Newman to lend his sanction to your brand. That's what a leading French skincare brand (Lux Ligne) has done: they merely asked Newman to appear as an airport passenger who happens to pass by a lovely Lux Ligne user (female, naturally). As he passes he says absolutely nothing; by merely lowering his sunglasses and momentarily admiring the Lux Ligne woman, his big blue eyes say it all! The lesson in this example is simply this: if there's an endorser that you believe will make a big difference in the selling of your brand, then there's always a way to get his or her "seal of approval."

Of course, some advertisers and their agencies have found a better way of dealing with celebrity endorsers (who invariably require a "mating process" that is not without its frustrations and potentially enormous costs): **they create their own.** From Tony the Tiger to Joe Camel, these kinds of wholly owned properties can—over the long haul—become celebrities in their own right. Even better, they don't risk being overused by signing on with other brands. But, like real, live humans, they aren't foolproof—as the demise of Joe Camel (who seemed to be encouraging youngsters to smoke) bears out. One has to wonder just what added reassurance for buying can really derive from, say, a fabricated personality who never does much except be "available," as in the case of Mr. Jenkins, the ever-puzzling and aloof Tanqueray Gin personality. Remember the basics: endorsers work best when they are both relevant and credible. One could question how much Mr. Jenkins works against these requirements.

Crazy as it may sound, there are times when a celebrity surrounded by "bad news" can work wonders as an endorser. Consider how deftly advertising for New York's Helmsley Hotels has insinuated a quality endorsement—based solely on the notoriety of its owner, Leona Helmsley. In a print headline, the news that she allegedly abused her hotel staff was brilliantly turned from "lemons" into "lemonade" via the implied tough standards Leona sets: "Say What You Will, She Runs A Helluva Hotel." A tongue-in-cheek endorsement, to be sure, but somehow you can't help feeling that every Helmsley Hotel will take elegance and guest service to a new level.

So, celebrated personalities—from a wide spectrum of availability and reputation—can be incredibly effective in making a Campaign Idea sell harder. But, before jumping into the celebrity circus, it might make sense to review with your agency counterparts the plusses and minuses of committing to any "live" celebrity:

Celebrity Endorser Checklist

Plusses	Minuses
—Instant recognition	—Celeb is remembered more than the brand, can embarrass the brand, or can appear to have been "bought"
—Added trust in benefits	
—Can build brand character	
—Leverages what's topical; seems contemporary	—Negotiating is a big hassle
—Can endure and "grow" with the brand	—Costs are enormous (and only get bigger)
—Can bring "stature"	—Celeb can lose popularity
—In a competitive dogfight can be the point-of-difference	

Testimonials—Closely related to the endorsement is the testimonial. True testimonials differ from an endorsement in that they engage live brand users (or converted users) in on-camera or in-print "plugging" of the brand. In television's earlier days, it seems that by far the majority of testimonials were indeed done with real people, not actors posing as real people. Nowadays it seems that the reverse is more the norm. In either case, the selling power of a testimonial comes from its inherent "listen-to-someone-who-ought-to-know" appeal. The principle is akin to that used when seeking to hire someone: you do your homework and check references. In effect, that's what a testimonial accomplishes—it gives the prospective buyer a legitimate, some-one-like-me, reference.

One of the most understated—but nevertheless highly effective—print campaigns is for Rockport shoes. It typically features an amazingly durable pair of Rockport shoes—along with a hand-written note from the shoes' satisfied owner—but never shows us the actual person giving testimony! Yet it works beautifully: in a twist of the traditional testimonial form, the "visible evidence" of the product itself becomes, in effect, the strongest testimony.

As you might expect, when using testimonials—especially those that re-place real people with actors—the "make or break" of the sell lies in the cred-ibility of the testimony given. As a general rule, you're better off going with real people who have first-hand conviction in their testimony; actors some-how have a way of always coming across as, well, actors.

Challenge—A less frequently used way to add sell to a Campaign Idea is the challenge. Recall that most famous of all advertising challenges—the Pepsi Challenge—which ran during the 1970s and early 1980s and did much to in-flame the Cola Wars. For a considerable period of time, Pepsi-Cola was able to gain significant marketshare by employing the highly comparative and competitive challenge approach. As the term implies, it involves confronting real consumers of a brand or category and "challenging" them to test their commitment to a given brand. In the case of the Pepsi Challenge, Coke drinkers were asked to try two unidentified colas on camera and pick their favorite. Time and again the Coke drinkers surprised themselves (and the TV audience) by selecting Pepsi as their favorite. In a real sense, this famous cola challenge was a testimonial "as it happened." It therefore carried sub-stantial credibility along with it.

While this challenge case worked for a time, it's important to know the proverbial "rest of the story" before you jump too quickly at a competitive challenge. Coke responded most cleverly to the challenge by using an *endorser!* And not just any endorser, but good ol' Bill Cosby. Cosby's mission, which he carried out so deftly, was to use his immense personal credibility to cast doubt upon those quickie taste-tests run by Pepsi. In one Coke Response spot, for example, he simply wondered aloud how it could be that in all those side-by-side drinkings no one *ever* selected the Coke. Cosby's ultimate effectiveness forced the Pepsi Challenge into permanent retreat.

But challenges need not pit one brand against another to be effective selling. In fact, probably more successful challenges in advertising have pitted a *product improvement* or new form of a given brand against its *previous* one. Who can forget the times that detergent users were stopped on live camera and asked to "trade out" their favorite brand for a new, unidentified one—only to learn later that the unidentified one was merely a new version of their favorite?

"Halo"—This technique falls broadly under the endorsement umbrella, but it is typically more subtle than a "plug" from an endorser. It's basically the use of borrowed interest—especially interest from something/someone/some event that is currently topical. A great recent example was BMW's advertising (in television and print) of their special-edition, powder-blue, convertible sports coupe—the same one, incidentally, that was featured as James Bond's new toy in *GoldenEye*. As the movie was being promoted, BMW was taking orders for their special-edition Bond-mobile (of which only 25,000 were available). News reports indicated that orders far exceeded availability; and for BMW there was a tremendous "rub-off" or "halo" effect in the association with the new Bond movie. All of this goes to prove that your opportunity to sell can be dramatically enhanced by the associations you make, by the "company you keep."

Guarantee—When you get down to it, what better incentive to buy can you give someone than a money-back guarantee? It instantly takes all the risk out of the situation for the prospective buyer. Most reputable companies these days will, in fact, refund your money fully should you not be satisfied with their products; so you might say that guarantees are pretty much "price of entry" into most categories.

But not everyone's guarantee is necessarily as valuable as another's. In other words, there are still ways to leverage the notion of a special guarantee in a Campaign Idea as a means of selling harder. Old Spice personal care products have been touting their "what-have-you-got-to-lose" guarantees for several years now. And the result is that a tired, dated brand has given incentive to whole new generation of users to try the brand and to join the franchise. The other thing that Old Spice has done is to couple its satisfaction guarantee with a **demonstration** of superior performance (for example, a longer-lasting coverage effect versus other deodorant brands). This "double-whammy" effect makes the sale that much easier. Although often overlooked, the guarantee is something worth considering from time to time.

KEY PRINCIPLES

Summary

✔ "Telling" is never the same as "selling." Your words alone cannot be expected to make the sale; you and the agency must consciously build "seeing-is-believing" salesmanship into the Campaign Ideas you develop.

✔ There are at least nine "sure-fire," proven methods that successful advertisers have used and are still using to drive this salesmanship. To the extent you can "mix and match" them, your odds of closing a sale are so much the better.

✔ Primary among the methods is *visualizing* the benefit and reason-why. Make sure you are always pushing to make the visualization as compelling as it can be; don't just settle for something that does the job.

✔ The *demonstration* is perhaps the single most convincing way to make a sale. Get your R&D and agency teams to work together on inventing a distinctive demo for your campaign.

✔ Whether crafting a demo—or the more exaggerated "torture test"—make sure the end result is relevant and credible. Anything less will backfire.

✔ Endorsements and testimonials come in a variety of forms; carefully consider the pros and cons of each before using them—especially with celebrities.

✔ Consider the benefits of creating your own brand celebrity. Such a personality will never get beyond your control.

✔ If you pursue a challenge, remember that you need not pit your brand against another; challenges against your former self can work well too.

✔ If you do elect to challenge another brand, think through how that brand might respond, as it surely will. Where is your challenge vulnerable?

✔ Consider the "Halo" and Guarantee as often-overlooked means of bolstering your salesmanship.

CHAPTER 15

Executing TV and Print Campaign Ideas: All You Need to Know

"When I was a young assistant on my first brand, my brand manager laid out the boundaries for me: 'If the execution is on strategy, legally supportable, and in good taste, you have no basis for comments,' he said."

The question is, "What, if anything, do we as client-advertisers need to know about advertising execution—specifically, television or print production?" Indeed, our agency colleagues might hastily cut off our response with, "Not much—that's what you pay *us* for!" Hard to argue with such a curt cut-off as that, but there must be some "middle ground" between the roles of becoming wanna-be experts at production and placing total (even blind) reliance on our agency teammates. After all, the parameters set by the brand manager above seem suspiciously ill-advised.

As the ones who are ultimately responsible for what happens in our business, we client-advertisers have a duty regarding *advertising execution*—one that goes beyond merely "policing" it for legality or tastefulness. The fact is that *execution* is the one and only way we have of delivering our hard-crafted Campaign Idea to our customers, so it's incredibly important to us that it succeeds. Stop and think about how many page-turner books you've read that somehow slow to a snail's pace when executed as movies. A lot can happen between nailing down the big idea and running it for the first time before our customers' eyes. To be more precise, much like the proverbial "three things that can happen when you throw a football (with two of them being bad)," there are really five things that can happen between settling on a Campaign Idea and completing its execution—with only two of them being acceptable:

Campaign Idea versus Execution—Things That Can Happen

Campaign Idea	Execution	Result
1. Bad	Bad	This is the worst (a disaster!)
2. Bad	Good	Almost as bad
3. Good	Bad	Inexcusable (time for a new agency!)
4. Good	Good	What we and agency get paid to do
5. Great	Great	Ultimately, why we're all in this business

Clearly, if you and your development team are unfortunate enough to start out with a "bad Campaign Idea," nothing that happens in the execution is going to salvage things. Though you sometimes hear our agency colleagues urging that we withhold final judgment on the Campaign Idea until the execution "works its magic," if you strongly suspect the Campaign Idea is fundamentally flawed, this is the time to speak up!

If, on the other hand, it should happen that you *do* have a strong (even great) Campaign Idea, but the execution fails to deliver it, that's not only inexcusable, but it's time to seriously question what expertise your agency partners are really bringing you.

Where you want to be, of course, is in the situation of having both a good Campaign Idea and good execution. (No, you actually want to be beyond even this, almost "off the chart" as it were, with a great Campaign Idea and a great execution.) You'll probably never have a better opportunity to influence those off-the-chart odds than during the execution planning phase of the development process.

Execution Planning versus Execution

There's an old model out there when it comes time to execute television and print advertising. The model is based on the tacit assumption that once a "board (or comp) is approved, we're into pure execution," and the agency takes over. In this context, the client-advertiser usually takes on the singular role of brand overseer. He or she attends the pre-production meeting and the shoot, but, not being trained technically for all the mechanics of the production, reserves comments or direction for such things as product placement, logotype accuracy, and the like. In short, the client-advertiser is of limited added-value at this point.

But, thanks mainly to smaller and more time-constrained marketing groups these days, this old model is being used less and less. The new model that's replacing it is based on these assumptions:

- The time to discuss and assess broad executional issues (such as *optimal executional format*) is right when the Campaign Ideas and storyboards are being debated and approved; it's really a "ripe time" for execution planning.
- When it comes time for actual filming or photography, the agency part-ners are also competent as brand overseers.
- And, finally, execution planning is cyclical. As new creative material is needed for the campaign, there will be a need for further reconsideration of executional issues.

This new model view can perhaps best be seen in the diagram on the next page—a venturi tube of sorts—that summarizes the television production-execution process. The client-advertiser has a key role at the "intakes" and "out-takes" of the tube; the agency, however, runs the "fast and furious middle":

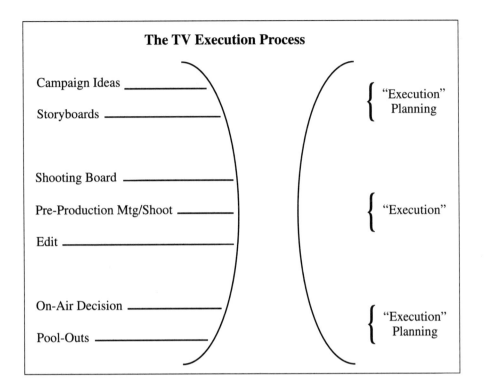

The TV Execution Process

Campaign Ideas _____

Storyboards _____

Shooting Board _____

Pre-Production Mtg/Shoot _____

Edit _____

On-Air Decision _____

Pool-Outs _____

"Execution" Planning

"Execution"

"Execution" Planning

Execution Planning: The Five Formats (Television)

Probably the most important executional issue that you should deal with in any execution planning phase is: "What's the optimal *format* for conveying the Campaign Idea?" And the main reason why such a question is so important is that the format you and the agency choose for the campaign will have a great deal to do with how well it meets those critical criteria for great advertising (see Chapter 12): relevance, credibility, ownability, and memorability.

What kinds of *formats* are we talking about here? We're talking about kinds of communication devices (as a book, or audiotape, or comic book might be communication devices or "formats" for a novel). There are five distinct devices that advertisers draw from, occasionally in combination, to execute a Campaign Idea:

TV Execution Formats

1. Presenter/Announcer Voiceover

2. Slice-of-Life

3. Vignette

4. Animation

5. Pure Demonstration

Sometimes you will hear people talk about a sixth executional format, the so-called problem-solution. This is really more a way to "make the argument for the sale" than it is a device for filming the advertising (in fact, problem-solution would work in any of the five formats). Let's take a look at each format-type and consider some of the prevailing pros and cons.

Presenter/Announcer Voiceover—It could be argued that these two really represent distinct formats in themselves, but they actually have much in common. Probably one of the oldest forms of communicating known to man (including any salesman), the *presenter* is sometimes derisively referred to by agency creatives as the "talking head." Despite slurs like these, the *presenter format* seems remarkably alive and well; some categories of consumer products, in fact, are totally dependent on it. Take analgesics or the new acid blockers—virtually every major advertiser in these categories has elected to serve up its message via some variation of presenter (celebrity; actor trying to look like an authority; actor trying to look and sound like a real customer).

It is in category situations like these where client-advertisers simply must keep raising the execution-planning question: "Are we as competitive as we can be with our Campaign Idea served up in the same format as everyone else's?" Such a question clearly requires a careful consideration of the pros and cons offered by the approach:

Presenter/Announcer Voiceover

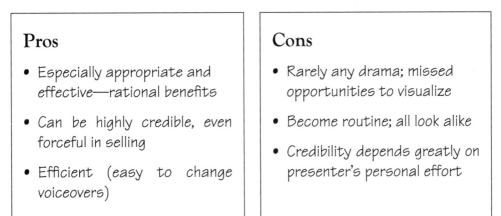

Pros	Cons
• Especially appropriate and effective—rational benefits	• Rarely any drama; missed opportunities to visualize
• Can be highly credible, even forceful in selling	• Become routine; all look alike
• Efficient (easy to change voiceovers)	• Credibility depends greatly on presenter's personal effort

Slice-of-Life—As the name implies, this format-type intends to communicate a selling message to customers in the context of (presumably) their everyday lives. The idea is to create a mini-plot of sorts—to tell a story. Like the presenter format, *slice-of-life* has deep roots in the history of television advertising.

And *slice-of-life* has come a long way in terms of development and "involvement power." Originally, the format could be type-cast as: two people (usually women) at home (usually in the kitchen) in which one of the two has a problem (dish-pan hands) and the other has the solution (Palmolive Liquid). While such a formula might have reflected many customers' lives in the 1950s and 1960s, it obviously falls well out-of-touch with today's customers.

Something else has happened to push the *slice-of-life* evolution along: brands selling largely emotional benefits (jeans, soft drinks, beer, greeting cards, athletic gear) have employed the format in great numbers. One of the foremost examples of an enduring *slice* campaign has to be "The Pepsi Generation." In all its moves from celebrities like Lionel Richie to Michael Jackson to Michael J. Fox, the brand consistently told captivating stories that centered around the choice of Pepsi. The campaign also included numerous clever demonstrations of choice for Pepsi over Coke. (Of course Coke itself also has a rich history with the *slice* format; from landmark campaigns like "Have a Coke and a Smile" to "Coke Is It!"—and all the heart-grabbing special spots in between, such as "Mean Joe Greene.") For sales such as these, it's no wonder that America's "most liked" commercials are typically *slice-of-life*. Still, as the potential cons illustrate, *slice* is not without its risks:

Slice-of-Life

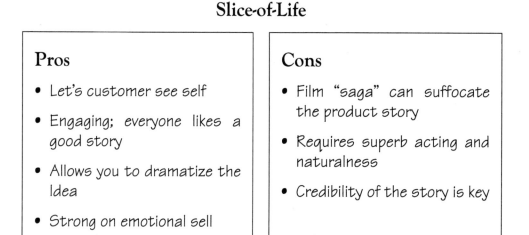

Pros	Cons
• Let's customer see self	• Film "saga" can suffocate the product story
• Engaging; everyone likes a good story	• Requires superb acting and naturalness
• Allows you to dramatize the Idea	• Credibility of the story is key
• Strong on emotional sell	

Vignettes—From the French word for "small portraits" comes this format-type that typically involves tedious editing to piece together a series of quick shots or incidents all related to the use (and sale) of the product being advertised. It's a type that's particularly well-suited to brands selling lifestyle; but it also can make good sense for "corporate brands or trademarks" that need to sell a wide-ranging line of goods or services.

Regardless of the objective, however, there is typically one element that all *vignette* advertisers share in common: **a driving, get-inside-the-mind, memorable piece of music.** With so many images passing by the customers' view, it's the music (lyrics *and* melody) that holds it all together. In many cases, the music is a primary conveyor of the emotional benefits.

You would expect that the same advertisers who use *slice-of-life* effectively also might use *vignettes*. They do. But the latter can work well for *any* brand trying to contemporize itself and **update its brand character.** A great example of exactly this is in some of Hanes current advertising. For many years an almost commodity-like brand of men's underwear, Hanes has not only significantly expanded its line to include all kinds of active-wear for men and women, but it has also become more competitive with other leisure brands (such as Champion, Dockers, and even Nike). How? By the invention of a new Campaign Idea—with key copy words, "Just Wait 'til We Get Our Hanes on You," and by the shift from *presenter/AVO* format to upbeat *vignettes*, driven by a catchy piece of country-rock music. Here, in summary, are the upsides and downsides of using the *vignette* format:

Vignettes

Pros	Cons
• Strong sale of lifestyle and action	• Hard to link with the brand
• Can help update a brand character	• Sense they've "all been seen before"
• Allows for multiple products and targets	• Can be costly shoot: often need 15 vignettes to get 10 "editable"

Animation—Who doesn't know what *animation* is all about? Better yet, who doesn't find it appealing? After all, since childhood we have all been treated to the fun and imaginative powers of *animation*. Oddly enough, there's the "rub." While we are universally fond of its ability to entertain, we are also typically wary of it when used in conjunction with advertising—at the very least, we give it cautious consideration.

As an executional format, *animation* has at least two basic "sub-forms": as a full, 30-second spot; and as a considerably shorter "middle cut-away." This "middle" may show up as line drawings, claymation, or computerized graphics; in each instance, its purpose is to somehow demonstrate "in the lab" what apparently cannot be effectively demonstrated in "live action." This kind of animated device shows up often, especially in *presenter/AVO* formats. Not so the full, 30-second animated commercial; rather, its use over the years has tended to be cyclical (often coincident with the latest technology in animation)—mainly as a way to get instant customer "engagement" and talked-about-ness in the marketplace.

Thinking about a change from any of the other format-types to *animation* is a lot like thinking about bringing on a celebrity. Both decisions stem from an apparent need to refresh a brand's advertising; and both, in a sense, end up relying on a kind of "borrowed interest" to supply that freshness. Finally, both can offer a much-desired dose of **ownability** (with *animation* offering the better odds of sustaining that ownability, because celebrities do have a habit of huckstering other brands). Of course, if you really were faced with a decision to sign a celebrity or create your own in *animation*, keep in mind that the animated ones are much easier to control.

Ultimately, the choice in executing all or part of your ad campaign should be a well-thought-out one. Something beyond merely "adding a fresh look" needs to be at stake. It must be a seamless fit with your Campaign Idea. As a rule of thumb, it makes good sense to "raise the animation question" every couple of years or so, just to ensure that you're not missing any opportunities to get a leg up in ownability or memorability. Some key considerations for animation:

Animation

Pros	Cons
• Highly memorable	• Fit with brand character?
• Can do demos more easily (especially hard-to-visualize live-action ones)	• "Real" target unseen
	• Humor can overshadow the product story
• Ownable, controllable "celebrities"	• Cost of new technologies

Pure Demonstrations—Of all the formats available for execution, perhaps *demonstrations* are most overlooked. The truth is, almost no one is doing the 30-second demo these days. It's probably because they require so much raw creativity. Imagine the challenge of filling a full 30 (not to mention 60!) seconds with an extended product performance "story." Yet the power of this format remains impressive.

As we noted in Chapter 14, in the early days of television, it wasn't uncommon to see live-action *demonstrations*—as part of the live broadcast! Talk about convincing! Even when the product somehow "failed," you couldn't help having some empathy for its having been tried. But the deterrent today has nothing to do with avoiding embarrassing failures; no, it has to do with the hard work required in inventing the knock-you-out-of-your-chair *demo*.

When BMW introduced power steering for its mid-range line, some creative team invented the idea of having a white mouse sniff its way to the steering wheel and proceed to get the wheel spinning by running its circumference. Wouldn't it have been easier to do a computerized cutaway to illustrate the new components? Easier, perhaps . . . but also deadlier. The mouse was a hit.

Another recent success in *extended demonstration* has to be what Dove did with its litmus test (as detailed in Chapter 14). By simply showing—with no announcer voiceover—what happens to a piece of litmus when dipped in a household cleanser (it darkens) versus distilled water (it remains light), Dove has executed the most brilliant of (unexpected) ideas. And the ensuing comparison among three or four leading "beauty bars" is a slam-dunk win for the brand: only on Dove does the litmus remain unchanged. No wonder a great demo is often the key to great advertising. Here, then, are the main strengths and possible shortfalls of doing pure demonstration on page 204.

Execution Planning: Print Principles

If dealing with what format to use is the focal point for executional planning in television, then where should the client-advertiser's focus be when planning for a print effort? Well, thinking (and talking with your agency) about the TV format-types is also useful in print campaign planning. You *can* do

Pure Demonstration

Pros	Cons
• Can lend the ultimate in credibility (seeing *is* believing)	• They don't come easy; require separate creative "exploratories"
• Captures people's imagination	• Have to guard against being too "techy"
• Can become a legitimate brand equity	• Often require breaking some rules

slice-of-life, vignettes, animation, pure demonstration, and even off-shoots of stand-up presenter in print. As with television execution, it's always a good idea to assess the relative competitiveness of your Campaign Idea's format vis-à-vis the category at large (or, better yet, your intended competitive framework).

Having acknowledged this, it's also true that print is a quite different animal than television. Maybe it's because print has more of a lingering effect: it literally "stares back at you" and can be studied at will; television moves too quickly for such immediate scrutiny. Or maybe it's more basic than even this. Print (particularly the more common kind in magazines and journals) operates within much less *space*. As such, really great print advertising demands maximum "economy of the page." And that means that each of the print ad's "page-parts"—the headline, visualization, and body-copy/layout design—simply must carry its weight. As client-advertisers, we need to appreciate and adhere to some basic principles for executing these print "page-parts."

Headlines

Anyone who reads a daily newspaper knows the power of headlines—to *arrest attention*, to *involve and encourage further readership*, to *complement related pictures*, to *sell!* Print advertising headlines must serve these self-same roles, plus one other: hard-working print headlines *set up*, or *lead to* (sometimes even directly *deliver*) the brand's benefit. Let's take a cursory look at some technical aspects of headlining (some technical tips, really) that can enhance the effectiveness of print execution.

Getting Headlines That Arrest Attention, Flag Down the Target, Provoke Interest in Further Reading of the Ad—Agency creative people experienced in the crafting of print advertising typically draw from a big bag of tricks when it comes to writing arresting, provocative headlines. The smart client-partner rightly gives these talented people wide berth in their headlining. But, once in a while, that same client-partner might want to suggest some exploratory headline approaches to his creative team, in the interest of stopping, intriguing, even enticing prospective target readers.

✔ *Play with the Unthinkable*—In 1997, an ad for the Life and Health Insurance Foundation for Education carried a simple but stark black-and-white headline: "It's 1999. You're Dead. What Do You Do Now?" Talk about stopping power! It's often said that we live every day of our lives as if there will always be another one coming, but it also seems universally true that very few of us can ignore the prospect of not being here when prompted to consider it. Accordingly, very few readers might guess who sponsors such an ad, but few could resist the temptation to read on and find out. What would be an "unthinkable provocation" for your brand?

✔ *Challenge Conventional Thinking*—If playing with the unthinkable seems a stretch, maybe you can take a more direct approach in provoking interest with your headlines: playing with the "thinkable." That's what a relatively new pharmaceutical brand has done with considerable success. Propecia (from Merck) is the first pill designed to reduce hair loss in men. Perhaps because male pattern baldness has for so long seemed genetically linked, most men who face it feel powerless to stop or retard it (let alone reverse it). The conventional thinking centers around resignation, which is why the headline for one of Propecia's introductory ads works so well; it challenges that very thinking head-on: "If You Think Losing More Hair Is Inevitable, Think Again." In a straightforward statement Propecia calls out to balding men, "Stop a minute! Nothing's Inevitable!"

✔ *Pose a Revealing Question*—Particularly for those brands engaged in on-going competitive battles, headlines that coyly question a competitor's product or positioning can be insidiously effective. Take, for instance, the hard-waged analgesic wars. Specifically, with nearly every major brand taking shots at the leader, Tylenol, consider what Tylenol has cleverly done in raising a previously unasked question about Excedrin's caffeinated formulation. By posing an "exposing" question—"Do You Want Caffeine . . . or Decaf with That Headache?"—superimposed on a photo of an Excedrin bottle hanging alongside coffee mugs, Tylenol fights back ever so deftly. Such an unexpected, even intriguing, question as this cannot help getting a reader's attention (and getting him or her to re-think their analgesic choice).

Getting Headlines That Set Up, Lead To, and Even Deliver the Brand's Benefit—As we've seen already, within a Campaign Idea it's the key copy words that deliver the brand's benefit (in written form, anyway). Because of this, a good many brands will include their campaign key copy words somewhere in their print executions as well—but typically *not* as the headline. Why? It comes back to those multiple roles a good headline has to fulfill; more often than not you seek more flagging-down power in a headline than most key copy words can provide. Still, though, the headline *should* be a conduit to the brand's benefit, at the very least. Here are a few ways this can happen.

✔ *Play with the Suggestive*—Playing with sexual innuendo (across all media forms) has probably become an end in itself these days. But there actually *are* some categories of products where sensual suggestiveness is an important part of the selling approach. Take bras—more specifically, the Bijou Bra from Triumph International in the U.K. Bijou's main benefit is its invisibility under even the tightest clothing, providing a more natural look. In a recent print execution (proving via photograph that Bijou *isn't* visible under a T-shirt-type top) the headline leads right to this benefit: "If I Want a Man to See My Bra, I Take Him Home." What more need be said in today's post-sexual-revolution society?

✔ *Lead with the Ridiculous*—Crazy as it sounds, the absurd is not only an effective way to attract attention, it can also bolster your benefit. There's a long-running print ad for a little-known golf ball company (so little known, in fact, they don't technically use a brand name for their balls) that has been calling out to hackers everywhere: "Small Company's New Golf Ball Flies Too Far; Could Obsolete Many Golf Courses." Ludicrous? Insane, even? Of course. Which is exactly why so many golfers have stopped to read on and then sent in anywhere from $24.95 to $109.00 for several dozens of these incredible balls. Probably no one who orders thinks for a minute that the balls will "obsolete their golf course"; but just as probably, most who order get the point—these balls just might give them the extra distance they're forever seeking (the benefit!).

✔ *Exploit Ambiguity*—It's hard to find someone who isn't attracted to word play, particularly double meanings. Such devices appeal to the craftiness in all of us. They can work wonders in a headline, especially when one of the meanings carries your brand's benefit. Vivarin, a SmithKline Beecham brand that acts as a safe stimulant, recently advertised to the college market (in *Rolling Stone* and *Spin*) with the following headline: "Stop Sleeping with Your Professors." The line carries at least two meanings, including the brand's main benefit: with Vivarin you can study late and still stay alert at next morning's lecture. Catchy. Target-relevant. To the point. All the things you want in a great headline.

Visualizations

From just these foregoing headline examples, you can see that, as compelling as they are, each is made even more so by a strong visual to accompany it:

• In the Propecia ad, a young man looking in his bathroom mirror imagines what he might look like in another five years with less hair;

- In the Tylenol ad, the half-exposed Excedrin bottle hangs prominently among the cupboard's coffee mugs;
- And in the Bijou ad, a young woman displays her snugly fitting T-shirt, without displaying the bra underneath.

In each of these cases the visualization fulfills many of the same roles that headlines do. But visuals go even further: they *dramatize* the sale. In fact, the hardest-working print visuals will involve the intended target-reader emotionally and demonstrate the brand's benefit(s). That's the drama.

This eye-catching, emotionally involving, and benefit-demonstrating drama can be set up in many creative ways. Here are a few of the ways that you might consider when doing the executional planning for your next print campaign:

✔ *Make a Real-Life Photograph the Focal Point*—Exactly what many not-for-profit advertisers do to capture a reader's heart. A recent ad for The Catholic Charities places an actual-sized Polaroid-like black-and-white at the center of the page, a photo of a homeless woman wrapped in plastic garbage bags. Combined with the headline, "Bosnia? Gaza? Try 10 Minutes from Your House," the emotional effect is powerful indeed. One such real-life picture *can* take the place of many, many words.

✔ *Do a Side-By-Side Comparison (with a Twist)*—Not long ago Healthy Choice Frozen Dinners created a most compelling (and competitive) comparison with its Lean Cuisine counterparts. But the twist came in the basis for the comparison: the grams of fat per box. On that basis—four grams per box—Healthy Choice wins hands-down; as a matter of fact, the only way that Lean Cuisine can compete as four grams per box is with half of their 8 grams per box. Guess which visual Healthy Choice went with? (A full box of Healthy Choice versus only half a box of Lean Cuisine.) Nice dramatic effect from a visual as simple as one-and-one-half boxes side by side on the page.

✔ *Create Your Own Drawings*—It's more and more rare in these days of computer graphics to find an advertiser who returns to pure illustration (as in drawings) for visualizations. That rarity alone, however, provides some of the inherent appeal of drawings: they can stand out in a crowd of photos and computerized graphic effects. Even better, if done distinctively, pure illustrations can become ownable and therefore synonymous with a brand. Prozac's now multi-year effort is living proof of these brand-enhancing effects; with illustrations that look to have been drawn by children, the simplicity of Prozac's efficacy stands out: "Depression Saddens. Prozac Can Help." What a great way to treat such a highly emotional and touching subject.

✔ *Create a Visual Pun*—Probably no other advertiser has created a more famous (or effective) long-running visual pun campaign than Absolut's. In their case, it's that distinctive Absolut bottle-shape that cleverly adapts itself into so many well-known scenes and situations, creating not play on *words*, but a play on *situations*. But visual puns can happen in many ways. In fact, Volvo has been running its own version of the visual pun lately: simply re-inventing the safety pin, but in the unmistakable shape of a Volvo sedan. No headlines. No copy. The instant recognition of the pin gives away the famous Volvo benefit—instantly.

(Note: A more commonly used offshoot of the visual pun approach is the *visual metaphor*. It seems to be especially prevalent among emerging pharmaceutical products aiming to make their technically based and highly FDA-regulated benefit stories easier to grasp. Among the longest-running and best-recalled visual metaphors within the Rx categories is the "Apple" for Rocephin, symbolizing the apple-a-day effect of the cold and flu treatment drug.)

Body-Copy/Layout Design

It's not the aim of this book to turn client-advertisers into art directors. But in those execution planning discussions with your agency creative team, it makes good sense to talk *with* their art directors about good body-copy and layout principles. Luckily, you don't need any special training (or even an art director) to know the two most basic principles:

1. Print layouts should make the ad and its body-copy *inviting to read.*
2. Even more crucial, layouts should make the ad *easy to read.*

These principles seem so intuitively obvious that you would think they go without saying. But with creative people being, well, creative by nature, they're always looking for ways to push the boundaries of the printed page. That means that on occasion, you may have to question the trade-off between creative design and simple readability. Take, for instance, a recent, highly dramatic, double-paged spread for Andersen windows: nearly 80 percent of the two pages features a startling photograph of an electrical storm in progress—as seen in natural clarity through an Andersen window. Stopping power? You bet. Visualized benefit? Right again.

But the design falls short when it comes to the body-copy. It's printed in black typeface on top of a dark-brown background, making it virtually unreadable.

So, in the spirit of our two principles above, here are some easy tips for improving the odds of quality readership:

✔ *Use Layouts That People Are Used to*—Most people read from top-to-bottom and from left-to-right. You can't go wrong with a layout that works that same way. Just as a good retailer knows how to draw his customers to the back of the store, so does a good print ad draw readers from the headline through the visual and into the body-copy.

Think about other familiar formats that work. There's the magazine-cover format that so effectively splits up storylines into eye-catching sound bites. In fact, Pond's has developed a print campaign that literally copies the magazine cover format; the result is an eye-appealing and highly readable piece of advertising. There's also the direct-mail, "catalogue" format. Not only does Land's End follow this format in their own catalogues, but when they place print ads they make them look like they came right out of the catalogues too. This approach fits their image and helps to sustain an ownable look.

✔ *Break Your Body-Copy into Digestible Pieces*—Both Pond's and Land's End accomplish this well: the former by the snappy sound-bites; the latter by short, one- to two-sentence paragraphs. Another technique that works is to simulate questions your intended reader might pose, and then answer them in individual, stand-apart blocks. It's a great way to serve up a lot of information without overwhelming the reader. Plus, particularly when speaking to potential new users of a category or brand, it's a comfortable way of inviting them in. Tampax has done just this with their ads aimed at teenaged girls who haven't yet used tampons. Using language that's authentic, Tampax simulates a young girl's innermost questions about first-time tampon usage: "Is It Gonna Hurt?"; "But Won't It Feel Funny In There?" and the like. And the answers are crisp and credible.

Yet another approach that makes for easy comprehension of a lot of material is the *call-out*. It's a layout device that's probably been around as long as salesmen have been selling because it really derives from the old-fashioned sales fliers and brochures. You know the ones—with product drawings or photos surrounded by a series of bullet-pointed features and benefits (often with arrows pointing to just that place on the product where each specific feature applies). Take a look at any current airline or computer magazine; you'll find plenty of print ads using call-outs to convey a lot of information in a little space.

One last thing to keep in mind about the "digestibility" of your print copy: just as most people read from top-to-bottom and left-to-right, they're also accustomed to seeing their sentences end at some point. Said another way, seemingly endless copy "columns" that run the breadth of a full page—or worse yet, a full double-paged spread—probably don't get read. The reader just tuckers out with all the work it takes to scan across all that space. Encourage your creatives to keep the columns "normally readable," along the lines of newspaper columns. You can't go wrong (as in too long) that way.

✔ *Make Sure Your Typeface Is Readable*—It's so tempting to let color patterns and unusual layout designs dictate, say, a *reverse-out* typeface. You know, where the headline or body-copy print is white on a darker background, often black. But legibility studies abound that show most people have a difficult time reading reverse-out print. If your intended target reader is, say, over 35, you can pretty much forget about using reverse-out. Beyond that point, the eyeballs typically don't want to work that hard! Does this mean that you can't be a little creative or even occasionally vary the typeface styles and colors for effect? Of course not. But just remind yourself that when you and your creatives go after these "effects," there are likely to be some "counter-effects" worth considering.

All You Need to Know About Execution: A Story and Some Final Thoughts

At the outset of this chapter we acknowledged, rightly so, that our agency-partners are the real experts when it comes to making advertising execution happen. But we also noted the heavy final responsibility that we client-advertisers have in delivering the "goods" on our brands. In looking at the five format types in television execution and at the three page-parts of print execution, we've probably just scratched the surface of all that we would *like* to know about developing those great executions for our great Campaign Ideas. It seems we can never know enough, which brings to mind a personal story about advertising execution:

> In my early days as a Procter & Gamble brand manager, we had the good fortune to introduce a new, superior-performing product: Puffs LF, as we coded it. Because the technology behind the tissue delivered a dramatically softer feel on the skin (especially below the nose), we wanted to launch it into test with an equally dramatic trial device—the first-ever, Sunday-insert-delivered, ten-sheet sample packet. Getting the tissue from plant to assembler-wrapper and then on to the individual newspapers involved a rather complex execution (not to mention the actual packing of the ten-sheet samples). I wasn't well-versed in those executional processes, but my able assistant brand manager oversaw the day-to-day flow and periodically updated me. On the weekend of the "drop" we had delivered the samples to the newspapers.

That fine, cold Sunday morning started out calmly enough for me; but shortly after mid-day, the phone rang and a P&G customer service rep told me that their phones had been flooded with complaints that morning about our new tissues! Forget that they were the softest thing known to human noses. These tissues smelled bad! (They smelled like news ink.) Near panic, I called my assistant at home to see what could have happened. Puffs were always perfumed at that time and had a reputation for smelling very pleasant. Unfortunately, neither of us knew enough then about the complete execution process for our sample pack. Had we known, for example, that Sunday inserts typically arrive at a newspaper on the Thursday before and then sit stacked among all the other free-standing inserts for the weekend, we would have seen the potential for ink-dye-odor transfer. Which is exactly what happened because our rather flimsy ten-sheet tissue packets lacked the barrier protection to fight off the strong color-dye odor of all the other inserts.

So, now you know the true story about how it was I came to leave Procter & Gamble! No, not really. In fact, because P&G is and always has been such a committed learning organization, we chalked that mini-fiasco up to good learning. We went on to big success with our sample pack (in a heavy-gauged cellophane wrapper!) in subsequent markets. Even better, both my assistant and I had learned a valuable lesson about the role of execution in bringing to life *any* big idea.

Curiosity is a good thing in business: it keeps us looking for new, different, and better ways to sell. Trouble is, few client-advertisers have the luxury of time to pursue all their curiosities; they're too busy general-managing. That's why we have experts to serve us. But it's always better to know enough to ask the right questions, to pose some alternative approaches to advertising execution. You can and should use the execution planning phases of the advertising development process to do these very things. It's during those phases when you have every right (and responsibility) to revisit what format type(s) make most sense for your brand and in your category; and to revisit the basic principles of print that gets read and that sells. When you get down to it, that is pretty much all you need to know.

KEY PRINCIPLES

Summary

✔ As client-advertisers, we have a key role to play in seeing the Campaign Idea come to life. The execution is the "movie" for our book, after all. Our primary concern is to guide the development team toward the power of a great Campaign Idea and a great execution.

✔ One of the ways we can best provide this guidance is to separate out the execution planning phase from the pure execution phase of the process. In the former, which should begin in earnest at Campaign Idea and storyboard session, we should be raising broad executional issues—especially ones that pertain to the long-term campaignability of the work.

✔ We should also take the lead in understanding (and questioning) the agency's recommended execution format. If nothing else, we should assess the merits of one format vis-à-vis another in the context of the category (what format are the other guys using, and how effective do we think customers find it?).

✔ From time to time, it makes sense to consider how *animation*—even as a part of the whole—might be worthwhile; if nothing else, get a feel for the latest techniques and who's using them.

✔ Consider assigning a totally separate creative team to the task of inventing a provocative, extended demonstration for your brand. Chances are your competitors are overlooking such a device, and you could catch them unaware.

✔ When executing Campaign Ideas in print, focus your thinking around the three "page-parts" that can maximize your economy of the page: the *headline*, the *visualization*, and the *body-copy/layout design*.

✔ Hard-working headlines serve a number of important roles: they *stop the reader* and pique his or her interest; they *encourage further reading*; they *fit with their visualizations;* and they *set up and sometimes deliver the brand's benefit(s).*

✔ Hard-working visualizations fulfill these same roles, plus one other: they *dramatize* the benefit(s).

✔ Hard-working body-copy and layout designs have to be *inviting to read* and *easy to read.*

✔ When honing in on a specific execution (once it shows up in a "produced form"), consider these key questions for quick assessment guidance:

Execution—Assessment Tool

• What happens in the advertising? — How clear or confusing? — How central is product to action?	
• How is the advertising credible or incredible?	
• Is the main benefit visualized? How?	
• If there is a reason-why, how is it visualized?	
• Are words and picture in sync?	

As a shortcut, use the **3 C's**: is the execution **Clear, Credible, Compelling?**

PART FOUR

Processes That Work

CHAPTER 16

Moving ASAP
from Strategy to
Successful Advertising

"Follow the yellow brick road." Or, if you don't heed this advice:
"DO NOT PASS GO. GO DIRECTLY TO JAIL!"

The third key responsibility of the effective client-advertiser is to establish and nurture an efficient process that will leverage creative development against strategy. Unfortunately, most processes that we encounter tend to be outmoded, ineffective, and inefficient practices that have just been "the way things have always been done around here." The client takes care of the strategic side—which is most often non-existent, or simply not bought by agency or senior client management. The agency is responsible for coming up with the creative genius—which is lacking when you don't provide sound strategic thinking or clear strategic ad direction.

So, how do we get from start to finish (great advertising) without going to jail? We need a process. And, we have a process, not just any process, but a process that works! Our yellow brick road. A process designed to improve the likelihood of efficiently developing great advertising. Who could ask for anything more?

This process works because it: a) is anchored in a strategic discipline; b) clearly spells out client and agency roles; c) focuses on those key factors for successful advertising; and d) encourages development of a bevy of creative ideas that are tied to the ad strategy. Let's examine it.

Strategic Discipline and Client–Agency Roles

By now you should be familiar with the strategic discipline. We start at the beginning with the development of the **Brand Positioning Statement.** It provides the blueprint for the development and franchise building of the brand. It represents our strategic vision for the brand in terms of how we want customers to think about our brand relative to competition. Brand positioning must precede the development of all sub-strategies such as pricing, distribution, and packaging, to name a few of the many marketing mix elements.

Smart client-advertisers, those who appreciate the critical importance of positioning in creating a brand, will take the role of creating the Brand Positioning Statement upon themselves. Even smarter client-advertisers will lead the development of the Brand Positioning Statement but will also include their advertising agency personnel as partners in this undertaking, which will include up-front homework using available marketing research, or getting it. It also includes a thoughtful evaluation of proposed positionings in the context of competitive positioning statements utilizing the **Positioning Matrix.**

Next, we move to the development of the **Advertising Strategy Statement.** The Ad Strategy Statement provides guidance and direction for the development of the brand's advertising campaign. It provides a common basis upon which to assess all of the agency's advertising recommendations. It consists of the: **Who** (target); **What** (benefit); and **Why** (reason-why support for the benefit) in addressing a specific brand marketing issue or objective.

The Ad Strategy Statement is built upon a meaningful **customer insight.** This requires an understanding of *consumer and competitive purchase dynamics and attitudes.* The key customer insight is strategic-based and must lead to a change in behavior that enables the brand to achieve its desired purchase behavior and marketing objective. Again, the smart client-advertisers, those who appreciate the importance of the ad strategy, will take the role of creating the Ad Strategy Statement upon themselves. Even smarter client-advertisers will lead the development of the Ad Strategy Statement including their advertising agency personnel as partners in this undertaking too.

The *smartest* client-advertisers don't just include agency account managers in the strategic process, they find a way to get the creatives involved. Let's face it. Good strategists are creative, and good creatives are strategic. The creatives may not approach strategy development in a linear way, but they get there. Edward DeBono, a leading authority in the field of creative thinking, calls it "lateral thinking." Whatever you call it, the result is beneficial to your brand. What's more, the earlier the client-advertiser gets the creatives involved, the more immersed they become in the brand and target, and the earlier they begin to get creative. In this way the creative team goes beyond creating on demand, to creating based upon insights and intuition established from real understanding. So the strategic-process steps and roles look like this:

Strategic Process Step	Role
Brand Positioning Statement	CLIENT/Agency
Ad Strategy Statement	CLIENT/Agency

Note that we have identified the primary mover by use of uppercase letters. Remember that agency personnel, both account and creative, must be involved in the process to add value and improve the likelihood of developing more effective advertising.

Creative Development

Now that the strategic work is behind us, it is time to get on with creative development. Presently, most processes call for the hand-off of the Advertising

Strategy Statement (when one is made available) to the agency. Where an Advertising Strategy Statement is not created by the client and/or client–agency team, the agency will usually develop a creative brief of their own to guide the creatives. Some four weeks, four months, or four years later, the agency returns with an armful of storyboards or rough print ads. In most instances, when the client reviews a dozen or so storyboards or rough print ads, he or she is getting to see only three, maybe four, Campaign Ideas. Most of the presentation is mired in execution. As such, the client-advertiser isn't really given many options.

To make the process more efficient and effective, we propose **ASAP** (Applied Strategic Advertising Process). In ASAP, the agency shares Campaign Ideas before ever going to storyboard or print executions. As you will recall from the previous chapter, the Campaign Idea is a way to dramatize the brand's ad strategy (especially the benefit) in provocative customer terms. The Campaign Idea manifests itself in two essential ways: a) key copy words (e.g., "If it's got to be clean, it's got to be Tide."); and b) core dramatization (e.g., Tide demonstration of newer-looking clothes washed in Tide versus frayed, color-faded clothes washed with a competitive brand).

In this way, the client truly leverages the creative and nurtures the development of a wide variety of options to deliver against the Ad Strategy Statement in a compelling, customer-appealing manner. Also, this process of assessing Campaign Ideas before storyboard/print execution development enables the client to get involved in creative development in a non-threatening, significant manner. Finally, it will ensure that the advertising has a Campaign Idea. Assuming you have done your strategic homework correctly, the Campaign Idea is your road to more successful advertising. If the advertising doesn't have one, it is highly unlikely it will be effective.

Instead of viewing a dozen storyboards or rough print executions with only three or four Campaign Ideas, the client is able to assess a dozen or more Campaign Ideas. The agreed-upon best of the lot (by client, agency, and senior management, explored through market research) can then be translated into storyboards utilizing a variety of executions to showcase the Campaign Idea. The current process and proposed **ASAP** practice are illustrated here:

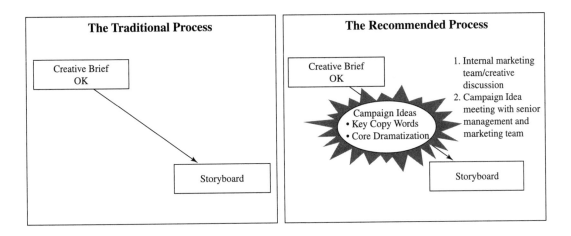

Perhaps the best way to approach **ASAP** is to schedule two meetings to review Campaign Ideas. The first meeting is a work session to be conducted upon the agency's hallowed ground. At this meeting the agency would share "tissues" (i.e., rough Campaign Ideas captured on flimsy tracing paper with markers) with the client. We recommend this work session be conducted at the agency in order to nurture a real dialogue. We have found that if the agency is asked to appear at the client company they will tend to undertake more finished work and arrive with a "sell" mindset as opposed to being open to ideas and future direction.

At the work session, the client can coach the agency as it relates to the scope as well as the specific elements of the Campaign Ideas. For example, if a specific idea pool is missing that the client believes to be important, you may direct the agency to undertake this new area. If the key copy words for a specific Campaign Idea need strengthening, now is a great time to identify the direction for the agency to pursue. Or, perhaps, a particular idea pool might be a font for the development of many more creative options in the form of new Campaign Ideas. This is your opportunity to be creative, provide additional direction, and coach the agency to success.

The second meeting is an agency presentation of the Campaign Ideas to you and your management (i.e., the key individuals who need to buy-off, or sign-off, on the advertising). This meeting can occur at the client company.

The Campaign Ideas are likely to be more refined and displayed on boards versus tissues. Here the added direction you provided to the agency at the work session will be reflected in the presentation. You and your management will be focused upon the Campaign Ideas—as opposed to being mired in executional issues of lesser substance.

The ideal Campaign Idea presentation meeting will be marked by the client understanding and visibly becoming excited by the Campaign Ideas. Agency morale will swell by the positive energy of the meeting, as contrasted to (the so-called constructive) criticism of most agency presentation meetings. Also, various client team members will have different Campaign Ideas they favor. In this case, the client has an abundance of riches. These alternate Campaign Ideas may be checked out with customers via market research. The whole process is iterative, enhancing knowledge and encouraging refinements the customer will find more compelling.

Now We Bring You . . . A Touch of Reality

It is time to come back down to earth. Some agencies will resist this approach to Campaign Ideas. They want to show you storyboards or semi-rough print executions. Digging deeper, you will find this resistance may be attributable to two potential sources of contention. The first is that the agency may have a creative review board that requires all work be reviewed by them before it can be presented to the client. The second influencer is that the agency may have a limited view of the client-advertiser's ability to rasp an important idea with just a set of key copy words combined with a visual of the core dramatization. In other words, they do not believe the client will appreciate the idea without 16, 32 or 48 frames, or finished print ads.

These represent formidable barriers to **ASAP** . . . but they are not insurmountable. In fact, they are easily overcome in those cherished instances where the process is adopted and institutionalized by senior client management. In the majority of instances where **ASAP** is not institutionalized by senior client management, the individual client-advertiser will need to overcome these barriers on the basis of his or her relationship with the agency. Stated another way, the client-advertiser will need to accomplish this by way of earning the agency's trust in his or her ability to grasp and distinguish among Campaign Ideas. This is no small feat, but it can be accomplished.

A Case History

We have used **ASAP** throughout our client and consulting careers with exceptional success. I first established this practice while assigned to the Sinex Nasal Spray brand. I was moved onto the brand following two recalls: one, from retail shelves when bacteria was found in the product; and two, from distribution warehouses when the FDA ruled that an ingredient in the formulation was judged to be of questionable safety. The second recall came on the heels of the first. I was brought onto the brand to breathe new life into it (if you will excuse the pun).

During my first week on this new assignment, the agency was presenting finished TV commercials for a new campaign. At this time, the agency had been unsuccessfully engaged in new campaign development for about two years. The presentation was made to senior management (i.e., the general manager of the division and the vice president of marketing). The agency's goal was to get approval to proceed to copy testing.

The agency started the presentation by taking management through each storyboard, followed, in turn, by the finished TV commercial. After the presentation was made the agency awaited approval, which was not forthcoming. Senior management stated that they wanted to scrap these commercials and begin campaign development anew. The agency was visibly distressed. I could see them sink deeper into their seats and their voices grow faint.

Recognizing a potential morale problem, and feeling that the finished commercials captured the same storyboards that management had approved, I stepped up to the plate. I stated that the commercials were faithful to the boards and, as such, we should proceed to copy testing. Management ignored this suggestion. I then took it upon myself to play "Let's Make a

Deal!" I got the agency to agree to pay for one-half of the copy testing costs. But management vetoed this idea. I stated the agency's case more forcefully by saying it was the judgment of many, including my own, that the commercials captured the storyboards and, therefore, we owed it to the agency to proceed to copy testing. Management, too, responded more forcefully by stating that some of us get paid for their judgment and I was not one of them—so shut up!

Well, the agency personnel gathered around me following the meeting and thanked me for my support. They stated that while my comments may not have helped my career with the company, they really appreciated my efforts. They also looked to me for direction for new campaign development. Reviewing the advertising strategy, I suggested we work on Campaign Ideas. We undertook **ASAP.**

A few weeks later the agency returned with some twenty or so Campaign Ideas. They presented each with enthusiasm and conviction. Management quickly became enthused with the ideas and began supporting their personal choices. We went with a campaign in which the key copy words were "A second of O-o-o-h. Ten hours of A-h-h-h." The campaign helped us achieve 85 percent of pre-recall levels in the first year. The campaign lasted for several years until that time when the active ingredient was changed.

Additional Suggestions

The aforementioned is not an isolated incident. Many agency executives claim similar successes. In speaking candidly with agency top management, we have learned that many follow a similar approach with more savvy clients, and enjoy success on a more consistent basis. But there are a few more pointers for helping you make this work: a) think ideas, Campaign Ideas, not execution; b) get your senior management involved with assessing Campaign Ideas; c) be open to investing in ideas that make you uncomfortable; and d) don't just settle for a clever set of copy words and predictable visual. Push the envelope!

Skillful Means

Buddhist teachers use the term "skillful means" to describe a way to make decisions, address problems and/or work in a way that resolves the issue without causing harm or further problems. How often do we step up to meet a challenge head-on in the short term but leave another, perhaps more significant, challenge to be managed in the long term? We get that new advertising campaign, but in its wake we leave a strained relationship that drowns any attempt at creating new successes.

ASAP will help the client-advertiser manage creative development with skillful means. It provides a process to facilitate skillful means. However, it requires the client-advertiser to change his or her mindset and management style from the old way of control to the new way of creation. It requires the client-advertiser to:

Skillful Means			
	Old (Control)		New (Creation)
• Move from managing	people	to	RELATIONSHIPS
• Move from managing	products	to	INNOVATION
• Look at assignments not as	transactional	but	TRANSFORMATIONAL
• View oneself not as	independent	but	INTERDEPENDENT
• Taking responsibility not to	delegate	but	COLLABORATE
• Ensuring one does not	evaluate	but	COACH
• Move from	exchanging information	to	SHARING UNDERSTANDING

This represents a seismic shift in attitudes, behavior, and skills. **ASAP** can make this shift easier, but the client-advertiser needs to follow up by seeing things through the right lens and taking the right action. A creative process managed with skillful means will result in more effective advertising on a consistent, predictable basis.

KEY PRINCIPLES

Summary

✔ The third key responsibility of the effective client-advertiser is to establish and nurture an efficient process that will leverage creative development against sound strategic thinking.

✔ In order to work, the process needs to: a) be anchored in a strategic discipline; b) clearly spell out client and agency roles; c) focus on those key factors for successful advertising; and d) encourage development of a bevy of creative ideas that are tied to the ad strategy.

✔ The smart client-advertisers, those who appreciate the importance of strategy in the development of great creative, will take the development of all essential strategic work upon themselves. *Even smarter* client-advertisers will lead the development of the strategy, but will include their advertising agency personnel as partners in this undertaking too. The *smartest* client-advertisers don't just include agency account managers in the strategic process, they find a way to get the creatives involved.

✔ The strategic process steps and roles look like this:

Strategic Process Step	Role
Brand Positioning Statement	CLIENT/Agency
Ad Strategy Statement	CLIENT/Agency

✔ To make the creative process more efficient and effective, use **ASAP** (Applied Strategic Advertising Process). In **ASAP,** the agency shares Campaign Ideas before ever going to storyboard or print executions.

✔ Assuming you have done your strategic homework correctly, the Campaign Idea is your road to more successful advertising. If the advertising doesn't have one, it is highly unlikely it will be effective.

✔ The best way to approach **ASAP** is to schedule two meetings to review Campaign Ideas. The first meeting is a work session with client-advertiser managers who are responsible for managing the process on a daily basis. The second meeting is an agency presentation of the Campaign Ideas to you and your management.

✔ The client-advertiser will need to earn the agency's trust, by his or her ability to grasp and distinguish among Campaign Ideas, to execute **ASAP.** This is no small feat, but it can be accomplished.

✔ The effort is worth it. In speaking candidly with agency top management, we have learned that many follow a similar approach to **ASAP** with more savvy clients and enjoy success on a more consistent basis than utilizing the standard approach.

✔ To make **ASAP** work, keep in mind these additional pointers: a) think ideas, Campaign Ideas, not execution; b) get your senior management involved with assessing Campaign Ideas; c) be open to investing in ideas that make you uncomfortable; and d) don't just settle for a clever set of copy words and predictable visual. Push the envelope!

✔ A creative process managed with skillful means will result in more effective advertising on a consistent, predictable basis.

CHAPTER 17

Client–Agency Relationship:

Practices for Making Beautiful Music Together

"The agency is our partner in the business."

As we stated in Chapter 2, no two words receive more play in advertising than "great advertising." If we had to pick another set of overused, hyped and misleading words in the world of advertising we would have to say "agency-client partnership." What kind of a partnership is it when one side gives orders? When that same side makes all the decisions? When they also set the fees? And, the same side can hire or fire the other? We call this a partnership? It certainly isn't one we would gladly enter into, nor is it likely that you would either.

We won't even try to dignify the word partnership in this case. It really doesn't exist. It is more along the old management model we shared with you earlier, "control!" Instead, what we have is a business relationship. Like all relationships it can be either highly productive and beneficial, somewhat productive and beneficial, occasionally productive and beneficial, not too productive or beneficial, or not at all productive nor beneficial. Believe it or not, the choice is largely ours.

There are books written on the subject of agency-client relationships. There are also books you might read regarding the development, maintenance, and growth of relationships. Just substitute the word "client" for "men," "agency" for "women," and John Gray's best seller might be titled *Clients Are from Mars, Agencies Are from Venus*. We can probably learn from it. What we are talking about is basic relationship building, particularly between two parties that are more dissimilar than similar. These two parties, clients and agencies, must come together to form one healthy whole, in order to make really beautiful music together (i.e., create really great advertising that reaches, engages, and turns on customers to our brand).

The client–agency relationship is the glue that holds this whole together. It must be productive if we are going to be successful in creating brand loyalty. It is hard enough to create brand loyalty in the marketplace when both groups are working well together. It is virtually impossible when they are not. But then an unproductive client–agency relationship is probably indicative of more deep-seated organizational and management problems.

It Takes Two to Tango

When we ask client managers about their relationships with their agencies we usually have to brace ourselves for a torrent of complaints. On a scale of 1 (poor) to 10 (excellent) the vast majority of ratings fall below 6. At best they are good. But all too often they are rated as poor. We hear that agencies don't understand our business, or that they are simply not creative. We are also told that the agencies are unresponsive to requests and oblivious to deadlines. Worse yet, client managers claim that often they cannot get the attention of their agencies because the same agency team is too busy with a larger brand or client. (Ah, the wonders of the new fee systems—which is to say, "it is hard to expect more service, people, and attention for less fees.")

But it is not all the agency's fault. The client must accept some of the blame. It really does take two to tango. We are not sticking up for agencies. We have had our share of problems with them, too. What relationship doesn't encounter its share of problems? But like any relationship, even a marriage, one has to take care of preserving and doing what is best for the relationship. You need to make sure you are doing your part. You need to make it work for the sake of the business and the brand. Adopt an attitude that you are going to make the relationship work for richer or poorer, in sickness and in health. It is the only way we know how to start!

Common-Sense Principles

We are not experts in client–agency relationships. Nor are we going to attempt to tackle the major organizational hurdles (such as fee structure) that block the way to a productive relationship. Organizational issues are the province of senior client management. But we have had more than our fair share of making the client–agency relationship, as well as other creative relationships, work. For the advice of experts, read one of their books. For a simple set of common-sense principles, read on and reflect upon how you might put them to use.

Define Expectations—Let's get it out on the table. What are your expectations regarding the agency? What do you expect them to accomplish over the next six months and year? Is it a new campaign? Pool-outs to the current campaign? Development of print ads to complement a TV campaign? What level of quality are you looking to achieve and how will you assess the work to ensure that your quality goals are met? In terms of expectations, we are attempting to define quantity and quality of work, and how we will work together.

But it is not just about our expectations. This is a good time to get the agency to define its expectations regarding us. Perhaps, the agency might identify the time they need for campaign development prior to airing. Or they might want to know what services you really need in this age of diminished fees. Their expectations might also include your giving them access to information and/or internal support groups (such as product research and development).

Whatever the expectations, this session, or sessions, should be a dialogue, not a laundry-list of demands. What we are attempting to do is begin a quality process of defining expectations that can be monitored and, in some way measured, to improve and multiply the fruits of the relationship. It is always a good idea to ask your counterparts, "What can we do to strengthen the relationship and improve the quality of our work?"

Honor Thy Role—Let's start at the beginning by defining key activities and roles. The specific steps and roles look like this:

Key Activities/Steps	Role
Brand Positioning Statement	CLIENT/Agency
—Positioning Audit	
—Positioning Matrix	
Ad Strategy Statement	CLIENT/Agency
Campaign Idea Development	AGENCY/Client
—Storyboards	
—Print Ads, etc.	
Execution	AGENCY/Client
—Production	
Market Assessment/Leanings	CLIENT/Agency

As you can see, both client and agency should be involved in each key activity step. However, you will also note that one name comes before the other and is in uppercase letters. This denotes the primary mover. So, in the case of developing the Brand Positioning Statement, it is the client. When it comes to developing Campaign Ideas, it is the agency. The primary mover has the ultimate responsibility and must assume ownership for that activity.

While the strategic activity steps, the brand positioning, ad strategy, and market assessment, are the responsibility of the client, the agency needs to be an integral part of your team. The Campaign Idea and advertising development, including execution, is the province of the agency. But just as smart clients know to integrate the agency in strategic development, smart agency managers will include the client in advertising development and execution. We are referring to the agency going beyond merely seeking client approval during these activity steps. It is important for the agency to seek out client creativity in the co-creation of advertising.

Each of the aforementioned activity steps and ASAP, discussed below, enable client and agency to iterate their way to success. Each step along the way is a meaningful whole yet each is integrated, building off and back against the previous step. For example, moving from the Brand Positioning Statement to the Positioning Audit to the Positioning Matrix provides an opportunity for new learnings to assist you in revising and strengthening the Brand Positioning Statement.

Follow ASAP—In the previous chapter we introduced you to ASAP. The primary currency in ASAP is the Campaign Idea. We talked you through the structure of work sessions to be conducted. If you want to create a climate for a productive client–agency relationship and improve your prospects for success, then adopt and follow ASAP. It will contribute to management through skillful means. It will take you out of the outmoded and inefficient practice of control and into the practice of creation, co-creation.

Woo the Agency—Whoa now, you are probably thinking that we have gone too far. Woo the agency? You have got to be kidding. We are the clients. We are the bosses. They ought to be licking our boots, not the other way around!

Wooing is not about that. It has to do with respecting, motivating, and showing your appreciation for others. It is about winning them over to the brand and business. Back in my days at the Coca-Cola Company the irascible worldwide creative director of McCann Advertising, John Bergin, used to say to me, "Czerniawski, if I have to be at the commercial shoot so should you." No, not really. I was fortunate to have a commercial production staff of experts. But if John Bergin wanted me on shoots, because he believed it was important enough for him to be there, then who was I to argue? So, I attended out of respect for him and his beliefs, and the agency team. I also used the time to strengthen relationships and engage in dialogues regarding the business, specific brand opportunities, ideas, and potential directions we might take. It was time well spent.

My partner, Mike, has a wonderful way of making people feel appreciated and, therefore, motivated to give him their best work. When he was vice president of marketing, salty snacks, for Frito-Lay, he employed my services on a number of important consulting projects. Following the work he took special care in selecting and gifting me with a book, knowing we share a love for books. Additionally, he took time to write in his own hand a thank-you note for my services. He was employing me but that didn't stop him from wooing me.

Fred Walker, a group product director at McNeil Consumer Products Company, makes it a practice to do some one thing that his agency creative director will appreciate. He tells of learning which special mechanical pencil his creative director favors and gifting him with one. The creative director evidences his appreciation and the acknowledgment of Fred by telling those who want to borrow the pencil, "Don't touch that one. Fred gave it to me." Little things can make a big difference.

Just asking questions of others, seeking their advice, and being open to their responses, can show that you respect agency people. Everyone likes to feel important. When you show interest in what someone else thinks, it makes that person feel important. So stay awake. Be sensitive. Do some small thing(s) on a consistent basis, to show you care for, respect, and appreciate agency team players. Woo the agency. They will pay you back a hundred-fold!

Coach for Success—This is the fourth core responsibility of the effective brand builder and client-advertiser. A coach's job is to get the personal best out of the individual and team. It is to find a way to get everyone to achieve more than she or he ever thought possible in accomplishing a meaningful goal.

It is much more than sitting in judgment of another's work. For one, it is more productive. For another, it builds a concept of team and, as such, contributes to strengthening relationships.

Successful coaches have a vision of what they want to achieve. For the late coach Jimmy V., Jim Valvano, whose North Carolina State team captured an NCAA championship, it was playing Madison Square Garden on Friday night with tip-off starting at 9:00 p.m. It was prime time. What it meant to him and his team is that the team made it into big-time college basketball. The effective client coach has a vision for her brand and advertising.

Coaches need to motivate their players. It is said that great coaches are great motivators. Motivation comes from inspiring, not criticizing. Sure, coaches identify weaknesses but, more important, they identify those areas of play the individual and team can build upon. Great coaches identify where everyone must go and devise a plan for getting there.

The effective manager coaches, not criticizes. The words "constructive criticism" is a sugar-coated vehicle to deliver criticism. It is nothing more than dressing up a wolf in sheep's clothing. While it is draped in a positive cloak, it is illusory. It still looks, sounds, smells, and feels like a wolf to us, and to agency creatives. Instead of building up a relationship, it allows doubts to creep in, morale to falter, and trust to erode.

Another important element of coaching relates to how we communicate—more specifically, how we say what we say to others. If we utilize the learnings and tools, we will be directing the agency's efforts toward important strategic elements. But if we are unable to articulate our feelings and direction, and/or fail to encourage and inspire, then the creative output will suffer. While we will cover the subject of how to comment in Chapter 18, it is important to take note of the following:

- **Provide an overview**—The typical response of the client following an agency presentation is very revealing. Even the most enthusiastic of agency presentations are met with the proverbial "pregnant pause" by the client. Whether one responds verbally or not, a statement of sorts is being made. Imagine that you have just shown a photo of your new baby to a friend. You ask him what he thinks. The response you receive is the pregnant pause. He continues to stare at the photo but no words are forthcoming. Now what do you think he thinks about your new baby? It's ugly!

  When we fail to respond to the agency's presentation, they probably think that we don't think too much about their work. This may, in part, be true. But far more often, clients don't know where to start with comments. The best place to start is at the beginning. Start with the big picture.

Tell the agency what you think of their work. Let them know where you stand. Are you pleased? Is there something of value with which you can build with the agency? Is the work promising but in need of additional work? Let them know how you feel. If you are unduly slow to respond, or don't tell them how you feel (but instead jump into "concerns" and "dislikes"), you communicate that you don't think their work is good. If that is the case, then tell them. But, if it isn't, you will need to learn to speak sooner and deliver the right kind of comments. Let them know what you truly think about the creative they have shared with you.

Also, much of what we communicate is communicated through body language. So try your best to relax while the agency presents creative to you. Don't be afraid to show your emotions. If you find something humorous about the work, then laugh. If it is poignant, then shed those tears. My friend Brad Moore gave me a reel of a pool of the emotion grabbing advertising from Hallmark. I told him how the spots evoked a range of emotions. Some made me laugh. Others brought on the tears. I asked him if he thought this might be a bit strange. "No," was the reply, "I find myself overcome with emotion, tears pouring down my cheeks, when the agency acts out some of these tear-jerker stories for me." Try smiling, too. It will help keep the meeting from feeling like a courtroom.

- *Provide specific comments*—Find something to like and build upon it. If there is something you like, that's great. But if there is nothing you like, look for a germ of an idea you can like. Hopefully, there is something in the presentation that you can build upon. If you cannot find anything to like, then you have a problem. But you have to own the problem. The fault cannot lie solely with the agency. Perhaps, the ad strategy was not made incapable of being misunderstood. Or maybe you just don't understand the idea as presented. Also, avoid telling the agency about your dislikes. Instead refer to what would please you. It puts your comments regarding direction in a positive context.

- *Identify and agree upon next steps*—Never leave a meeting without agreeing upon next steps, even if the next step is to get back to the agency in 24 hours with specific comments. You are coaching. You are managing. So you need to make it clear to all what are to be the next steps.

However, you do not have to be the sole originator of the next steps. Use your team, combined client and agency, to help identify and gain agreement on the next steps.

Review the Relationship (versus Expectations)—It is time to complete the circle and get back to the first point. We want to review the relationship against those expectations that we have established between the client and agency. The client reviews the agency and the agency reviews the client. It takes guts to have the agency review your part in the relationship. But it is a tremendous growth opportunity. Certainly there should be a formalized review at least once per year. (After all, isn't his what we expect our managers to do for us?) If you don't have one, put a formal review process in place.

Review of the relationship goes beyond a formal program. It needs to be administered in real time. This means feedback, immediate and frequent. Let the agency know how you feel they are doing. If a problem arises, bring it to their attention and request their assistance in getting it resolved. We are not looking to gig the agency. Our interest is to strengthen our relationship so we can create really great advertising. It takes open communication and plenty of it!

Making beautiful music with your agency doesn't require some magical practice. The results can be magical but the practices are just common sense. However, as Will Rogers put it, "Common sense is uncommon." On top of it all, it requires attentiveness, sensitivity, and hard work. We can make it happen if we want it to. Give it a try. It's worth it!

KEY PRINCIPLES

Summary

✔ The client-agency relationship can be highly productive and beneficial, somewhat productive and beneficial, occasionally productive and beneficial, not too productive or beneficial, or not at all productive nor beneficial. The choice is largely ours.

✔ The client–agency relationship is about relationship building between two parties that are more dissimilar than similar. However, they must come together to form one healthy whole if we are going to be able to satisfy customers and create brand loyalty through the development of really great advertising.

✔ Make sure you are doing your part. You need to make it work for the sake of the business and the brand. Adopt an attitude that you are going to make the relationship work.

✔ The first practice is to define expectations for the relationship that can be monitored and, in some way, measured. It is always a good idea to ask your counterparts, "What can we do to strengthen the relationship and improve the quality of our work?"

✔ Client and agency should be involved in each key activity step. However, the primary mover has the ultimate responsibility and must assume ownership for that activity step.

✔ Smart clients will involve the agency in strategy development activities from day one. Smarter clients will ensure that members from the creative team are also involved.

✔ Iterate your way to success. Each activity step along the way is a meaningful whole yet each is integrated, building off and back against the previous step.

✔ Wooing the agency is about respecting, motivating, and showing your appreciation for others. It is about winning them over to the brand and business.

✔ Coaching is much more than sitting in judgment of another's work. For one, it is more productive. For another, it builds a concept of team and, as such, contributes to strengthening relationships.

✔ When commenting on agency creative submissions, provide an overview. Tell the agency what you think of their work. Let them know how you feel.

✔ Next provide specific comments. Find something to like and build upon it. If there is something you like, that's great. But if there is nothing you like, look for a germ of an idea you can like. If you cannot find anything to like, then you have a problem. But you have to own the problem.

✔ Also, try to avoid telling the agency about your dislikes. Instead refer to what would please you. It puts your direction in a positive context.

✔ Identify and agree upon the next steps, the specific actions client and agency will take as a result of this meeting. Never leave a meeting without agreed-upon next steps, even if the next step is to get back to the agency in 24 hours with specific comments.

✔ Remember, you do not have to be the sole originator of the next steps. Use your team, combined client and agency, to help identify and gain agreement on the next steps.

✔ Review the relationship against those expectations established between the client and agency parties. The client reviews the agency and the agency reviews the client.

✔ Review of the relationship should include, and go beyond, a formal program. It needs to be administered in real time, too. This means feedback, immediate and frequent. Let the agency know how you feel they are doing.

CHAPTER 18

Mastering the Language of Storyboards and Coaching Creative Presentations

"I majored in English as an undergrad, but I also speak fluent French and Japanese. Oh, and I'm also learning to speak in storyboards."
                                                —*Entry-level Marketing Assistant*

Face it, *storyboards*—those comic-book-like frames agencies use to lay out the flow of a commercial—are a language unto themselves. And not one that most of us speak with fluency. But, having the perceptive skills to understand what's being communicated, or "see the film" in a storyboard, is an absolute requirement for any client-advertiser looking to achieve great television advertising. Attaining such skills takes years of practice; however, there are some other things you can and should do along the way to increase your facility (and confidence) in working with storyboards, namely:

- Use a storyboard process that everyone understands;
- Maintain a disciplined approach to your own mental evaluation of storyboards;
- Take the time to think about *how* you can most effectively comment on agency work.

The Storyboard Process Made Painless

At a lot of customer companies, the news of a major storyboard presentation is call for high excitement for some and high anxiety for others. That's because many blue-chip marketing departments have viewed such presentations as a legitimate "baptism-by-fire" way of training their junior people (by having the junior folks respond first to the agency's material). If longevity is any indicator, this Socratic approach has worked pretty well for many years.

Of course, there are probably many more customer companies—some marketing giants in their own right—who take another viewpoint: the purpose of storyboard presentations is to make decisions about the brand's new advertising (and any training that results is purely serendipitous). These companies don't stand on formality when it comes time to review the agency's storyboard work; anyone may respond or comment as the spirit moves them.

Which of these philosophies about the storyboard process is more effective? The answer, of course, is that either one can be effective, depending on how well it suits the way the company likes to do business. Procter & Gamble is a company devoted to building its business by growing people from within; it makes sense for them, then, to operate more effectively with a more formal, by-rank storyboard-response process. Pepsi-Cola, on the other hand, prides itself on fast-thinking and quickness in the market; in such an environment, the free-for-all storyboard response is a better fit. In short, it's really not which approach one uses that's important; rather, it's that all the players involved *understand* the approach (and get comfortable with it). And the "players" include the agency!

Once everyone is comfortable with how the client responses will be coming out, the rest gets easier. But there are still a few *process facilitators* that the agency can provide for you. Specifically, the agency should:

- *Lay out their "batting order"*—When presenting a series of campaign boards, they should explain up-front how they've sequenced them. Maybe they're in order of campaigns that could be considered "close-in" to the current campaign, all the way to those that are "further-out." Or perhaps they intend to show "lead" campaigns first, and "back-ups" last. Whatever their sequencing rationale might be, it helps if they tell you about it at the outset (as opposed to remaining coy, or even worse, trying to read your body language before deciding which one(s) to officially recommend).

- ***"Billboard" each Campaign Idea/campaign with key copy words***—It sounds like such a simple thing to do, but much like chapter titles in a book, it's a great device for keeping things straight, particularly when the agency is laying out anywhere from five to fifteen ideas.

Key Copy Word Billboards	"Lite Beer from Miller—Tastes Great, Less Filling"	"Lite Beer from Miller—It's It and That's That"

- ***Dramatize the board!***—This is an emphatic way of saying, "Help me see the film!" Most agencies have some "stand-up talents" on staff, creatives who might otherwise have gone into show business. These people are gifted not only at staging the storyboard out for you (complete with camera angles, sound effects, and lighting techniques), but also at acting out what happens in the board. Naturally, you would like to have creatives like these present all your boards to you, but sometimes you have to settle for someone less charismatic. Whomever you find standing before you, at the very least make sure they:

    ✔ Take you through the "what happens" sequence of the board (more than once, if desired);

    ✔ Read the copy, frame-by-frame, indicating which visuals it accompanies;

    ✔ And, as much as possible, show live examples of any special effects or dramatic techniques they intend to use (using "clips" from existing movies, for example).

If you have your agency do these things consistently, it will make your job of assessing the work and responding in a constructive manner painless and more effective.

The Disciplined Approach to Storyboard Assessment

There's no magic in developing a disciplined approach to assessing a storyboard. But there is a trick, of sorts, to it. And the trick is none other than this: *You can never go wrong by focusing your thoughts first on the* **Campaign Idea.** Sounds relatively easy, but you would be surprised how equally easy it can be to get sidetracked into a consideration of some minor copy point in the middle of Frame 7. To avoid this trap, you have to develop a discipline.

A good way to develop a discipline for storyboard assessment is to work from a *checklist*—the way airline pilots do so they won't overlook something important in their cockpit procedures. The checklist below contains six bullets. Notice that the first five deal with technical questions regarding the board; also notice that most of these focus on (surprise!) the Campaign Idea. Bullet number six deals with the "bottom line" for any storyboard session: *Do You Like It?* While this is clearly the most important of the six bullets, it comes last because your judgment should be based on your responses to the first five.

How to "Think Through" Storyboards

1. Is there a Campaign Idea?
   —What are its *key copy words? Core dramatization?*
2. Is it on strategy?
3. Is the Campaign Idea:
   —Meaningful? Credible? Provocative?
   —Consistent with the brand's character?
4. Does the execution showcase the Campaign Idea?
   —Is the benefit visualized?

—Does it tell a picture story?

—Is it clear, credible, and compelling?

5. Does the board represent a commercial or a campaign?

—Does it have legs?

6. Do you like it?

—Does it "sell" versus "tell"?

With a checklist like this (or even one that you customize to better fit your needs) you can arrange your thoughts in a logical manner. Most important, you'll stay focused on the issues that really matter, which should contribute a great deal toward gaining (and retaining) the respect of your team and agency colleagues.

The Fine Art of Commenting on Agency Ideas

When you get down to it, knowing *how to comment* on the agency's work is an art. It takes a certain style, even at times a panache, to achieve maximum effect. At the same time, effective commenting is nothing more than good human relations. As we have seen in Chapter 17, and adhering to one of our four core responsibilities as client-coaches, we should *always* be engaged in building the team effort, as opposed to tearing it down.

Many volumes have been written and videos taped that offer techniques for better human relations or intercommunications. This is by no means an attempt at another of those. Rather, it is just some helpful-reminder advice that's worth thinking about in between Campaign Idea meetings and storyboard presentations. At one time or another, these reminders probably ran to a baker's dozen or so; but, in the interest of "what matters most," here are five "sure-fire" tips for better commenting (notice that two of these five are so critical as to be "repeats" from our commenting tips in Chapter 17):

1. *Listen carefully*—How often have you heard this advice, and then forgotten to take it? When you are being overwhelmed with a presentation of 20 storyboards, there is no better time than to relax and listen; nor is there any better time to *buy some time* by asking someone to present a board again

so you can listen clearly to what's being pitched. Never write or take notes when a board is first being presented. Instead, sit, watch, and listen. There will be plenty of time for note-taking later.

2. *Provide an overview*—This is where that storyboard evaluation checklist really pays off. It can lead you naturally to your *headline*. For example, your first response after seeing multiple campaigns might be something like, "The Campaign Ideas I've seen here represent an exciting range of work. Some stand out as being better strategic fits than others. I'd like to talk about those first."

With a few headline sentences like these, you give the agency the good news they hope for—you *like* some of the work! Even better, you've indicated some especially strong work without disparaging anything else; you've already begun to focus the team on a building process, not a fault-finding process.

3. *Be honest but keep it positive*—Notice we don't say, "Be positive and try to keep it honest." Being positive is important, for all the reasons we've already mentioned, but absolutely nothing substitutes for honesty. A high-ranking executive with a worldwide customer goods company once remarked, "There is so much collective talent assembled at most agency presentations that some of the work must have merit; find that merit and build on it!" This is, of course, wonderful perspective for keeping things positive.

But should you find yourself facing a creative effort that somehow doesn't meet your expectations, you have to be truthful. A good way to diffuse an awkward situation like this is to: (1) tell the agency in your headline that you're surprised and concerned that the work isn't what you had anticipated; (2) if you can do so honestly, shoulder some of the blame for the shortcomings—as in, "Maybe I'm missing something here," or "I may not have given you the best direction when we last met"; and (3) call a "time-out" to huddle with a smaller team (client–agency) to work through what went wrong and to set some reasonable next steps. This should help get everyone back into a building process.

4. *Find things to build upon*—Echoing the sentiments of our high-ranking executive, you simply have to keep the team building and making forward progress. If you focus on the Campaign Ideas with some merit and enumerate ways to make them more compelling (for example, visualizing the benefit), you will contribute to this building approach. At all costs, avoid the "nitting and nibbling" kinds of comments—usually about executional matters—that will only signal you're more into finding fault than building constructively.

5. *Provide direction*—At the close of every storyboard meeting make sure you—or someone on the client team—writes down the agreed-upon next steps. Make a point to do this someplace where everyone can see them (like on an easel pad). This not only helps cement key agreements, but it ends things in a decisive, action-oriented manner. It's positive!

These steps will help you, the client-advertiser, turn into a better coach—guaranteed!

KEY PRINCIPLES

Summary

✔ Storyboards are a language unto themselves; they require a different perspective to understand and appreciate them.

✔ There are a number of things you and the agency can do to facilitate the storyboard process. Agencies need to consistently: *lay out their "batting order" or sequencing rationale for boards presented; "billboard" each campaign with key copy words; and dramatize each board effectively.*

✔ As a client-advertiser, you can provide the most effective response to agency submissions by developing your own disciplined approach to thinking through the merits of the work. This should always include as a basic precept: *start by focusing on the Campaign Ideas;* you'll never go wrong doing this.

✔ When you comment on agency work, keep in mind that your primary role is to *coach* and motivate the team to reach yet another "personal best."

PART FIVE

Post-Production

Chapter 19
"What Think?" Again

"What Think?" Again

"It's déjà vu all over again."
—*Yogi Berra*

 We have come full circle. We are back to that basic question at the beginning of this book, and your journey, to find *the way* to create brand loyalty through the development of a brand and more effective advertising, **"What think?"** Only this time we are better prepared to tackle the question. We have a deeper understanding of the strategic and executional issues dealing with brand building and advertising. We can, therefore, handle this question as marketing professionals!

A Final Tool for Responding

Whenever we are asked the question, "What think?" regarding advertising we reply to five basic areas:

1. Overview
2. Advertising Strategy
3. Campaign Idea
4. Execution
5. Implications

The **overview** is a crystallization of the perceived effectiveness of the advertising from your standpoint. It is *not* about whether you "like" or "dislike" the advertising, unless this is tied to your perception of its effectiveness. More important, your point-of-view regarding the effectiveness of the advertising needs to be supported with a rationale rooted in strategic as well as executional factors. This is the time to note strengths and weaknesses of the ad in both the strategic and executional realms. Finally, one may note the degree of perceived issues and potential impact on your brand's health and business prospects.

In order to provide an overview relating to the ad's effectiveness, one needs to identify and assess the importance of the **advertising strategy.** Who is the advertising targeting? We have learned in Chapter 5 that the ideal target definition contains a demographic, cites usage behavior, and identifies the need of the target customer group which the product can address through its promised benefit. Another key element to the ad strategy is the benefit, the payoff to the customer, or the desired belief. It should lead the customer, via a meaningful point-of-difference revealed by the customer insight, to realize the marketing objective (e.g., choose the brand versus competitive brands). The final key element of the ad strategy is the support for the benefit. It is the element that lends credibility to the promise. It serves to help convince the target that the product will deliver the promised benefit or reinforce the desired belief.

But identification of the ad strategy is just one facet of the effective advertiser's assessment of an advertisement, albeit an important one. Now comes the time for your particular insights regarding whether or not you believe your inferred ad strategy is strategically sound. It is one thing to tell what you see, it is another, more difficult yet more professional response, to explain what you think about it. Those client-advertisers who can do this, and be right about it, are going to contribute and be worth more to the business.

Next comes the **Campaign Idea**, the heart of the execution. Again, like the ad strategy, you need to identify the Campaign Idea and then assess its effectiveness. Look for the set of key copy words and the core dramatization. If they are not apparent then there is a potential problem with the advertisement, a big one! If they are readily identifiable then ask yourself whether it delivers against the ad strategy. Now, putting yourself in the role of the target customer, identify whether you find this compelling, and explain your reasoning for this particular assessment.

Now that we have the strategic core (advertising strategy) and key executional translation of it (the Campaign Idea), we are ready to delve deep into the **execution**. If you are assessing a television commercial then you will want to note the executional format being used (i.e., stand-up presenter, slice-of-life, vignettes, etc.). If it is a print ad, you will need to deal with those technical factors that enhance the impact, readability, and comprehension of the advertisement (namely, the size of ad, impact of the headline, stopping-power of the core visual, the role of the layout in encouraging readership and comprehension, readability of body type, etc.). The most important issue to address, regardless of the advertising media vehicle, deals with your perception of the effectiveness of the execution in showcasing the Campaign Idea. Specifically, determine whether the execution serves to make the Campaign Idea more understandable, memorable, and credible. Additionally, the execution should serve to capture the attention of the customer and encourage her/his interest in the ad, and more important, in the brand. Also, you will want to ensure the ad message is linked with the brand name. Finally make sure the ad is in keeping with the brand character (as noted from its positioning in the marketplace).

The final piece of your assessment of the advertising gets at **implications**. What are the potential indicated actions based on your assessment of the ad? This is a critically important question to get into the habit of asking yourself . . . and answering. This question is important regardless of whether you are assessing your own advertising or that of a competitor. The answers to this question could very well go beyond advertising to include other elements of the marketing mix. For example, if you are assessing a competitor's ad whose claim does not appear to be supportable by product performance, an indicated action may be to investigate the claim with your product research & development team and/or challenge it through legal means.

Now, we are ready to assess any advertising in a highly professional manner. Let's prove it. While doing so, we may also chart the progress of our professional development. If we have worked our way through this book, taking time to apply the tools we presented, then we will have a basic guideline for assessing any advertising and the skill foundation to do it thoughtfully and intelligently. This assessment will also serve to evidence improvement through our journey to become a more effective client-advertiser and brand builder.

Déjà Vu

What better way to demonstrate that we have made progress and are client brand advertising professionals than to re-tackle the TV ad for Kellogg's Frosted Flakes cereal appearing in Chapter 1, "What Think?". The photoboard for the ad spot appears again. Use the Advertising Assessment Tool below to guide your review and to provide your assessment. One note, it helps to start an ad assessment by identifying and assessing the advertising strategy or Campaign Idea before crystallizing your thoughts for the overview. This will enable you to provide a more intelligent and meaningful overview. However, when you report your assessment, follow the proscribed sequence starting with the overview and ending with implications.

Advertising Assessment Tool

1. *Overview*—Effective? Rationale. Key strengths/weaknesses? Remember to explain your point-of-view.

   _____

   _____

   _____

   _____

2. *Advertising Strategy*—What is it? Be as specific as possible. Is it strategically sound? Explain. What brand objectives and issues might it address? How valid/important are these to the ultimate success/competitiveness of the brand?

   _____

   _____

   _____

   _____

Kellogg's Frosted Flakes Cereal
(Silhouette Testimonials—"Joseph" Priest)

JOSEPH: Everyone calls me, Father. And I love a kids' cereal.

MALE ANNCR: Brave adults

wrestle with the notion that Kellogg's Frosted Flakes

is just for kids.

LISA: I work with tigers.

I never thought I'd love one. MALE ANNCR: That

delectable frosting,

that incredible crunch.

No wonder adults never outgrow the taste.

GEORGE: Oh, I'm guilty, guilty, guilty.

TONY: It's no crime. Frosted Flakes have the taste

adults have grown to love. They're great!

3. **Campaign Idea**—What are the key copy words? What is the core dramatization? Do they deliver against the ad strategy? Are they in sync? Are they compelling? Campaignable?

    _____

    _____

    _____

    _____

4. **Execution**—What is the execution format? How well does the execution deliver the Campaign Idea? Is the execution arresting? Memorable? If a print ad, what do you think about technical factors such as headline, etc.?

    _____

    _____

    _____

    _____

5. **Implications**—What are the indicated actions for us (as the advertiser or competitor)?

    _____

    _____

    _____

Take another moment to edit what you have written. Make sure you have addressed all the elements and issues of assessing an advertisement in a professional manner. When you have completed, see below to compare your assessment with ours.

Advertising Assessment Tool

(Kellogg's Frosted Flakes® Cereal)

1. **Overview**—This TV spot, and flanker campaign, appear to be very effective in recapturing lapsed and/or infrequent adult consumers of Kellogg's Frosted Flakes cereal. The ad strategy, with its tight target focus, is directed against a meaningful and achievable marketing objective and built from a strategic customer insight. The Campaign Idea is strong,

linking key copy words, core dramatization, and equity in a single-minded proposition. Finally, the execution is outstanding in engaging the target customer group and delivering a compelling message. Basically, we would run with this spot. With the exception of exploring for the future, we would not propose any changes to the campaign.

2. ***Advertising Strategy***—The ad strategy grows out of an inferred marketing objective to recapture and/or increase frequency of eating Kellogg's Frosted Flakes cereal among lapsed and infrequent adult consumers. The specific ad strategy appears to be to:

CONVINCE: Adult cereal eaters who grew up on Kellogg's Frosted Flakes cereal and may currently purchase the brand for their children but no longer eat it themselves (frequently), even though they still favor its taste, because they believe it is for children and lack the permission to indulge.

THAT: It's okay to indulge in the great taste of Kellogg's Frosted Flakes cereal.

BECAUSE: The support for this benefit is:

- Delectable frosting and incredible crunch
- You liked it as a kid and still like it today
- Other adults like and eat it too

The ad strategy appears to be very sound. It is rooted in a meaningful marketing objective to recapture those consumers who enjoy the taste but have basically left the franchise in favor of cereals they perceive to be more for adults. The target, lapsed or infrequent users who grew up eating Kellogg's Frosted Flakes cereal, is highly strategic and built upon a revealing customer insight. It was probably identified by research which indicated that many former brand users have fallen out not because they prefer the flavor of some other cereal but because of a perception that Kellogg's Frosted Flakes cereal is for kids. Perhaps, these consumers feel they should be eating more health-oriented cereals such as oatmeal.

The desired belief that it's okay for adults to eat Kellogg's Frosted Flakes cereal provides needed permission for lapsed or infrequent adult target consumers to indulge in the brand.

The support for the belief is its least-strong platform, but it appears sufficient. The "delectable frosting and incredible crunch" does support the promise of great taste (and eating experience). But there does not appear to be meaningful support to alleviate guilt. While German Chocolate Cake tastes sinfully wonderful to a dieting chocoholic who has strayed, that fact does little to alleviate the guilt s/he feels after eating it. (Although, if one is going to stray from a diet, there should be some compelling appetizing benefit.) However, rational support is, admittedly, probably less important in an indulgence product and target where emotion plays a large role in selection. In fact, rational support could interfere with the basic desired action and, in this case, may very well clash with the brand character and brand positioning.

3. *Campaign Idea*—The campaign idea is responsible adults, cloaked in anonymity, confessing their love of eating what they perceive to be a kid's cereal, Kellogg's Frosted Flakes cereal. The Campaign Idea is comprised of the key copy words "The taste adults have grown to love" with the equity copy "They're G-r-r-eat!," the core dramatization of seemingly responsible adults, whose identities are protected, confessing to eating Kellogg's Frosted Flakes cereal and, finally, reassurance that it is okay through the equity of the Tony the Tiger animated character.

The key copy words, "The taste adults have grown to love," appears to be highly relevant to the strategic target. It suggests that the target loved the brand as a child and has not outgrown its taste. The promise of "They're G-r-r-eat!" is also meaningful in that it confirms the adult target's decision and behavior in choosing to continue eating Kellogg's Frosted Flakes cereal.

The core dramatization of responsible (and, perhaps, aspirational) adults with their identities protected confessing to eating the brand, confirms that Kellogg's Frosted Flakes cereal is irresistible to adults from all walks of life. It also serves to demonstrate that the viewing consumer is not alone in his/her appetite for indulging in the brand and, as such, further contributes to the notion that it's okay. This is an improvement on earlier executions that featured "quirky" adults.

Finally, the appearance and reassurance of the animated character, Tony the Tiger, builds off the brand's long-term equity and relationship with the adult consumer. Tony the Tiger is not only familiar but triggers many positive emotional feelings about the product and the consumer's relationship with it, and him.

4. *Execution*—The execution is an amalgamation of three different TV formats. Specifically it is a (pseudo) testimonial combined with announcer voiceover and animation. It serves in talking to the target group, defusing guilt and making it acceptable (even desirable) to eat Kellogg's Frosted Flakes cereal, reinforcing the basic promise, providing strong brand linkage, building upon the equity of the brand . . . all the while remaining true to its brand character. While it may seem like too much to accomplish, the folks at Leo Burnett USA do an outstanding job in pulling all of it off.

The opening with Father "Joseph" confessing, with his identity protected like someone in a witness-protection program, is provocative . . . particularly in this day of public confessions and apologies. It has both stopping-power and is highly engaging in an amusing, light-hearted vein. The additional (pseudo) testimonials by "Lisa" the zookeeper and "George" the judge serve to continue engaging viewership and interest in the spot. Moreover, the appearance of prominent, responsible roles casts a positive halo on the target's behavior and reinforces the decision that it is okay to consume Kellogg's Frosted Flakes cereal.

The bold, assertive voice of the announcer motivates confidence in the target customer group's behavior. The appearance of Tony the Tiger builds upon the brand equity and brand character. Additionally, Tony the Tiger, along with his rallying cry "They're G-r-r-eat," the package shots, AVO copy, and brand character, all serve to provide strong brand linkage.

5. *Implications*—If we were the Kellogg's Frosted Flakes cereal brand team, we would be very pleased with this creative. In fact, we would not want to make any major changes. Instead, we would choose to ride this campaign for as long as sales and marketshare continue to grow and consumer

research indicates that it is having the desired impact on the target customer group's attitudes and behavior. Rather, our coaching would focus down the road. Our interest would lie in ensuring that we could continue to build upon the campaign and keep it fresh. As such, we would want to explore the following:

- Investigation of a "bandwagon" executional approach. This approach suggests growing popularity with the idea that it is okay for adults to eat Kellogg's Frosted Flakes cereal. The identity of the adults would not only be shown, but heralded. This could take the form of testimonials of real people or, like the advertising for milk, popular celebrities.
- Investigation of executions whereby Tony the Tiger resolves conflict between adults and kids, or adults and their inner child, who are claiming the cereal to be theirs exclusively. However, we would want to ensure that this remains a flanker campaign for the adult target, not all family, to ensure that we do not dilute the effectiveness of the message.
- Investigation of alternate key copy words. If adults who formerly ate Kellogg's Frosted Flakes cereal as kids but don't eat it (as frequently) today, feel it is for kids, then perhaps we should reinforce this belief (albeit in a positive way) in the key copy words. As such, we might want to tap into the belief that there is a kid in all of us, regardless of our age. Kellogg's Frosted Flakes cereal satisfies and brings out our inner child.

In brief, our goal is to be prepared in the event of a slowdown in sales growth and to push the envelope regarding learning about ways to keep the campaign vibrant. Again, we are not interested in prematurely changing a campaign that is working well for the brand but in looking for ways to extend it into the future.

Seek Understanding Through the Customer

We now have a rich, thoughtful assessment of the Kellogg's Frosted Flakes cereal TV spot. But your judgment may be different from ours. It's okay. We don't have to argue our differences. We can seek a higher level of understanding through dialogue with customers. We can let the customer be the final arbitrator of the effectiveness of the ad. The customer can help us understand what is or is not working, and why. All we need to do is get out of our ivory towers and seek out the customer's input on key issues and relevant elements of the ad.

Interestingly, if you are keeping track of your initial response, what we have is a much more rich analysis of the ad versus what we were able to first do when we posed the question "What Think?" in Chapter 1. We are now focusing on the core strategic and executional elements in a disciplined and professional manner. This very process assists us in exchanging knowledge and enhancing learning about this ad, and about advertising in general.

Post-Production

Our instruction is complete. You may feel, however, that as much as you tried with the *"What Think?" Again* exercise, your assessment is not as comprehensive as ours. That's okay too. In fact, it is expected. Like the development of any skill, you have to work at it to get better. You have to work at it over and over again, in the right way, to gain mastery.

It is said that to master a physical skill requires about 5,000 repetitions. Not mindless, but mindful repetitions. While the number will vary based upon the individual, what it comes down to is that you cannot expect to become a great client brand builder and advertiser just from reading a book, this or any other. Nor can you expect to significantly improve your skills given the limited number of agency advertising presentations with which you are likely to be involved. So you'll have to find other ways to build your skill base. Here are a few suggestions:

- ***Discuss what is going on in the world of brand marketing and advertising with agency and marketing team members***—Learn what brands and advertising campaigns are winning in the marketplace and those that are failing. More important, go beyond the "what" to get at the "why." We need to appreciate and understand the key factors responsible for success and failure. You'll find that the effective marketing and agency people really know what is going on with a wide variety of business case histories and advertising communications.

- *Read books and articles on brand building and advertising*—There are plenty of them out there written by highly successful marketers and advertisers who have given their lives to the business. The more you read, the more perspectives you will get. The more you read, the more mindful you will be of ways to create brand loyalty through brand building, positioning, and advertising. The more you read, the more connections you will make in your mind that may be applied to your business.

- *Hold advertising luncheons within your company.* This is a great way to get together with fellow managers who share your interest in developing their skill base in the quest to become more effective client-advertisers. This could take the form of an informal luncheon, breakfast, or break. Have someone bring in advertising for all to review. Use the Advertising Assessment Tool provided in this chapter to do a professional quality assessment. Remember, don't just identify what you see in the ad but what you think regarding its effectiveness. Also, put yourself in the shoes of the advertiser to identify actions for improving the advertising. Or, better yet, study the advertising of your competitors and identify those actions that might be wise for your business. Finally, you might want to have managers take turns preparing and facilitating a team discussion regarding brand and advertising case histories. Do this routinely. Do it consistently, such as the first Friday of every month.

- *Assess commercials and print ads whenever you watch television or read magazines*—Don't leave at the commercial break for the kitchen or bathroom. Save that for the programming. Instead, try to identify the ad strategy and Campaign Idea for a given commercial and assess the effectiveness of it. Do this all the time. Soon you will find the task getting easier. One day it will become a habit if you do it often enough.

- *Make it a practice to assess competitive advertising campaigns in writing*—It is important to the business and will help improve your skills. Writing up your assessment will encourage a mindful analysis and establish a noteworthy discipline. Again, use the Advertising Assessment Tool provided in this chapter. Share the assessment with colleagues and advertising agency team members. Incorporate their thinking too!

- *Use tools from the toolkit*—These will serve a two-fold purpose. First, they will guide how you should think about advertising, strategy, and execution so that you may leverage your judgment. Second, they will reinforce a desired thought pattern to help you develop sound skills.

- *Find a mentor and seek her/his feedback*—This could be someone(s) from your management and/or agency team. Let them know you admire their skills and insights, and would like to learn from them. They will be flattered and, hopefully, they will provide a source of meaningful coaching for you.

- *Attend an advertising seminar to bolster your effectiveness*—There are many available. We, at BDN, could arrange a seminar for your organization. We have conducted scores of our three-day **Strategic Positioning & Ad College** throughout the world for leading client-advertising companies. Or, perhaps, you might want to attend one of our open (i.e., public) programs. If you would like more information, don't hesitate to give us a call or visit our website at www.adcollege.com.

Creating brand loyalty in this age of sameness doesn't just happen. It takes the management of Power Positioning and Really Great Advertising. This requires exceptional client marketing managers who know and dutifully undertake their responsibilities as they relate to brand building and advertising. And, it takes skills. All of which can be yours—with awareness, thoughtful insights, and some more work. It's worth it! Good Luck!

Invitation

We enjoyed sharing our learnings with you and hope they will prove to be of value in developing advertising that makes a difference, building profitable sales and marketshare, creating brand loyalty, establishing a healthy brand, and even in advancing your career.

We are interested in what you think about this book and how it impacts your performance. And, we are prepared to make it worth your while to tell us. Just visit our Web site **www.adcollege.com** and complete the brief questionnaire provided. For your troubles, we will provide you with a password that will allow you to download clean copies of the tools appearing in this book for your further use. Also, we will make available to you, through the Web site, any modifications and new tools we develop.

Finally, if you are interested in attending one of our open **Strategic Positioning & Ad College** programs and/or would like us to customize a program for your organization, visit our Web site and let us know.

Best wishes for your success in building power brands, developing really great advertising, and creating brand loyalty.

Richard D. Czerniawski   Michael W. Maloney

APPENDIX A

Glossary of Key Terms

Advertising Strategy   A written statement that provides guidance and direction for the development of a brand's advertising. As such, it should capitalize on a key customer insight in addressing the brand's marketing objective.

  The Ad Strategy thus provides a common basis upon which to assess and "coach" the agency's creative work.

ASAP (Applied Strategic Advertising Process)   A non-traditional approach to the development of advertising: one that consciously employs **Campaign Ideas** as its main "currency," rather than storyboards.

  The ASAP way builds in less formal, "on-the-agency's-turf" work sessions prior to the review of storyboards. As such, it is typically a more efficient use of creative resources; it is often more productive, too.

Benefit   One of the essential elements of a Brand Positioning Statement: the one that addresses, "What's in it for me?" for the intended brand Target Customer Group. May occur in any one (or combination) of three ways:

- *Customer*: a benefit that, literally, answers, "What's in it for me?" The direct, functional reward for the customer. For example, with Reach toothbrush, the customer benefit might be cleaner, healthier teeth.

- *Emotional*: a benefit that is, actually, another classification of a customer benefit, but that better answers the question, "How's it going to make me feel?" Again, with Reach such a benefit might be confidence.
- *Product*: The simplest form of benefit—answers the question, "What does this product do?" The Reach toothbrush does a number of things: reaches to clean back teeth; helps reduce plaque along the gumline; etc.

Brand Character   One of the essential elements of the Brand Positioning Statement: the one that addresses who your brand is as a personage. It represents the complexion, temperament, and spirit of the brand.

(Brand Character is a strategic element that is intended to last, unlike "tone," an executional element which refers to a specific, shorter-term attitude or style of a particular ad.)

Brand Positioning   A written statement that clearly articulates the way we want customers to perceive, think, and feel about our brand versus our competitors' products. The statement should include six key elements: Customer Need, Target Customer, Competitive Framework, Benefit(s), Reason-Why, and Brand Character.

Campaign Idea   The provocative expression of a brand's benefit(s) in customer language (it is therefore *creative material*). It uses both Key Copy Words and a Core Dramatization to communicate the benefit(s).

Competitive Framework   One of the essential elements of the Brand Positioning Statement: the one that enables the intended customer to understand, "What should I use this instead of?"; and the one that answers the marketer's question: "From which other products/brands will I source my brand's volume?"

Customer Insight   As the name implies, an understanding of the "inner nature of things"; a revelation that follows the act of "seeing intuitively." Such understandings and revelations should link the brand's marketing objective and advertising strategy to qualify as a true Customer Insight.

C'mon. You haven't heard about Dri-weave?

DRI-WEAVE IS
WHAT ALWAYS IS ALL ABOUT.
IT'S A CLEANER, DRIER
KIND OF PROTECTION.

Only Always® has Dri-weave.
Dri-weave has unique cone-shaped holes that let moisture flow
in and then help keep it there. It's what makes Always maxis
cleaner and drier.* And that's what our protection is all about.

IT'S CLEANER. IT'S DRIER. IT'S ALWAYS.

Extra Strength Excedrin: *Woman In Attic*

WOMAN: Tylenol. Yeah, I use it

SUPER: TYLENOL IS A REGISTERED TRADEMARK OF JOHNSON & JOHNSON.

for aches, pains, fever

that kind of thing. But headaches are another story. For headaches I use

Excedrin,

'cause Excedrin relieves headaches better then Tylenol.

SUPER: USE ONLY AS DIRECTED.

They did clinical research

to prove it.

But you know that's for doctors,

so I did my own kind of research.

I tried it on my headache, that proved it.

Excedrin. The headache medicine.

Also available in geltabs.

SUPER: 1997 BRISTOL-MYERS SQUIBB CO.

Hallmark

Funny how finding this on the back can make any parent feel special.

Pepsi: *Shady Acres Switch*

(MUSIC IN) (SFX: WOMAN SINGS)

(MUSIC/SFX CONTINUE) WOMAN (VO): Rock and roll

is okay, but I prefer rap.

MAN: Awesome!

(MUSIC/SFX CONTINUE)

DELIVERY MAN #1: Wait a second, Sandy Acres was supposed to get the Coke and the frat house

was supposed to get the Pepsi. DELIVERY MAN #2: Coke, Pepsi-- what's the difference?

(MUSIC CHANGES: CLASSICAL) MALE COLLEGE STUDENT: I24.

(SFX: SLURPING IN & OUT)

(SFX: SNORING IN & OUT)

(MUSIC CHANGES: RAP) MAN SINGS: Movin', grovin', I'm... (SFX: MAN SINGS IN BKGD)

MAN: This is radical. (SFX: SINGING OUT) (MUSIC OUT)

STOP SLEEPING WITH YOUR PROFESSORS.

Is it the sound of that whispery voice, or those big, intellectual words?

If your professors are putting you to sleep, Revive with Vivarin®.

Don't let fatigue get the best of you. Vivarin's® the safe

way to stay mentally alert, with the same caffeine as about

two cups of coffee. So stay sharp in class. Don't sleep

your way to the bottom.

Revive with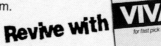

VIVARIN®
for fast pick up—safe as coffee

© 1995 **SB** *SmithKline Beecham*
Consumer Healthcare
Each tablet contains 200 mg of caffeine, equal to about two cups of coffee. Use only as directed.

This advertisement prepared by
GREY ADVERTISING INC.
Client: SmithKline Beecham
Product: Vivarin
Job No: **045-55-289**

Space/Size: Pg. 4C bld. (5⅜x7½)
Pubs: Marketsource Term Planner
Issue: 1995

There.

4g. Fat per box.

4 8g. Fat per box.
half

Now we're
even.

	Healthy Choice	Lean Cuisine® Comparable items
Beef Pepper Steak Oriental	4	8
Cheese Pizza	4	8
Cheddar Broccoli Potatoes	5	10

(total fat in grams.)

HEALTHY CHOICE®   EAT *what* YOU *like*

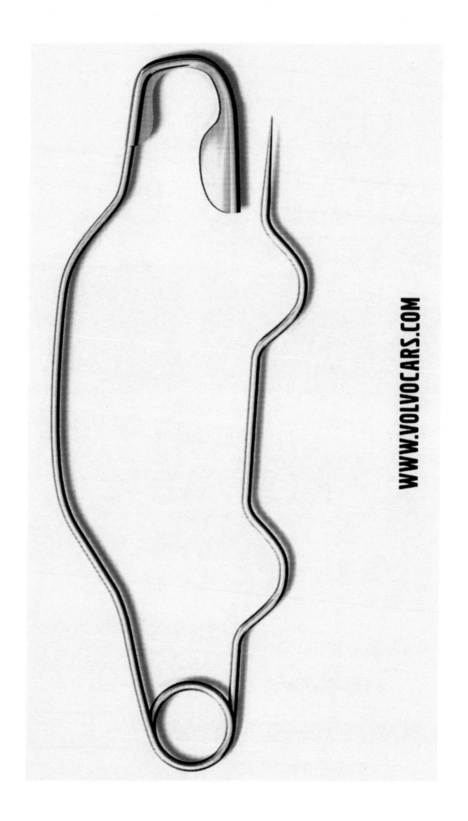

WWW.VOLVOCARS.COM

POND'S
INSTITUTE

HELP BOTH
PREVENT & CORRECT
THE APPEARANCE OF
WRINKLES AND OTHER
SIGNS OF AGING

ONE BOTTLE, TWO SEPARATE MOISTURIZERS
BOTH SIDES OF THE
AGE DEFYING STORY

PREVENT	CORRECT
LOTION WITH	LOTION WITH
SPF	ALPHA HYDROXYS
EACH DAY	EACH NIGHT

WHO KNEW?
90% OF SIGNS
OF PREMATURE
AGING
ARE CAUSED BY
SUN AND
ENVIRONMENT

POND'S
 PREVENT
& CORRECT
LOTION

POND'S INSTITUTE
1-800-34-PONDS

ALSO AVAILABLE IN CREAM

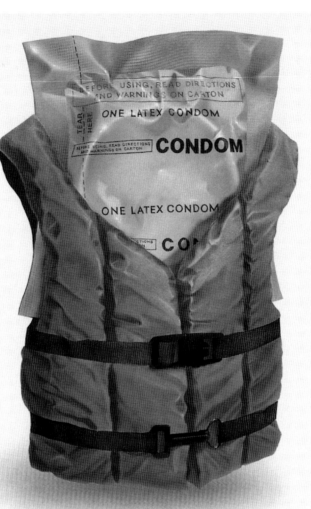

K-Y PLUS.

PROTECTION FOR YOUR PROTECTION.

K-Y® Plus with Nonoxynol-9 isn't just excellent lubrication. It's added safety for your condom. Because it's water based, it guards your condom against the friction that can cause tears.

 And Nonoxynol-9, a highly effective spermicide, offers backup protection for additional peace of mind. These days, it's smart to use a condom. It's even smarter when your condom has a partner.

Protect your condom, protect yourself with K-Y Plus with Nonoxynol-9.

A Customer Insight that works will effect a change in current customer attitudes and behaviors regarding your brand.

Core Dramatization   One of the two components of a Campaign Idea. This one is the visual-audial-ization of the brand's benefit(s). Examples include: demonstrations, product switches, reactions to product usage, a unique plot twist, and even ownable iconography, among others.

Customer Needs   One of the essential elements of the Brand Positioning Statement: the one that identifies the specific rational and emotional wants, desires, and needs your intended Target Customer is looking to have (better) satisfied. Typically require a blend of customer research and entrepreneurial intuition to determine.

Execution Planning   That phase of any television or print advertising development process that directly precedes and follows the filming/photo-shooting/editing phases. It is a good time to raise broader executional issues, such as which TV formats to pursue or which print layout guidelines to follow.

Key Copy Words   One of the two components of the Campaign Idea. This one translates the brand's strategic benefit(s) into compelling, provocative language for the intended customer. Oil of Olay's "A Lifetime of Beautiful Skin" is an example; so is Miller Lite's "Tastes Great. Less Filling."

(Note: Don't confuse Key Copy Words—which always state or imply the benefit(s) with occasional "tag lines" that do not.)

Permission to Believe   An aspect of credibility that one can build into the brand positioning; a type of Reason-Why, if you like. It typically involves the use of outside or external forces to provide that credibility—such as a hospital or athletic endorsement.

Positioning Matrix   A "displayed thinking" tool that literally lays out any number of Brand Positioning Statements (actual and/or inferred) side by side for more thoughtful assessment. An essential tool for understanding how competitive your brand is relative to your competition.

Reason-Why   One of the essential elements of the Brand Positioning Statement: the one that supports the benefit(s) by providing credibility
for it. It is typically something internal to the brand—a design feature
or formulation, a unique process. The Reason-Why helps close the
brand sale.

Single-Minded Proposition   Creative material—an executional device, really—
that permits a brand with multiple benefits to communicate them
succinctly, and memorably. Lexus's use of "The Relentless Pursuit of
Perfection" as their Key Copy Words represents a highly successful
example of a Single-Minded Proposition.

Target Customer Group   One of the essential elements of a Brand Positioning Statement: the one that defines the most likely prospects—who
have a similar set of needs and concerns—that your product or service
(brand) can satisfy.

   An effective expression of the Target Customer Group includes three
components: need mindset; current usage habits/ behaviors; and
demographics.

Forms, Tools, Templates

Customer Needs

Physical/Rational	Psychographic/Emotional
•	•
•	•
•	•
•	•
•	•
•	•
•	•
•	•
•	•
•	•

Target Link

Demographics	Usage Behavior	Needs
•		
•		
•		
•		
•		

Strategic Targeting

	"Convince . . ."
Pepsi-Cola	Heavy cola drinkers who purchase both Pepsi and Coke interchangeably (based on lowest price or availability of preferred package type) . . . and who generally think that the taste of Coke and Pepsi, being similar, there is little basis for difference between them THAT_____
Kellogg's Frosted Flakes (Adult)	Adults, 25–49, who grew up with Frosted Flakes as one of their favorite cereals and who currently buy it for their children . . . but rarely eat it now because they think it's mainly for kids THAT _____ _____

People/User Type (Demographics) _____

_____

_____

Who Use (Behaviors) _____

_____

_____

And Who Think (Attitudes/Needs) _____

_____

_____

Target Customer Profile

Name: _____

Gender: _____ Age: _____

Marital Status (Married to/# years): _____

Children (Ages): _____

Occupation: _____

Education: _____

Personal Auto: _____

Currently working on: _____

_____

My favorite leisure activity is: _____

_____

I stay home to watch (on TV): _____

_____

Last good book I read: _____

_____

The newspapers/magazines I usually read include:

_____

(Continued)

My favorite music/performer is: _____

The last vacation I took was: _____

_____

What my friends say about me (when I'm not in their presence) is: _____

_____

_____

If there was one thing I could change about myself it would be: _____

_____

_____

A really good evening to me is: _____

_____

_____

My dream in life is: _____

_____

_____

_____

_____

The reason(s) I choose _____
(versus competitive brands) is: _____

_____

_____

_____

_____

Competitive Framework
Option Tool

Ways to Establish	**Options**
1. Versus a Contiguous Category	_____ _____
2. Versus the Gold Standard	_____ _____
3. Versus the "Rat Pack"	_____ _____
4. Versus an All-New Frame —e.g., What it isn't	_____ _____
5. Versus the Unexpected "Further Out" Category (but with a benefit you can win on!)	_____ _____

Benefit Laddering Tool

Target:
Demo:
Usage Behavior:
Need:
Product Benefit
Customer Benefit
"Emotional" Benefit

Reason-Why Tool

Benefit: _____

_____

_____

Reason-Why Options:

  Design: _____

  _____

  Formula/Ingredients: _____

  _____

  Endorsement: _____

  _____

  Claim Research: _____

  _____

  Source: _____

  _____

  Other: _____

  _____

Brand Character Tool

- Celebrity: _____

  _____

- Characteristics:

  —

  —

  —

  —

  —

  —

  —

  —

  —

  —

  —

Brand Positioning Statement

To _____

                     (Target Customer Group-Need)

_____

_____ is the brand of _____

       (Brand)   (Competitive Framework)

_____

that _____

         (Benefit)

_____

The Reason-Why is _____

                       (Reason-Why)

_____

_____

The brand character is _____

                       (Brand Character)

_____

Brand Positioning Statement
Audit Tool

Target Group-Need	Rating	Needed Adjustments
• Demographics • Usage behavior • Ownable need • All 3-dimensions	_____ _____ _____ _____	• • • •

Competitive Framework	Rating	Needed Adjustments
• Too broad/restrictive • Meaningful frame-of-reference	_____ _____	• •

Benefit	Rating	Needed Adjustments
• Clear customer take-away • Meaningful point-of-difference	_____ _____	• •

Reason-Why	Rating	Needed Adjustments
• Aligned with benefit • Intrinsics consistent with product • Utilizes extrinsic credibility aid • Easily understood/appreciated by target	_____ _____ _____ _____	• • • •

Brand Character	Rating	Needed Adjustments
• Identifies celebrity • Contains personality characteristics/values meaningful and consistent with brand bundle and desired image • Clearly communicates brand character	_____ _____ _____	• • •

Positioning Matrix

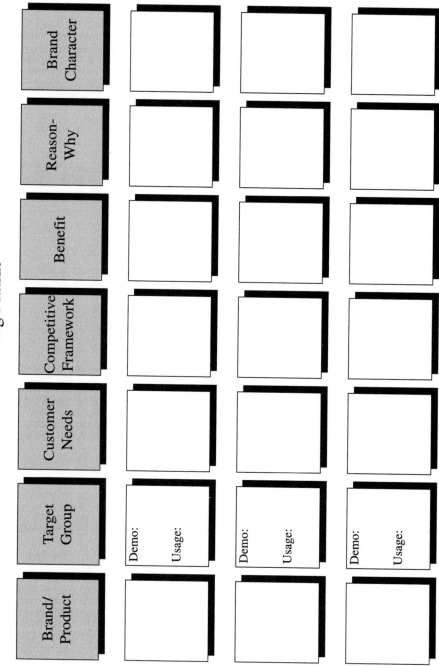

Customer Insight Thought Process (Tool)

Target: _____

_____

_____

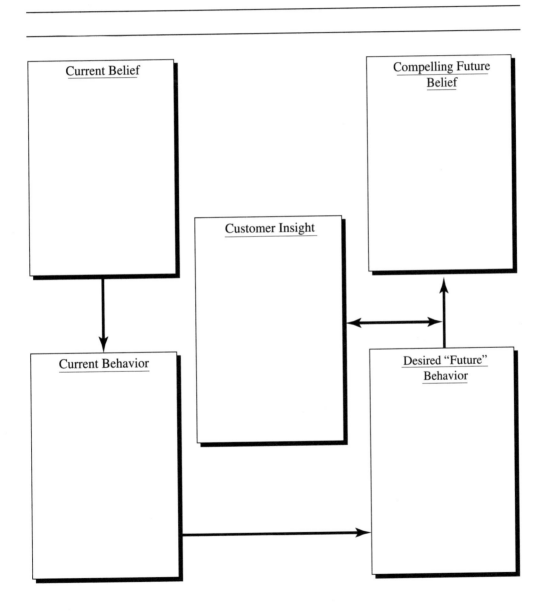

Ad Strategy Statement

Convince (Who):
(Target)

- **Demo:**

- **Usage:**

- **Need:**

That (What):
(Benefit)

Because (Why):
(Reasons-Why)

Agency Brief

Marketing Objective:

Assignment:

Customer Insight:

Ad Strategy Statement:

- **Convince** (Target)

- **That** (Benefit)

- **Because** (Support)

Brand Character:

Legal/Regulatory Mandatories:

-

-

-

The Campaign Idea

One-Sentence Encapsulation:

Core Dramatization:
(Visual/Illustration)

Key Copy Words:

Campaign Idea Assessment

A Campaign Idea is the provocative expression of a brand's benefit(s) in customer language. It uses key copy words and a core dramatization to communicate the benefit(s).

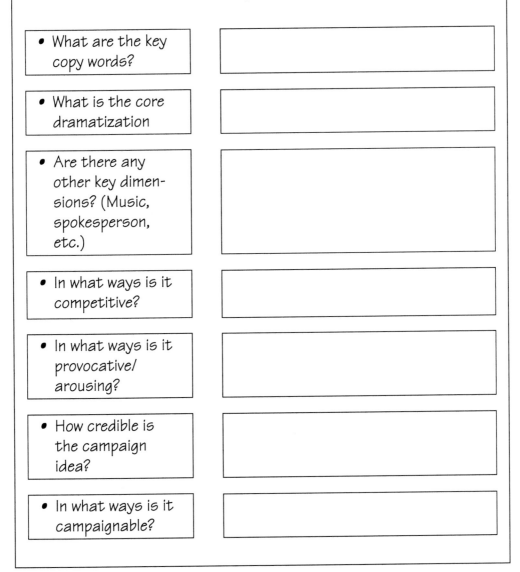

• What are the key copy words?	
• What is the core dramatization	
• Are there any other key dimensions? (Music, spokesperson, etc.)	
• In what ways is it competitive?	
• In what ways is it provocative/ arousing?	
• How credible is the campaign idea?	
• In what ways is it campaignable?	

Execution Assessment Tool

• What happens in the advertising? —How clear or confusing? —How central is the product to action?	

• How is the advertising credible or incredible?	

• Is the main benefit visualized? How?	

• How is the Reason-Why visualized?	

• Are words and pictures in sync?	

Storyboard Assessment

• Is there a Campaign Idea?	
• Is it on strategy?	
• Is the Campaign Idea: —Meaningful? Credible? Provocative?	
• Does the execution showcase the Campaign Idea? —Is the benefit visualized? —Does it tell a picture story? —Is it clear, credible and compelling?	
• Does the board represent a commercial or a campaign? —Does it have legs?	
• Are the ideas communicated clearly in visual-audio elements?	
• Do you like it? —Does it "sell" versus "tell?"	

Competitive Advertising Assessment Tool

1. ***Overview***—Effective? Rationale. Key strengths/weaknesses? Remember to explain your point-of-view.

   _____

   _____

   _____

   _____

2. ***Advertising Strategy***—What is it? Be as specific as possible. Is it strategically sound? Explain. What brand objectives and issues might it address? How valid/important are these to the ultimate success/ competitiveness of the brand?

   Target

   - Demo

   - Usage

   - Need

   Benefit

   _____

   _____

   Reason-Why

   _____

   _____

3. **Campaign Idea**—What are the key copy words? What is the core dramatization? Do they deliver against the ad strategy? Are they in sync? Are they compelling? Campaignable?

_____

_____

_____

_____

4. **Execution**—What is the execution format? How well does the execution deliver the Campaign Idea? Is the execution arresting? Memorable? If a print ad, what do you think about technical factors such as headline, etc.?

_____

_____

_____

_____

5. **Implications**—What are the indicated actions for us (as the advertiser or competitor)?

_____

_____

_____

_____

Index

About the Authors

Richard Czerniawski and Michael Maloney are principals with Business Development Network, Inc., a marketing consulting firm with a long-term track record of developing marketing strategies and initiatives that create brand loyalty and grow businesses. They are both successful former brand marketing managers and advertisers with Fortune Top 100 companies. Together they represent more than 50-years of marketing management experience.

Richard Czerniawski has held key marketing management positions with Procter & Gamble, Johnson & Johnson, Richardson-Vicks, and The Coca-Cola Company (where he served as director of marketing for all soft drink brands in the United States). Most recently, he assumed the role as chief marketing officer for a start-up company in the natural healthcare category, where he managed the development of successful ad campaigns to consumers and healthcare professionals. He also served on the board of directors to that company prior to its sale. Richard has contributed to the successes of well-known brands such as Folger's Coffee, Reach Toothbrush, Band-Aid Brand Adhesive Bandages, and Coca-Cola Classic.

Mr. Czerniawski holds a BS in Education and an MBA. He is a former naval aviator and officer who served as an instructor pilot. Additionally, he is the author of numerous articles on marketing management (*Journal of Consumer Marketing*) and publishes *DISPATCHES*, a newsletter to the marketing community. He has served as a guest lecturer for the MBA programs at DePaul University, Lake Forest College, and Thunderbird International School of Management.

Michael Maloney has held key marketing positions with Procter & Gamble, the Coca-Cola Company, Tropicana Products, and PepsiCo. During his seven-year tenure with PepsiCo he worked in both the domestic and international snack businesses. At Frito-Lay, he served as vice-president of their "Salty Snack" portfolio; he also served as the general manager of their overall snack operations in the Northeast and Midwest territories of the United States. And, with PepsiCo Foods International (now known as Frito-Lay International), he led the worldwide marketing team. Mike has contributed to the successes of such well-known brands as Puffs Facial Tissues, Sprite, Coca-Cola, Tropicana Pure Premium Orange Juice, Doritos Tortilla Chips, and Ruffles Potato Chips.

Mr. Maloney holds an MA in English and an MS in Personnel Counseling. He is a former Air Force instructor pilot, and he has taught English at the U.S. Air Force Academy. More recently, he has served as an associate board member to the Cox Business School at Southern Methodist University.